HELP ME UNDERSTAND, LORD

Prayer Responses to the Gospel of Mark

By
NEELY DIXON McCARTER

THE WESTMINSTER PRESS

PHILADELPHIA

BOOK DESIGN BY DOROTHY ALDEN SMITH

First edition

Published by The Westminster Press ®
Philadelphia, Pennsylvania

PRINTED IN THE UNITED STATES OF AMERICA

9 8 7 6 5 4 3 2 1

Library of Congress Cataloging in Publication Data

McCarter, Neely Dixon, 1929–
  Help me understand, Lord.

  1. Bible. N.T. Mark—Devotional literature.
2. Prayers. I. Bible. N.T. Mark. English.
New English. 1978. II. Title.
BS2585.4.M25   242'.8   77–14511
ISBN 0–664–24180–8

*To the memory of one whose life often embod-
ied the struggle of prayer but whose death was
an answer to her prayer that God would send
his angels to take her home quickly*
NELL DIXON MCCARTER

CONTENTS

PREFACE

Prayer is a problem for many people. Maybe because prayer is crucial for Christians, it is a painful problem. I suppose real prayer has never been easy, but in our own time it has tried the souls of many who would call upon the God and Father of our Lord Jesus Christ.

Why is prayer a problem? I am not sure anyone really knows. Shifting world views, our concomitant commitment to secular modes of thought and to the Christian faith, the depersonalization rampant in society—all of these and perhaps others agitate the issue. But for whatever cause, many people wrestle with the form and reality of prayer.

I am aware that for large segments of the believing population, prayer is no problem. It remains a vital and lively experience. But as T. S. Eliot once said, there are others who are like "children at the gate / who will not go away and cannot pray" (*Ash Wednesday,* V).

Many years ago while working among the students at the University of Florida, I discovered a little book by Alan Richardson, *A Preface to Bible-Study.* He suggests a kind of dialogue with the Scripture as a part of study. Years later I came to love the writing of Søren Kierkegaard and profited from his prayer dialogues with the word.

9

From these two sources and my own struggles I have developed this "dialogue with Scripture" approach to prayer. It is an effort to avoid simply talking with myself and to focus on a word from the outside. It is not an effort to find God or to hear him in my own consciousness or selfhood, but an effort to hear God speak to one's consciousness and then reply. Obviously one's subjectivity plays a role even in the hearing, but at least there is some promise of a balance.

A few more words may help the reader in the use of the book. First, the passages of Scripture are printed. I realize that some prefer to force the reader to examine the Bible itself. In this case, however, since the response is primarily devotional and personal, not technical and critical, I find the words of Mark helpful when they are placed immediately prior to the response. I have selected *The New English Bible* because of its freshness. Having said this, I trust that the critical Biblical scholar will find that I have not strayed too far from the truth. The responses are based on some relatively serious study of the text.

Second, I find as I reread the prayer responses a strange shifting of pronouns. Sometimes *I* is used; other times *we*. This change may occur within a paragraph. I account for this variation by realizing that while these words were written in private for personal use, I cannot separate myself from the body, the church. Therefore, I speak for myself and for our family, the church, simultaneously.

Third, as you read the prayers, you will find that I follow the Christian tradition of addressing both the Father and the Son. Lord, Lord God, God our Father, and similar expressions are used, depending on the context and meaning.

A final word. When I decided to put these prayer responses in print, I reworked them. I was constantly caught by the urge to leave concrete places, persons, and events in the text; otherwise, prayer becomes vague and general. On the other hand, the specifics for which I prayed during these past years may no longer be issues or may even be unknown to the reader. So I have compromised and taken out some of the particular references and left others. I hope that the reader will be assisted in being specific even though the writing varies with respect to particularity. After all, these pages do not contain your prayers; they are words to get you started on a dialogue. For this reason primarily, *the book should not be read straight through.* A sense of sameness will develop. Read it in small portions as occasions for reflection.

I wish to express appreciation to President Fred R. Stair, Jr., and the Faculty of Union Theological Seminary in Virginia for the sabbatic which provided occasion for my completion of the manuscript. I am also grateful for the loyal, consistent, and patient work of my secretary *par excellence,* Mrs. Grace Cosby.

N.D.M.

HELP ME UNDERSTAND, LORD

1 / MARK 1:1

Here begins the Gospel of Jesus Christ the Son of God.

The beginning seems so long ago, Lord. For most of us it is an old, old story. Sunday school pictures, strange names, portions of parables, fragments of events, litter our memories, providing us with some vague imagery of Jesus, his life and message. Lord, through this haze of familiarity, enable us to perceive the majesty of the gospel. Let that good news which has transformed the possibilities for human life break through to us. Let the humanness of Jesus as he fulfilled the role of the Anointed One reveal the Son of God to us again and again.

And so, Lord, we stand before the witness of Mark. We are a little afraid that our reading will fall into the patterns of the past and there will be no lively dialogue with the One who both spoke the gospel and was the good news. As we begin at the beginning of the Gospel, may the presence of the Son conform our lives to the good news of Jesus Christ.

In the prophet Isaiah it stands written: "Here is my herald whom I send on ahead of you, and he will prepare your way. A voice crying aloud in the wilderness, 'Prepare a way for the Lord; clear a straight path for him.' " And so it was that John the Baptist appeared in the wilderness proclaiming a baptism in token of repentance, for the forgiveness of sins; and they flocked to him from the whole Judaean country-side and the city of Jerusalem, and were baptized by him in the River Jordan, confessing their sins.

John was dressed in a rough coat of camel's hair, with a leather belt round his waist, and he fed on locusts and wild honey. His proclamation ran: "After me comes one who is mightier than I. I am not fit to unfasten his shoes. I have baptized you with water; he will baptize you with the Holy Spirit."

Lord, while some of us do not understand all the allusions to earlier promises, we do sense your faithfulness and consistency in dealing with your people. As you promised, so you have acted. You sent your servant John to pave the way. He made it clear by his preaching of repentance, by his strange dress and life habits, by his baptizing in the river, that what followed involved a turning around, a crossing of the sea, a washing away of the old, a new beginning, a new way.

Lord, this day we are grateful that we are among those who seek to walk in the new way. We confess that the leeks and garlic of the old country still beckon us; that comfortable, establishment religous leaders and patterns of life still suit us best. Yet you have touched our lives through your promise-words; you called us through the preaching of humble persons like John, so that our lives seek a different master. We are restless when we merely conform to the

14

world about us. We struggle in the lonely isolation of our hearts and with the community of faith in seeking to be disciples of the Way.

And so we pray for a clearer vision of your work and promise, for a better grasp of the differences between your way and the ways of destruction, and for that personal strength to join ranks with those who follow Jesus Christ, the Son of God.

3 / MARK 1:9–11

It happened at this time that Jesus came from Nazareth in Galilee and was baptized in the Jordan by John. At the moment when he came up out of the water, he saw the heavens torn open and the Spirit, like a dove, descending upon him. And a voice spoke from heaven: "Thou art my Son, my Beloved; on thee my favour rests."

Lord, Mark skips the mystery stories of your birth and references to your childhood—those things which we feel we need in order to understand a person. He skips them in order to focus on rebirth, the great turning around, the pushing in of the new order. The very dwelling place of God was opened to you, Lord; the very power of God descended upon you and the mighty voice of God crowned you king. All this happened to you, Lord, while you stood dripping by the river, surrounded by nondescript persons and a fanatical preacher. Your ways are full of contradictions and surprises, for here you blend the servant and the king. Lord, many of us have no spellbinding stories to tell about the moment of our rebirth, or ecstatic experiences of being lifted into the third heaven; we're only plodding disciples. So, Lord, we're grateful for the memory of your baptism in water and by the

Spirit, for we know that you did it for us. Your acts give new hope to our lives, for because of you, we also are children of God and know his favor.

4 / MARK 1:12–13

Thereupon the Spirit sent him away into the wilderness, and there he remained for forty days tempted by Satan. He was among the wild beasts; and the angels waited on him.

Just at the moment when the symbol of rebirth was fresh and the words of the Father offered assurances of Sonship, just at that moment you, Lord, were driven into the wilderness to fight with Satan. So it is with us, for no sooner has the Spirit descended on us than we are driven to wrestle with evil. Lord, as children of God, it would be nice to have positions of honor, not a lifetime of fighting on our hands. And yet, it is true, Lord, we have to deal with the evil that emerges in the wilderness of our own lives—those temptations and sins known only to us and to you. We are compelled to struggle with the injustice in our communities, the hunger of the world, the pain of the poor, the emptiness of life for so many. Lord, perhaps the real temptation for those of us in the wilderness is not to fight, but to relax, protect ourselves and let Satan have his way in the affairs of life.

But thank you, Lord, for the Spirit who sends us out to do battle, who will not let us fall into complacency, but keeps edging us out. And thank you, Lord, for the sure knowledge that your struggle was victorious, that even as you moved toward the cross, the demons knew you had authority over them. Give us new confidence, Lord, in your power over evil, that the battle with Satan's temptation will not immobilize us. Give us eyes of faith, we pray, to see the angels, those messengers of your grace, even while we are among wild beasts. Give us most of all, we pray, a sense of the presence of the One who overcame even death itself and has promised to be with us, as we follow the way of the cross.

5 / MARK 1:14–15

After John had been arrested, Jesus came into Galilee proclaiming the Gospel of God: "The time has come; the kingdom of God is upon you; repent, and believe the Gospel."

Lord, not even John's fate slowed you down. In fact, the way Mark has it, John's removal from the scene appears to have been your cue. Despite the dangers, you knew it was time to tell about the crumbling of the forces of evil and the beginning of the reign of God. That is good news, Lord, and it is also hard to believe. Even a shallow memory retains visions of a seven-day war, Vietnam, Watergate, economic crunch, starvation, and much more. Is this the reign of God? One indeed has to turn around, alter one's perception of reality; one has to believe, Lord, for it is not self-evident that the kingdoms of this world are becoming the Kingdoms of our God. We believe, Lord, or we would not be praying; help our unbelief.

6 / MARK 1:16–20

Jesus was walking by the Sea of Galilee when he saw Simon and his brother Andrew on the lake at work with a casting-net; for they were fishermen. Jesus said to them, "Come with me, and I will make you fishers of men." And at once they left their nets and followed him.

When he had gone a little further he saw James son of Zebedee and his brother John, who were in the boat overhauling their nets. He called them; and, leaving their father Zebedee in the boat with the hired men, they went off to follow him.

Lord, one wonders how well these men knew you. What had they heard about you? Did they have reasons for having confidence in you? What possessed them to walk away from their families and sources of livelihood to follow you? How could they have known what the phrase "fishers of men" meant?

I suspect, Lord, that Mark has told it like it happened— both then and now. You call people and they follow you simply because you call. There may be no reason at first; we hear and respond without fully knowing why.

But the years make a difference, Lord. While we have heard your mysterious call in our inner selves, we still live with our families and seldom leave the old man sitting in the boat with the servants. We tend to respond in well-worn patterns.

Lord, we need to hear your call anew and perhaps in the midst of the commonplace and familiar. In the context of our familial, economic, and institutional life, let us, we pray, hear your voice in all of its personalness and authority. Grant freshness to that call so that the link between us may be strengthened, so that we may each day follow the One who calls, the One who guides the church, and the One who saves the world.

They came to Capernaum, and on the Sabbath he went to synagogue and began to teach. The people were astounded at his teaching, for, unlike the doctors of the law, he taught with a note of authority. Now there was a man in the synagogue possessed by an unclean spirit. He shrieked: "What do you want with us, Jesus of Nazareth? Have you come to destroy us? I know who you are—the Holy One of God." Jesus rebuked him: "Be silent," he said, "and come out of him." And the unclean spirit threw the man into convulsions and with a loud cry left him. They were all dumbfounded and began to ask one another, "What is this? A new kind of teaching! He speaks with authority. When he gives orders, even the unclean spirits submit." The news spread rapidly, and he was soon spoken of all over the district of Galilee.

Lord, we read that the man with the demon was in the synagogue on a Sabbath when you started teaching. That probably means he was just an ordinary man who had gone to church. Like us, he probably went to worship often but had no reason to assume you would be there authoritatively battling the demons in him with your words. How odd, Lord, that we should know so little about demons since we are apparently their hosts!

Now, Lord, we don't ask for some bizarre display of convulsions or fits, but we do need to discern the difference between the holy and the demonic. Our tendency is to assume that what we approve of is holy and what we disapprove of is demonic. And so some of us think you're fighting the demons of scholarship and formality, while others of us assume you're warring with the demons of ignorance and chaos. We are sure you're down on the demon of drugs—

19

at least the kinds of drugs other folks take, not the helpful and safe ones we use. We are sure you are against somebody else's sexual expressions but not our sexual repressions. Lord, we have reasons to believe you are clashing with the demons in the Communists that cause them to kill and destroy, but we feel justified in obeying the demons in us that lead us to maim and mutilate. We are sure you are depressed about those demons driving the Catholics and the Protestants to fight in Ireland, but we are sure you favor our defense of the truth that causes a little infighting in our own church.

We are so comfortable as a people with our demons, Lord, that we actually go to church thinking they will be at home there. Do battle with those spirits in us, even if it causes us to convulse and cry out.

Lord, so that we might pray like this and mean it, give us confidence in the graciousness and love of the Father as revealed in Jesus Christ.

8 / MARK 1:29–31

On leaving the synagogue they went straight to the house of Simon and Andrew; and James and John went with them. Simon's mother-in-law was ill in bed with fever. They told him about her at once. He came forward, took her by the hand, and helped her to her feet. The fever left her and she waited upon them.

Lord, even as you cast out the demon in the church, so in the quietness of a home you brought healing. We are grateful that your word sounds with authority in the midst of gathered believers and we are also thankful that your touch brings health and enables the healed to serve you. Bring healing to our homes, we pray, and make us your servants.

Now to tell the truth, Lord, when we pray for healing today, we do so with hesitant tongue. Are we asking you to work without doctors and medicines, psychiatrists and hospitals? Or are we asking for the healing that brings some wholeness to us and enables your modern therapeutic instruments to function effectively?

Lord, for some of us, these early stories do not help us believe in you. Our God doesn't have to be a miracle worker. But because we do believe in you, we seek to understand and to be a part of your healing ministry this day.

9 / MARK 1:32–34

That evening after sunset they brought to him all who were ill or possessed by devils; and the whole town was there, gathered at the door. He healed many who suffered from various diseases, and drove out many devils. He would not let the devils speak, because they knew who he was.

At the close of the Sabbath, Lord, when persons were freed from the numerous laws of the day, they came to you. They brought the sick and the crazy for you to restore. At an early service that day a demon had announced your identity; now you tell them to be quiet. Did you not want your name known? Hadn't you in fact conquered their lord in the wilderness and now should you not be recognized as the Lord? Is this Mark's way of reminding us that you do not want a following made up of those who have heard amazing stories? Maybe Mark tells us about these miracles, Lord, primarily to point to your personal encounter with people which makes them whole.

Lord, if the devils aren't to speak, help us who know you are Savior to share the truth with others.

10 / MARK 1:35-39

Very early next morning he got up and went out. He went away to a lonely spot and remained there in prayer. But Simon and his companions searched him out, found him, and said, "They are all looking for you." He answered, "Let us move on to the country towns in the neighbourhood; I have to proclaim my message there also; that is what I came out to do." So all through Galilee he went, preaching in the synagogues and casting out the devils.

Lord, amid the excitement you created but did not want, you returned to the wilderness—that symbol of struggle. This time you did not wrestle with the devil, but sought to clarify your own purposes in dialogue with the Father. The clamor and even popularity must not cause you to forget your message or forsake your mission.

Lord, to be alone in prayer is difficult. Most of us tend to think and ask for things we want, favors we'd like done. Prayer ceases to be a step along the way of the cross, finding your will, message, and mission for us; rather it becomes a kind of indulgence of the self. Some even believe that prayer changes things, but, Lord, I suspect its real purpose is to change us into your servant disciples.

Once he was approached by a leper, who knelt before him begging his help. "If only you will," said the man, "you can cleanse me." In warm indignation Jesus stretched out his hand, touched him, and said, "Indeed I will; be clean again." The leprosy left him immediately, and he was clean. Then he dismissed him with this stern warning: "Be sure you say nothing to anybody. Go and show yourself to the priest, and make the offering laid down by Moses for your cleansing; that will certify the cure." But the man went out and made the whole story public; he spread it far and wide, until Jesus could no longer show himself in any town, but stayed outside in the open country. Even so, people kept coming to him from all quarters.

Once again, Lord, the motif appears: the healing of a person and the effort to keep sensational stories quiet so that people would not follow you only for this.

Lord, most of us have never seen a person with leprosy —at least with the disease. But as in your time upon the earth we do know people who are forced to live in loneliness, cut off from established and proper religion, isolated from families, and helplessly outside the affairs of the community. You restored a person like that and he had to tell it. You touched the untouchable, taking upon yourself his curse. Now if we really pray to be your servant disciples, we had better be willing to take upon ourselves some of the curse that has fallen on others in our society. Help us, Lord, to find the wisdom and courage we need to restore the oppressed and helpless in our midst.

When after some days he returned to Capernaum, the news went round that he was at home; and such a crowd collected that the space in front of the door was not big enough to hold them. And while he was proclaiming the message to them, a man was brought who was paralysed. Four men were carrying him, but because of the crowd they could not get him near. So they opened up the roof over the place where Jesus was, and when they had broken through they lowered the stretcher on which the paralysed man was lying. When Jesus saw their faith, he said to the paralysed man, "My son, your sins are forgiven."

Now there were some lawyers sitting there and they thought to themselves, "Why does the fellow talk like that? This is blasphemy! Who but God alone can forgive sins?" Jesus knew in his own mind that this was what they were thinking, and said to them: "Why do you harbour thoughts like these? Is it easier to say to this paralysed man, 'Your sins are forgiven,' or to say, 'Stand up, take your bed, and walk'? But to convince you that the Son of Man has the right on earth to forgive sins"—he turned to the paralysed man—"I say to you, stand up, take your bed, and go home." And he got up, and at once took his stretcher, and went out in full view of them all, so that they were astounded and praised God. "Never before," they said, "have we seen the like."

Lord, the crowds came around you now. The word was out! They, like us, no doubt came for many reasons—curiosity, wanting to see a good show, feeling a need for wholeness. The five friends, Lord, had fearsomely aggressive faith and they heard the good words: "My son, your sins are forgiven." As they had torn off the roof, so you, Lord, threw open the gates of the Kingdom.

Lord, the good people—the lawyers—thought you were blaspheming, for you were assuming the role of God. Like most of us, these people constantly had the words of faith on their lips, but they seldom tore up roofs, ran risks, or carried their friends to the Savior. They were blind to the presence and power of God in the simple man Jesus.

And so we pray, Lord, for healthy skepticism, lest we be led astray by wandering miracle workers—of which there seems to be no end. But also, Lord, grant us that sensitivity to your presence and openness to your will, that we might discern your mighty acts, even when they arise from unexpected sources. May your mercy and power be incarnated ever afresh so that wholeness might be enjoyed by the forgiven. And, Lord, grant us the ability to be astounded by your actions and enable us to exercise the gift of praise.

13 / MARK 2:13–17

Once more he went away to the lake-side. All the crowd came to him, and he taught them there. As he went along, he saw Levi son of Alphaeus at his seat in the custom-house, and said to him, "Follow me"; and Levi rose and followed him.

When Jesus was at table in his house, many bad characters—tax-gatherers and others—were seated with him and his disciples; for there were many who followed him. Some doctors of the law who were Pharisees noticed him eating in this bad company, and said to his disciples, "He eats with tax-gatherers and sinners!" Jesus heard it and said to them, "It is not the healthy that need a doctor, but the sick; I did not come to invite virtuous people, but sinners."

Lord, our inclination on reading such a passage is to imagine that Jesus was really telling the scribes, perhaps indirectly, that they were sick and needed a physician. And maybe he was, but Levi was sick also. He must have had an incredible thirst for money to have turned upon the customs of his people, collected money for an oppressor, isolated himself from the fellowship of his own people. He was left with bad characters as friends. And you, Lord, ventured into that company, identifying with crooks, even sharing a meal with them as a sign of brotherhood.

Lord, it is not easy for us to do like that. Social pressure is bad, but probably not as powerful as it was in your day. But among such, we tend to share their sin, not bring healing. Our own lust for money, the exercise of power, the satisfaction of the flesh, cause us to join the sick—just a little of that money, just sharing the power for an evening, just an occasional affair, not a life-style. Oh, we know the risks you took, Lord, in being with those people.

And so, Lord, we tend to become like the scribes, wondering how you can be a part of their company and really not share in their sin. How difficult it is to believe that you can be a physician to the sick and the sick can actually come into your Kingdom!

The circle is complete; we are back again thinking about the identification of the sick—who then are the sick? The tax collectors or the scribes? The answer is really no mystery, for we recognize that the sophisticated, urban, cultured, and religious are just as sick as the cunning, crude, blatant offenders. We all need the same doctor. In no other area of our lives do we share such a common denominator. With no other One can we sit at the banquet table with joy.

Once, when John's disciples and the Pharisees were keeping a fast, some people came to him and said, "Why is it that John's disciples and the disciples of the Pharisees are fasting, but yours are not?" Jesus said to them, "Can you expect the bridegroom's friends to fast while the bridegroom is with them? As long as they have the bridegroom with them, there can be no fasting. But the time will come when the bridegroom will be taken away from them, and on that day they will fast.

"No one sews a patch of unshrunk cloth on to an old coat; if he does, the patch tears away from it, the new from the old, and leaves a bigger hole. No one puts new wine into old wine-skins; if he does, the wine will burst the skins, and then wine and skins are both lost. Fresh skins for new wine!"

As in the dinner party scene before, so here, Lord, there are people who cannot imagine that your presence brings joy. Surely doing without food is more pleasing to the Almighty than enjoying a stag party!

But, Lord, you have made it clear that it is not so in the new Kingdom. Even though you—and now we—walk the way of the cross, there is joy and rejoicing with our friends. We may fast, but that's because there are others in the world who are starving and we need to share the food of the earth. We do not fast because you have left us, or to earn your favor, but because your presence and grace make us conscious of the needs of others.

It was difficult for those Pharisees of old, and it is hard for us to accept the newness of your reign. The somber religious patterns are familiar and feel good, Lord. The new and exciting are suspect and better kept at arm's length. We really do prefer old wine. Help us, Lord, to be fresh enough of spirit to hold the new expressions of your grace and thus be helpful channels of joy, not old coats full of holes.

15 / MARK 2:23–28

One Sabbath he was going through the cornfields; and his disciples, as they went, began to pluck ears of corn. The Pharisees said to him, "Look, why are they doing what is forbidden on the Sabbath?" He answered, "Have you never read what David did when he and his men were hungry and had nothing to eat? He went into the House of God, in the time of Abiathar the High Priest, and ate the sacred bread, though no one but a priest is allowed to eat it, and even gave it to his men."

He also said to them, "The Sabbath was made for the sake of man and not man for the Sabbath; therefore the Son of Man is sovereign even over the Sabbath."

Lord, the stories have a cumulative effect; they sparkle with joy, freedom, and conflict. The leper and the tax collector were welcomed into a new fellowship; the lame man walked and your disciples ate well—and all of this goodness caused pain to those regular, dedicated preservers of the faith.

We are not surprised, Lord, that your disciples nibbled on corn as they walked on the Sabbath. We are amazed that someone could see this as a violation of the Ten Commandments, some serious affront to God. And you, Lord, had to point them beyond their crusty rules to David's act of human necessity and even beyond to your sovereign reign.

It is our own attitude and behavior that bothers us, Lord. There are a few Sabbatarians left, but they have seemingly little impact on us and our world. There are many happy heathen who do as they please on Sunday and suffer no pangs of conscience. And there are those of us somewhere in between. Every so often, Lord, we have to vote on blue laws and have to struggle with forcing others to rest on our holy day or causing people, especially the poor, to have to work seven days a week. To honor you and make life more humane are our goals, Lord, but it is not always clear how best to act on the Sabbath.

And so we pray to the Lord of the Sabbath to help us become models of that joyful existence of freedom in your presence that makes every day worth living aright.

16 / MARK 3:1–6

On another occasion when he went to synagogue, there was a man in the congregation who had a withered arm; and they were watching to see whether Jesus would cure him on the Sabbath, so that they could bring a charge against him. He said to the man with the withered arm, "Come and stand out here." Then he turned to them: "Is it permitted to do good or to do evil on the Sabbath, to save life or to kill?" They had nothing to say; and, looking round at them with anger and sorrow at their obstinate stupidity, he said to the man, "Stretch out your arm." He stretched it out and his arm was restored. But the Pharisees, on leaving the synagogue, began plotting against him with the partisans of Herod to see how they could make away with him.

Lord, they were appalled when you said, "Your sins are forgiven"; they were scandalized when you ate with sinners; they were irritated when you and your disciples broke the

Sabbath laws; and they were driven to murderous plotting when you healed a man who had come to church on the Sabbath.

It is difficult for us to grasp all of this, because most of us do not take our faith with the earnestness that gripped the Pharisees. Their whole lives were wrapped up in the preserving of their heritage, while we tend to live without much sense of history and an eager willingness to discover the new, especially if it tastes good, feels good, or makes life a bit nicer.

But you, Lord, are still a revolutionary. No doubt you still look with anger and sorrow at our obstinate stupidity, for we also fail to do good and to save life on the days you have given us. It is not that we are busy holding on to the past—not many of us, anyway. It is that we are preoccupied with other things—our stocks, the state of the economy, finding a golf partner, keeping the boat repaired, complaining about the government, trading cars, arranging flowers for the altar, and all the other lovely, harmless-in-themselves things that keep us from noticing and doing something about the people with withered arms in our midst.

Lord, grant that we may be restless until doing good and saving lives become the theme of the days you have given us.

17 / MARK 3:7–12

Jesus went away to the lake-side with his disciples. Great numbers from Galilee, Judaea and Jerusalem, Idumaea and Transjordan, and the neighbourhood of Tyre and Sidon, heard what he was doing and came to see him. So he told his disciples to have a boat ready for him, to save him from being crushed by the crowd. For he cured so many that sick people of all kinds came crowding in upon him to touch him. The unclean spirits too, when they saw him, would fall at his feet and cry aloud, "You are the Son of God"; but he insisted that they should not make him known.

When we read these words, Lord, we are invaded by the uncomfortable feeling that nothing much has changed. Despite the empires built by science, the volumes written by philosophers, the ebb and flow of political power, people still gather around one who speaks and acts with authority. The sick are still desperate for someone to heal them; they grasp at any straw that may restore life. And it is hard to fault them for it. However we may interpret it, unclean spirits still work havoc in individual and corporate lives.

As we read these words again, Lord, the crowd seems faceless, apparently motivated by curiosity or the all-consuming hope of being cured. Only the unclean spirits realized that a new age was dawning, that reality would never be the same again, and you told them to be silent.

Lord, for whatever reason, we find ourselves among that great number who have been called out to look to you. Grant that we may not be content merely to gaze in amazement or simply to seek healing for ourselves. May we see at least as clearly as the unclean spirits. Give us the grace to behold the Son of God in our midst.

18 / MARK 3:13–19

He then went up into the hill-country and called the men he wanted; and they went and joined him. He appointed twelve as his companions, whom he would send out to proclaim the Gospel, with a commission to drive out

31

devils. So he appointed the Twelve: to Simon he gave the name Peter; then came the sons of Zebedee, James and his brother John, to whom he gave the name Boanerges, Sons of Thunder; then Andrew and Philip and Bartholomew and Matthew and Thomas and James the son of Alphaeus and Thaddaeus and Simon, a member of the Zealot party, and Judas Iscariot, the man who betrayed him.

Lord Jesus, you left the curious and the demon-possessed, the halfhearted responders and unnamed masses by the sea for a rendezvous with the Twelve upon a hill. We long, Lord, for experiences like this, for mountaintops are special places where God leans out of heaven and touches the lives of human beings. And so on this hill, Lord, the New Israel was formed, Jacob created, symbolic patriarchs named, the Great Commission given.

It is with grateful hearts, Lord, that we acknowledge that you have made us part of your new family. And how like the Old Israel we are. The betrayer is ever in our midst; we look for privilege, not the way of the cross; we have a new name but the heart is slow to change.

Lord, call us once again, so that the routines of our lives can become mountaintops. Give us, Lord, love for one another so that the appointment to be your companions might be realized this day. Lord God, loosen our tongues to speak good news to a disinterested world and give us eyes of faith in order that we might perceive your power driving out devils in the midst of our technological age.

Make us conscious, Lord, that you are more willing to give to your disciples than they are to use what you have given.

He entered a house; and once more such a crowd col-lected round them that they had no chance to eat. When his family heard of this, they set out to take charge of him; for people were saying that he was out of his mind.

The doctors of the law, too, who had come down from Jerusalem, said, "He is possessed by Beelzebub," and, "He drives out devils by the prince of devils." So he called them to come forward, and spoke to them in parables: "How can Satan drive out Satan? If a kingdom is divided against itself, that kingdom cannot stand; if a household is divided against itself, that house will never stand; and if Satan is in rebellion against himself, he is divided and cannot stand; and that is the end of him.

"On the other hand, no one can break into a strong man's house and make off with his goods unless he has first tied the strong man up; then he can ransack the house.

"I tell you this: no sin, no slander, is beyond forgiveness for men; but whoever slanders the Holy Spirit can never be forgiven; he is guilty of eternal sin." He said this because they had declared that he was possessed by an unclean spirit.

Lord Jesus, they thought you were crazy. You ministered to others, not even finding time to eat, and even your own family wondered about that. Your shattering of demonic forces was seen as evil and God's victory over Satan was not recognized.

It is frightening, Lord, to think that the only unforgivable sin is calling the work of the Holy Spirit the work of the devil. But we confess, Lord, that we live in the shadow of this possibility. It is so easy to label others crazy when they do not conform to our version of the obedient life. It is so very easy and even comforting to interpret people, groups, and movements as demonic when they do not fit the patterns we think of as holy.

And so we are grateful for this testimony: you do have the power to enter Satan's domain and drive him forth! You are the Lord of life and the victor over death!

Grant us, therefore, O God, discerning eyes, mild but effective critical facilities, and wild zeal for your cause.

20 / MARK 3:31–35

Then his mother and his brothers arrived, and remaining outside sent in a message asking him to come out to them. A crowd was sitting round and word was brought to him: "Your mother and your brothers are outside asking for you." He replied, "Who is my mother? Who are my brothers?" And looking round at those who were sitting in the circle about him he said, "Here are my mother and my brothers. Whoever does the will of God is my brother, my sister, my mother."

What anguish your mother and brothers must have endured, Lord. Surely people spoke to them about your bizarre behavior and blasphemous claims. Though they questioned your sanity, Lord, they loved you and came to help you. Perhaps the Father was preparing them for the later anguish that comes to those who helplessly watch their loved ones suffer. We are thankful, Lord, for the tradition of caring for our families "according to the flesh." But we are also thankful for the new brothers, sisters, and mothers who are given to us by our Father, as we gather around you our elder brother, in the bosom of our mother, the church. This new family, Lord, enables us to live with the anguish and pain of life.

Grant, O Lord, that as we gather, you may be the center of our circle, that as a family we may ever seek to do the Father's will, and may we thus sense our sharing in the work of your Kingdom, our kinship with the apostles, and our membership in your family.

21 / MARK 4:1–9

On another occasion he began to teach by the lake-side. The crowd that gathered round him was so large that he had to get into a boat on the lake, and there he sat, with the whole crowd on the beach right down to the water's edge. And he taught them many things by parables.

As he taught he said:

"Listen! A sower went out to sow. And it happened that as he sowed, some seed fell along the footpath; and the birds came and ate it up. Some seed fell on rocky ground, where it had little soil, and it sprouted quickly because it had no depth of earth; but when the sun rose the young corn was scorched, and as it had no root it withered away. Some seed fell among thistles; but the thistles shot up and choked the corn, and it yielded no crop. And some of the seed fell into good soil, where it came up and grew, and bore fruit; and the yield was thirtyfold, sixtyfold, even a hundredfold." He added, "If you have ears to hear, then hear."

Lord, these words must have astounded the listeners. Could they grasp that your word—the voice of an unknown peasant—was going to issue in multitudes of believers?

Didn't they know the condition of people's hearts, even as you knew it? How could your simple word penetrate that thorny and rocky territory?

Yet, Lord, you spoke without hesitation or doubt. You knew with joy that the Father would give the increase.

And so, Lord, in our own day your word goes out through your servants, most of whom are unknown and unacclaimed by the world. That word falls upon the rocky ground and in brier patches of our hearts which are already hardened by the words about Alka-Seltzer and amused by the gospel of Peanuts. In this sea of words, can your simple word still reach the hearts of human beings? Can we believe that the foolish act of speaking the word of One who died upon a cross is going to make any difference in the lives of women and men?

I take it, Lord, that we are not so much called upon to have courage, to be clever and forceful, as to have confidence that the Father can give a thirtyfold, a sixtyfold, yes, even a hundredfold harvest to the scattered seed. Therefore, Lord, free us from the sense of competition with others who speak about different realities and deliver us from the success game of mounting statistics. Only make us mindful of our need to be faithful in witnessing to your word and trusting the fruit-giving power of the Spirit.

22 / MARK 4:10–12

When he was alone, the Twelve and others who were round him questioned him about the parables. He replied, "To you the secret of the kingdom of God has been given; but to those who are outside everything comes by way of parables, so that (as Scripture says) they may look and look, but see nothing; they may hear and hear, but understand nothing; otherwise they might turn to God and be forgiven."

I feel obliged to pause and reflect on these few words, Lord, even though they are a part of the larger story. There are two mysteries here, Lord, which baffle me. First, you seem to give the insiders a break by offering interpretations while leaving the outsiders to figure out the parables for themselves. Second, your tutoring of the disciples did not seem to help them very much. They looked and didn't see; they listened but didn't understand—at least until after the resurrection. How could they have been so dull?

Maybe, Lord, the two mysteries come together in that quiet, but productive work of the Spirit. For while the Spirit causes the seed to grow, we are clearly responsible for the condition of our hearts. And out of this strange duality emerge some who believe. But frankly, Lord, the most mysterious reality of all is that you have enabled us—with our hardness of heart and dullness of mind—to look and to see, to listen and to understand. And for this, we are grateful.

23 / MARK 4:13–20

So he said, "You do not understand this parable? How then are you to understand any parable? The sower sows the word. Those along the footpath are people in whom the word is sown, but no sooner have they heard it than Satan comes and carries off the word which has been sown in them. It is the same with those who receive the seed on rocky ground; as soon as they hear the word, they accept it with joy, but it strikes no root in them; they have no staying-power; then, when there is trouble or persecution on account of the word, they fall away at once. Others

37

again receive the seed among thistles; they hear the word, but worldly cares and the false glamour of wealth and all kinds of evil desire come in and choke the word, and it proves barren. And there are those who receive the seed in good soil; they hear the word and welcome it; and they bear fruit thirtyfold, sixtyfold, or a hundredfold!"

And now, Lord, we have to look at our own hearts, for Mark has turned his words on us. For some reason your comments about the first two groups do not bother us very much, for either they turned you off to begin with or they were only temporarily interested. The bird Satan grabs the seed before it can work into the hard heart and the others are believers only as a convenience. But that third group touches a responsive chord in many of us who seek to walk in the way of the cross. Your word has come to our hearts, but the thistles were already growing there and probably have deeper roots. Worldly cares, Lord, yes, worldly cares occupy our minds—we are so conscious of what we wear, how well we eat, the car we drive, the trips we take, and all the rest. The glamour of wealth may be false but it is seductive to one who has to worry about paying the heating bill or getting the children through college. Oh, we know, Lord, if we were not so full of evil desires for so many things, so many comforts, so much leisure and pleasure, these anxieties might not be there. But the truth of the matter is, Lord, that we are children of our age and culture. Therefore, these are real thistles that grow deeply in our hearts, choking the word.

But, Lord, we know our hearts are not so different from the hearts of others; we share a common human condition. And the wonder of it all is that you, Lord, found and find good soil. It is good because you yourself make it good, and the word bears fruit—the story is told again and again—your teaching is heard, and you, the very content of that teaching, are present. So be it.

24 / MARK 4:21–25

He said to them, "Do you bring in the lamp to put it under the meal-tub, or under the bed? Surely it is brought to be set on the lamp-stand. For nothing is hidden unless it is to be disclosed, and nothing put under cover unless it is to come into the open. If you have ears to hear, then hear."

He also said, "Take note of what you hear; the measure you give is the measure you will receive, with something more besides. For the man who has will be given more, and the man who has not will forfeit even what he has."

If only so many can hear, why do we teach your Word, Lord? Why should we scatter seed all over creation if there is only a certain amount of good soil? Your answer is clear: the word is like a lamp which has no place under a tub or a bed. Yea, the Word is the Light of the world. Help us, Lord, to learn to teach and speak your word. Is it false piety to say we do not really know how to relate your truth to the buying and selling of stock, death caused by cars, world hunger, or even the neighbor next door? Is it false humility to say we are not often certain our interpretation of Scripture is the true one? Deliver us, we pray, Lord, from the need for such certainty and enable us to spread the Word so that we can hear more clearly and fully and not forfeit what insights we do have.

25 / MARK 4:26–29

He said, "The kingdom of God is like this. A man scatters seed on the land; he goes to bed at night and gets up in the morning, and the seed sprouts and grows—how, he does not know. The ground produces a crop by itself, first the blade, then the ear, then full-grown corn in the ear; but as soon as the crop is ripe, he plies the sickle, because harvest-time has come."

Because you have taken responsibility for the growth of the Kingdom, Lord, we can go to bed at night and sleep. But grant, Lord, that when we wake, we may patiently work in your harvest fields, confident that you are performing the miracle of grace in our lives and in the lives of all who belong to your Kingdom.

26 / MARK 4:30–34

He said also, "How shall we picture the kingdom of God, or by what parable shall we describe it? It is like the mustard-seed, which is smaller than any seed in the ground at its sowing. But once sown, it springs up and grows taller than any other plant, and forms branches so large that the birds can settle in its shade."

With many such parables he would give them his message, so far as they were able to receive it. He never spoke to them except in parables; but privately to his disciples he explained everything.

Lord, in our age we wonder how things happen and with our coolly analytical minds we frequently can figure it out. Folks have wondered over the years about your creation of the universe out of nothing; we have our theories on this. We have wondered how the smallest seed could produce so large a tree; our botanists have helped us with this one. We also wonder how your Kingdom could have grown from so shabby a band with such a faint witness; our psychologists and sociologists have helped us with this one. We wonder *how* when perhaps the point of your parable is that we should wonder *at*. The two do not necessarily contradict each other. Our minds and spirits, conditioned as they are by this age, will continue to wonder how. But, Lord, grant us that gift of spirit to wonder at your great work—to stand astonished, to be amazed, to sense surprise, and to marvel in the face of your grace.

27 / MARK 4:35–41

That day, in the evening, he said to them, "Let us cross over to the other side of the lake." So they left the crowd and took him with them in the boat where he had been sitting; and there were other boats accompanying him. A heavy squall came on and the waves broke over the boat until it was all but swamped. Now he was in the stern asleep on a cushion; they roused him and said, "Master, we are sinking! Do you not care?" He awoke, rebuked the wind, and said to the sea, "Hush! Be still!" The wind dropped and there was a dead calm. He said to them, "Why are you such cowards? Have you no faith even now?" They were awestruck and said to one another, "Who can this be? Even the wind and the sea obey him."

At first, Lord, the passage causes a storm in our own hearts. Our boat will sink before we can solve the problem of miracles in this critical and scientific age. Maybe we

41

should look on this story as a parable, see the boat as the church in the wicked world. Maybe we should spiritualize the event and decide you were really only telling the disciples to be calm and trust you.

What do we do with it, Lord? Perhaps the story pictures for us our life in the world with you. Following you as those early disciples did we encounter danger. It's dangerous to turn the other cheek, to return good for evil, to love people more than possessions, to value obedience more than success, to love the Father more than country, to walk in the way of the cross. It's dangerous, Lord, and we are cowards. We forget that you are here; that you care; we lose faith. As we read the story, let us hear your voice again telling us to be still. Make us conscious that our lives are lived in the presence of the one who can still the winds and calm the sea.

28 / MARK 5:1–20

So they came to the other side of the lake, into the country of the Gerasenes. As he stepped ashore, a man possessed by an unclean spirit came up to him from among the tombs where he had his dwelling. He could no longer be controlled; even chains were useless; he had often been fettered and chained up, but he had snapped his chains and broken the fetters. No one was strong enough to master him. And so, unceasingly, night and day, he would cry aloud among the tombs and on the hill-sides and cut himself with stones. When he saw Jesus in the distance, he ran and flung himself down before him, shouting loudly, "What do you want with me, Jesus, son of the Most High God? In God's name do not torment me." (For Jesus was already saying to him, "Out, unclean spirit, come out of

42

this man!") Jesus asked him, "What is your name?" "My name is Legion," he said, "there are so many of us." And he begged hard that Jesus would not send them out of the country.

Now there happened to be a large herd of pigs feeding on the hill-side, and the spirits begged him, "Send us among the pigs and let us go into them." He gave them leave; and the unclean spirits came out and went into the pigs; and the herd, of about two thousand, rushed over the edge into the lake and were drowned.

The men in charge of them took to their heels and carried the news to the town and country-side; and the people came out to see what had happened. They came to Jesus and saw the madman who had been possessed by the legion of devils, sitting there clothed and in his right mind; and they were afraid. The spectators told them how the madman had been cured and what had happened to the pigs. Then they begged Jesus to leave the district.

As he was stepping into the boat, the man who had been possessed begged to go with him. Jesus would not allow it, but said to him, "Go home to your own folk and tell them what the Lord in his mercy has done for you." The man went off and spread the news in the Ten Towns of all that Jesus had done for him; and they were all amazed.

The madness of human beings is not foreign to us, Lord. There is something among us that far exceeds a poor environment or even manic depression. The faces of Hitler, Oswald, and a multitude of others flash before our minds. The silent graves of Martin Luther King, Jr., and Bobby Kennedy speak loudly of this madness which drives people to destroy themselves and others. It is frightening because we glimpse a touch of the madness in our own lives—that drink or drug, that greed or lust, that envy or pride—all drive us to cut ourselves and cry out in the night. That madness, Lord, that permits us to live in a place where babies can be bitten by rats, where people starve in a town where food is thrown away, that causes the strongest nation on the face of the earth to drop unnumbered tons of bombs on a little piece of Asian soil, that causes Catholics and Protestants to kill their neighbors—that madness we know about firsthand.

Lord, you are the only one who knows the names of the legions of demons which are our madness. Lord, you are the only one who can send the demons back to their home in the sea, though this may destroy some of our possessions and change our way of life. Now I do not pretend to know what all of this figurative language ultimately means or what it would look like for you to so act. But there is faith and hope that you will remove the madness from our lives and enable us to continue to live in these very places as your witnesses. And will you move through us to remove the madness of man and exercise your prerogatives as King?

29 / MARK 5:21–24, 35–43

As soon as Jesus had returned by boat to the other shore, a great crowd once more gathered round him. While he was by the lake-side, the president of one of the synagogues came up, Jairus by name, and, when he saw him, threw himself down at his feet and pleaded with him. "My little daughter," he said, "is at death's door. I beg you to come and lay your hands on her to cure her and save her life." So Jesus went with him, accompanied by a great crowd which pressed upon him.

44

*While he was still speaking, a message came from the
president's house, "Your daughter is dead; why trouble
the Rabbi further?" But Jesus, overhearing the message as
it was delivered, said to the president of the synagogue,
"Do not be afraid; only have faith." After this, he allowed
no one to accompany him except Peter and James and
James's brother John. They came to the president's house,
where he found a great commotion, with loud crying and
wailing. So he went in and said to them, "Why this crying
and commotion? The child is not dead: she is asleep"; and
they only laughed at him. But after turning all the others
out, he took the child's father and mother and his own
companions and went in where the child was lying. Then,
taking hold of her hand, he said to her, "Talitha cum,"
which means, "Get up, my child." Immediately the girl got
up and walked about—she was twelve years old. At that
they were beside themselves with amazement. He gave
them strict orders to let no one hear about it, and told
them to give her something to eat.*

Lord, Jairus was no doubt a man of honor, prominent, and
with power. He was just the kind of person who must have
looked on you with profound suspicion, if not righteous
indignation, for you were the one whose life and teachings
were breaking up his church.

But he was desperate, Lord. The life of his child was more
important than his position; his love for her was stronger
than his fear of you. So he threw himself at your feet. And
you, Lord, found faith in the heart of a natural enemy. You,
Lord, brought happiness and gladness to the home of those
who had a right to hate you. You turned their weeping into
laughter.

Lord, there seem to be two great possibilities here. Grant

that those of us who call ourselves by your name might be able to transcend our suspicions and fears of our enemies and perceive, as you did, the possibility of faith. No one is outside your love and care.

And, Lord, grant that we might see in every situation the hope of life over death. When disease preys upon a child, or boredom slowly squeezes the life from a body, or loneliness empties the life from our forms, give us a vision of the possibility of life—when you are in our midst.

You, Lord, can make enemies into brothers and weeping into laughter.

30 / MARK 5:25–34

Among them was a woman who had suffered from haemorrhages for twelve years; and in spite of long treatment by many doctors, on which she had spent all she had, there had been no improvement; on the contrary, she had grown worse. She had heard what people were saying about Jesus, so she came up from behind in the crowd and touched his cloak; for she said to herself, "If I touch even his clothes, I shall be cured." And there and then the source of her haemorrhages dried up and she knew in herself that she was cured of her trouble. At the same time Jesus, aware that power had gone out of him, turned round in the crowd and asked, "Who touched my clothes?" His disciples said to him, "You see the crowd pressing upon you and yet you ask, 'Who touched me?'" Meanwhile he was looking round to see who had done it. And the woman, trembling with fear when she grasped what had happened to her, came and fell at his feet and told him the whole truth. He said to her, "My daughter, your faith has cured you. Go in peace, free for ever from this trouble."

She was another unlikely candidate for faith, Lord. A penniless woman who had been taken to the cleaners by the doctors and who was still ailing. Yet in her desperate heart, there were still sparks of faith when she heard people talking about you. Lord, she was a nobody; the disciples could not recognize her in the crowd. Yet you knew the desperation of her heart and saw the flicker of hope. Lord, you are so wanton with your grace and we so niggardly. You are quick to turn fear to faith while we do not hesitate to create fear in order to gain followers. You care for the nobodies; we tend to look for the somebodies.

Lord, like the woman, we go to our doctors. The general practitioner, the orthopedic surgeon, the psychiatrist, and the eye-ear-nose folks—they are honorable for the most part and we are grateful for them. But, Lord, like the woman, we sometimes bleed deep within and no doctor can remove the uncleanness; money is impotent. Remind us, Lord, that we always live with the possibility of your cleansing. Heal us, Lord, and make us unruly in witnessing to your grace to all the other nobodies.

31 / MARK 6:1–6

He left that place and went to his home town accompanied by his disciples. When the Sabbath came he began to teach in the synagogue; and the large congregation who heard him were amazed and said, "Where does he get it from?" and, "What wisdom is this that has been given him?" and, "How does he work such miracles? Is not this

the carpenter, the son of Mary, the brother of James and
Joseph and Judas and Simon? And are not his sisters here
with us?" So they fell foul of him. Jesus said to them, "A
prophet will always be held in honour except in his home
town, and among his kinsmen and family." He could work
no miracle there, except that he put his hands on a few sick
people and healed them; and he was taken aback by their
want of faith.

It must have been a holiday! The local boy who was
reported to be making it big came home, and—whether they
intended to be or not—they are amazed at your wisdom and
power. But, Lord, they knew you too well: "Is not this the
carpenter?" "Don't his sisters and brothers live around
here?" Obviously God could not be working in such a person. In Moses, yes—but he was a somebody, trained in
Pharaoh's house. In David—of course, but he was a king.
But in a carpenter . . . ?

Lord, an enemy like the president of the synagogue or a
stranger like the sick woman could believe; they were desperate and you were their last great hope. But to those who
knew you, you were only a carpenter. Lord, we are more
like the latter group than the former. You are a household
word with us. Your symbols lace our architecture and literature; the Book that speaks of you outsells even *The New
York Times.* What do we expect from one we know so well?
The centuries have dulled our perception and lulled our
expectations into apathy; the Christ talked about in the
churches is like the carpenter: we really don't look for anything much to happen. And so I fear, Lord, that you are
taken aback by our want of faith.

On one of his teaching journeys round the villages he summoned the Twelve and sent them out in pairs on a mission. He gave them authority over unclean spirits, and instructed them to take nothing for the journey beyond a stick: no bread, no pack, no money in their belts. They might wear sandals, but not a second coat. "When you are admitted to a house," he added, "stay there until you leave those parts. At any place where they will not receive you or listen to you, shake the dust off your feet as you leave, as a warning to them." So they set out and called publicly for repentance. They drove out many devils, and many sick people they anointed with oil and cured.

Lord, you trusted those disciples! Even though you had given them private interpretations, it had not apparently helped very much. They were an undistinguished group, to say the least. Yet you gave them the power to restore people to wholeness; they were the symbols of the new Kingdom of twelve tribes; they carried staffs as undershepherds of your people. What honor was given to undeserving souls! But, Lord, that's your mode of operation and we are grateful for it.

Your telling them to travel lightly and depend upon the hospitality of the people is of concern, Lord. Should all of us who are your witnesses give away everything we have except the clothes on our backs? Or, are you saying that the way in which we walk, the way of the cross, must reflect that weakness in which there is strength? What does it mean, Lord, to live in weakness in the contemporary age where even a welfare check makes us strong in comparison to most of the people on earth?

Lord, help us to have one all-consuming passion and that is, to do your will in our time.

33 / MARK 6:14–16

Now King Herod heard of it, for the fame of Jesus had spread; and people were saying, "John the Baptist has been raised to life, and that is why these miraculous powers are at work in him." Others said, "It is Elijah." Others again, "He is a prophet like one of the old prophets." But Herod, when he heard of it, said, "This is John, whom I beheaded, raised from the dead."

Lord, you have a way of troubling our memories. When we hear about you and your work of grace, as with Herod, phantoms from our past begin to wander through the halls of our memory. We each have our John whom we fear will return from the dead to destroy us. Lord, Herod was fascinated with John but did not grasp his message; otherwise he would have recognized you and you are the only one who could have transformed Herod's nightmare into joy. But he only experienced guilt. Lord, though your presence causes us to remember our dark past, grant that our remembrance of your dark day upon the cross may bring us the light of a new day of hope. Free us from crippling guilt that we might join with those who spread your fame.

34 / MARK 6:17–29

For this same Herod had sent and arrested John and put him in prison on account of his brother Philip's wife, Herodias, whom he had married. John had told Herod, "You have no right to your brother's wife." Thus Herodias nursed a grudge against him and would willingly have killed him, but she could not; for Herod went in awe of John, knowing him to be a good and holy man; so he kept him in custody. He liked to listen to him, although the listening left him greatly perplexed.

Herodias found her opportunity when Herod on his birthday gave a banquet to his chief officials and commanders and the leading men of Galilee. Her daughter came in and danced, and so delighted Herod and his guests that the king said to the girl, "Ask what you like and I will give it to you." And he swore an oath to her: "Whatever you ask I will give you, up to half my kingdom." She went out and said to her mother, "What shall I ask for?" She replied, "The head of John the Baptist." The girl hastened back at once to the king with her request: "I want you to give me here and now, on a dish, the head of John the Baptist." The king was greatly distressed, but out of regard for his oath and for his guests he could not bring himself to refuse her. So the king sent a soldier of the guard with orders to bring John's head. The soldier went off and beheaded him in the prison, brought the head on a dish, and gave it to the girl; and she gave it to her mother.

When John's disciples heard the news, they came and took his body away and laid it in a tomb.

Lord, Herod was like so many of us. He had power and position; he appreciated John's simple but good life; he stood in awe of John and listened to him even though he could not accommodate John's words to his own life. He meant no harm to John. But when he was warmed by wine and the sensuous body of a girl, he made a foolish promise. And so, Lord, the surly woman got her way.

Lord, deliver us from mere fascination with faith in you.

How easy it is to appreciate the life of your simple followers; to listen to the words of your witnesses; to mean no harm; even to see ourselves as somehow among those who enjoy the things of faith. But like Herod, Lord, those of us who live on the level of what feels good or looks good are vulnerable in the presence of a person with a grudge.

Enable us, we pray, not to be like Herod or Pilate, who played around with the truth until, suddenly, there was a body to be carried to a tomb.

35 / MARK 6:30–44

The apostles now rejoined Jesus and reported to him all that they had done and taught. He said to them, "Come with me, by yourselves, to some lonely place where you can rest quietly." (For they had no leisure even to eat, so many were coming and going.) Accordingly, they set off privately by boat for a lonely place. But many saw them leave and recognized them, and came round by land, hurrying from all the towns towards the place, and arrived there first. When he came ashore, he saw a great crowd; and his heart went out to them, because they were like sheep without a shepherd; and he had much to teach them. As the day wore on, his disciples came up to him and said, "This is a lonely place and it is getting very late; send the people off to the farms and villages round about, to buy themselves something to eat." "Give them something to eat yourselves," he answered. They replied, "Are we to go and spend twenty pounds on bread to give them a meal?" "How many loaves have you?" he asked; "go and see." They found out and told him, "Five, and two fishes also." He ordered them to make the people sit down in groups on the green grass, and they sat down in rows, a hundred rows of fifty each. Then, taking the five loaves and the two fishes, he looked up to heaven, said the blessing, broke the loaves, and gave them to the disciples to distribute. He also divided the two fishes among them. They all ate to their hearts' content; and twelve great basketfuls of scraps were picked up, with what was left of the fish. Those who ate the loaves numbered five thousand men.

Hunger—Lord, the world is full of hunger. Multitudes will die this very day of hunger, while others will complain that the garbage has only been hauled off once. Hunger—Lord, the world is full of it. We hunger intellectually; we hunger for the beautiful; we hunger for companionship; we hunger for peace in our world and in our souls. We hunger for fame and fortune; we hunger for quietness and solitude. We hunger after righteousness—to be right with our God. I believe it is this hunger, Lord, which is the focus of our story.

Like sheep without a shepherd, we still run after persons, things, and places that might satisfy our hunger. TM, TA, yoga, therapy, scientology, and, Lord, you alone know all the others. How badly we seek someone who will lead us into green pastures and beside still waters. Our souls are restless, Lord, until they feed upon the Bread of Life.

And so in the midst of the assembled congregation, you took bread and broke it and gave to your disciples to give to the people. Lord, are you not saying that you give your broken body, the very Bread of Life, to those who hunger after righteousness?

We are grateful, Lord, for the Bread that feeds our souls, and we are grateful for your commingling the Bread of Life and physical bread. Make us better disciples, Lord, as we learn to share food with the hungry, to feed the bodies of the sick with medicine, to assuage the hunger for work with jobs, to mitigate loneliness with presence. Help us not to despise the myriads of foods with which you grace our world. Of these, there are many leftover full baskets. But also remind us, Lord, that as those first disciples had no bread of their own, not even a topcoat, we have nothing to give to those who hunger after righteousness save the body and blood given for us.

36 / MARK 6:45–52

As soon as it was over he made his disciples embark and cross to Bethsaida ahead of him, while he himself sent the people away. After taking leave of them, he went up the hill-side to pray. It grew late and the boat was already well out on the water, while he was alone on the land. Somewhere between three and six in the morning, seeing them labouring at the oars against a head-wind, he came towards them, walking on the lake. He was going to pass them by; but when they saw him walking on the lake, they thought it was a ghost and cried out; for they all saw him and were terrified. But at once he spoke to them: "Take heart! It is I; do not be afraid." Then he climbed into the boat beside them, and the wind dropped. At this they were completely dumbfounded, for they had not understood the incident of the loaves; their minds were closed.

This time, Lord, they were dumbfounded! Those disciples battling the waves—just doing what you had told them to do—were unaware that you knew their plight and were present with them. When they did perceive your presence and power in their midst, they were terrified and dumbfounded.

Lord, we are quick to condemn those poor disciples. They seem so blind; they did not grasp the meal which affirms your constant presence and power. When the external circumstances changed, they thought you were somewhere else.

But I suspect, Lord, that secretly many of us would like to have some weird experience, some multiplying of bread or calming of the winds, some incontrovertible evidence of your presence and power. Like closed-minded disciples or pagans, we cannot accept your unadorned word: "Take heart! It is I; do not be afraid."

37 / MARK 6:53–56

So they finished the crossing and came to land at Gennesaret, where they made fast. When they came ashore, he was immediately recognized; and the people scoured that whole country-side and brought the sick on stretchers to any place where he was reported to be. Wherever he went, to farmsteads, villages, or towns, they laid out the sick in the market-places and begged him to let them simply touch the edge of his cloak; and all who touched him were cured.

Lord, the disciples may have been terrified by your presence and power, but the sick people weren't. As in the feeding of the multitude, there seems to be a mingling of the spiritual and the physical in this healing. We are grateful for the healing brought about by medical science as an evidence of your grace. But we are also thankful that your grace can bring healing and wholeness to us as persons even while we suffer.

A group of Pharisees, with some doctors of the law who had come from Jerusalem, met him and noticed that some of his disciples were eating their food with "defiled" hands —in other words, without washing them. (For the Pharisees and the Jews in general never eat without washing the hands, in obedience to an old-established tradition; and on coming from the market-place they never eat without first washing. And there are many other points on which they have a traditional rule to maintain, for example, washing of cups and jugs and copper bowls.) Accordingly, these Pharisees and the lawyers asked him, "Why do your disciples not conform to the ancient tradition, but eat their food with defiled hands?" He answered, "Isaiah was right when he prophesied about you hypocrites in these words: 'This people pays me lip-service, but their heart is far from me: their worship of me is in vain, for they teach as doctrines the commandments of men.' You neglect the commandment of God, in order to maintain the tradition of men."

Lord, our religion like theirs is compiled of many habitual forms. Even though we follow you and you rebuked the teachers of the commandments of men, we know that we share the same sin. We engage in lip service also, for there are times when we go to church on Sunday, but do not worship; we bow, but do not pray; we sing, but do not praise; we labor as deacons, but not for your glory; we say grace before eating, but are not grateful. Lord, our drinking habits, our sexual behavior, our patriotism, and our investment procedures—are these controlled by your laws or the laws of men? There seems to be no simple answer, Lord, for over the years, like the Pharisees, our laws and your desires

56

have become commingled. The commandments of God do not stand naked before us, but are only seen through our history-laden eyes. But then, Lord, you never asked us perfectly to interpret the law and you warned of our inability to keep even those portions we do understand. You call, Lord, for singleness of purpose which causes the words of our lips and the intentions of our hearts to coincide in seeking to obey you, to transcend merely the following of the religious patterns we find around and within us. Lead us, Lord, beyond mechanical obedience to intentional service.

39 / MARK 7:9–13

He also said to them, "How well you set aside the commandment of God in order to maintain your tradition! Moses said, 'Honour your father and your mother,' and, 'The man who curses his father or mother must suffer death.' But you hold that if a man says to his father or mother, 'Anything of mine which might have been used for your benefit is Corban'" (meaning, set apart for God), "he is no longer permitted to do anything for his father or mother. Thus by your own tradition, handed down among you, you make God's word null and void. And many other things that you do are just like that."

Lord, we still use religion to get our way. Our desires turn out to be the important matters, even though they are covered with a veneer of gospel. We boast of our church work, but it is to get elected to public office; we labor long hours in the church, because we cannot get along in our own homes; we are regularly at the worship services, because it's good for business to be a law-abiding, churchgoing person. We use our interpretation of the commandments to get our children to behave in a manner pleasing to us. We use our giving to reduce our income tax. A bad temper we call righteous indignation. Repressed sexual desires we label a crusade against pornography. O Lord, help us to slice through it all and get to the heart of the matter. May we not make your word null and void by twisting it to fit our desires, but grant, Lord, that our lives may reflect the desires of your heart.

40 / MARK 7:14–23

On another occasion he called the people and said to them, "Listen to me, all of you, and understand this: nothing that goes into a man from outside can defile him; no, it is the things that come out of him that defile a man."

When he had left the people and gone indoors, his disciples questioned him about the parable. He said to them, "Are you as dull as the rest? Do you not see that nothing that goes from outside into a man can defile him, because it does not enter into his heart but into his stomach and so passes out into the drain?" Thus he declared all foods clean. He went on, "It is what comes out of a man that defiles him. For from inside, out of a man's heart, come evil thoughts, acts of fornication, of theft, murder, adultery, ruthless greed, and malice; fraud, indecency, envy, slander, arrogance, and folly; these evil things all come from inside, and they defile the man."

Lord, as we read these passages, we secretly rejoice, for you are repudiating the religious laws of men. You chastise the false shepherd who leads us into legalism. And, Lord, we don't like to be stifled by so many regulations. We enjoy being free to follow the inclinations of our hearts. But it is just here that you arrest our wandering minds with the reminder that we are judged by you according to the flow from our hearts. It's a shame, Lord, for the heart seems like such a good hiding place. Most of the time we can keep the outside of the self under control, and so we look like Christians and our reputations are in good shape. But deep within us—in that psychic space, that core of the self known as the heart—we mutter words of hatred, we pile up for ourselves great wealth, we engage in sinfully exciting activities upon the screens of our minds, we quietly envy, slander, and even murder.

Be merciful to us, we pray. Help us find cleansing from the inside out. Help us, O Lord, to be those who will to do one thing from the heart, and may that one thing be your will.

41 / MARK 7:24–30

Then he left that place and went away into the territory of Tyre. He found a house to stay in, and he would have liked to remain unrecognized, but this was impossible. Almost at once a woman whose young daughter was possessed by an unclean spirit heard of him, came in, and fell at his feet. (She was a Gentile, a Phoenician of Syria by nationality.) She begged him to drive the spirit out of her daughter. He said to her, "Let the children be satisfied first; it is not fair to take the children's bread and throw it to the dogs." "Sir," she answered, "even the dogs under the table eat the children's scraps." He said to her, "For saying that, you may go home content; the unclean spirit has gone out of your daughter." And when she returned home, she found the child lying in bed; the spirit had left her.

Lord, we know you were sent first to the Jews. It is not so odd that God should choose the Jews. He had to choose someone, for you, Lord, could not come in a vacuum. You had to be a part of a tradition or you would make no sense. We would not have had words, ideas, or pictures with which to understand you otherwise. And so we can comprehend your passion for feeding first the children of Israel.

But, Lord, we confess that it is odd that you should have called that good Gentile woman a dog. There are several characters on the pages of this Gospel for whom that title might have been most appropriate, including some of those law-abiding Pharisees. But for this simple woman, it is troublesome to grasp.

For whatever reason—and I guess we will never know—the woman responded with humility, hope, and faith. And you demonstrated that the love of the Father and his healing powers knew no national or racial boundaries. That lets us know that you intend good for all of us. For this, we are grateful, Lord.

42 / MARK 7:31–37

On his return journey from Tyrian territory he went by way of Sidon to the Sea of Galilee through the territory of the Ten Towns. They brought to him a man who was deaf and had an impediment in his speech, with the request that he would lay his hand on him. He took the man aside, away from the crowd, put his fingers into his ears, spat, and touched his tongue. Then, looking up to heaven, he sighed, and said to him, "Ephphatha," which means "Be opened." With that his ears were opened, and at the same time the impediment was removed and he spoke plainly. Jesus forbade them to tell anyone; but the more he for-

bade them, the more they published it. Their astonishment
knew no bounds: "All that he does, he does well," they
said; "he even makes the deaf hear and the dumb speak."

Such shocking contrasts between the duplicity of the lost
children of Israel and the simplicity of the Gentiles! Such a
disparity between the closeness of the Pharisees and the
openness of the outsiders! Lord, there was such a difference
between the obstacles built by the Jews to protect and purify
their faith and the facility with which you shared the goodness of God. All that you do, you do well.

Lord, help us remember that we are in this generation the
Israel of God and that we are no freer than the Old Israel
from the sins of duplicity and exclusiveness. As those who
have had their ears opened to hear the gospel and their lips
freed to sing, help us to praise you aright with singleness of
purpose.

43 / MARK 8:1–10

There was another occasion about this time when a
huge crowd had collected, and, as they had no food, Jesus
called his disciples and said to them, "I feel sorry for all
these people; they have been with me now for three days
and have nothing to eat. If I send them home unfed, they
will turn faint on the way; some of them have come from
a distance." The disciples answered, "How can anyone
provide all these people with bread in this lonely place?"
"How many loaves have you?" he asked; and they an-
swered, "Seven." So he ordered the people to sit down on
the ground; then he took the seven loaves, and, after
giving thanks to God, he broke the bread and gave it to
his disciples to distribute; and they served it out to the

people. They had also a few small fishes, which he blessed
and ordered them to distribute. They all ate to their hearts'
content, and seven baskets were filled with the scraps that
were left. The people numbered about four thousand.
Then he dismissed them; and, without delay, got into the
boat with his disciples and went to the district of Dalmanu-
tha.

Lord, once again you manifest the abundance of the Father's grace and the call of your disciples to feed the crowds, even the Gentile multitudes. In that lonely place as they ate, the desert rejoiced and blossomed. There are crumbs aplenty flowing from the inexhaustible bounty of the Father. Always there are some left over.

Lord, evangelism is such a rusty old word. Many of us are turned off by slick peddlers of the gospel who have answers for every question. But, Lord, we confess that as your disciples, we are not doing much about feeding the multitudes. Swarms of remedies are offered to the hungry people around us while we who are the church invest too much of our resources in providing for ourselves. Teach us, Lord, as you did those early disciples, so that we may know how to distribute the Bread of Life.

44 / MARK 8:11–13

Then the Pharisees came out and engaged him in discussion. To test him they asked him for a sign from heaven. He sighed deeply to himself and said, "Why does this generation ask for a sign? I tell you this: no sign shall be given to this generation." With that he left them, re-embarked, and went off to the other side of the lake.

The contrast is sharp, Lord, between those who with abandon received your words, were healed and fed, and those who needed more evidence. How easy it is for us to be a part of this group looking for signs! If the Bible is free of errors, that's a sign it's true. If some scientists can argue for missing time, it's a sign the sun stood still. If magic and spooky things can happen, it's a sign of your presence. If we can fall into a state of ecstasy and hear a voice out of the night, then we are sure it is a sign from you. We all ask for signs, Lord, each in our own way. But signs are miracles and there were then and are now miracles all around us, if we have eyes of faith. Lord, we do not ask for signs, but for open eyes to perceive the miracle of your presence and action in our midst.

45 / MARK 8:14–21

Now they had forgotten to take bread with them; they had no more than one loaf in the boat. He began to warn them: "Beware," he said, "be on your guard against the leaven of the Pharisees and the leaven of Herod." They said among themselves, "It is because we have no bread." Knowing what was in their minds, he asked them, "Why do you talk about having no bread? Have you no inkling yet? Do you still not understand? Are your minds closed? You have eyes: can you not see? You have ears: can you not hear? Have you forgotten? When I broke the five loaves among five thousand, how many basketfuls of scraps did you pick up?" "Twelve," they said. "And how many when I broke the seven loaves among four thousand?" They answered, "Seven." He said, "Do you still not understand?"

Lord, we confess that we still do not understand. We, like those other followers, worry about the externals—yes, even in the church. We worry about the family night supper, having good music on Sunday morning; we check the air conditioner and see that the ushers walk in step. We become so preoccupied on this level, Lord, that we forget your concerns. *You* can handle ordinary bread-needs, if *we* will only avoid that leaven of the Pharisees and Herod—that dependence on our religious status and forms, that snug relationship with political power, those demands for signs and proofs, those failures to perceive the real signs of your presence among us, that vain attempt to monopolize your grace. Lord, from such blindness, deafness, and lack of understanding, deliver us and allow us to feed on the Bread as we walk in the way.

46 / MARK 8:22–26

They arrived at Bethsaida. There the people brought a blind man to Jesus and begged him to touch him. He took the blind man by the hand and led him away out of the village. Then he spat on his eyes, laid his hands upon him, and asked whether he could see anything. The man's sight began to come back, and he said, "I see men; they look like trees, but they are walking about." Jesus laid his hands on his eyes again; he looked hard, and now he was cured so that he saw everything clearly. Then Jesus sent him home, saying, "Do not tell anyone in the village."

Lord, how weary you must become—always dealing with blindness: the blindness of the Pharisees with their stubborn hearts; the blindness of your own disciples who try to see, but whose vision is cloudy; the physical blindness that casts a cloak over the radiance of creation. You were sent, Lord, that the eyes of the blind might be opened. We are grateful for your powerful healing. And so take us, we pray, outside the crowd and deal with us individually. Lord, clarify our vision; we still confuse persons and trees. Lord, open our eyes to your presence; enable us to see you clearly and make a good confession; grant us a vision of the way in which we shall walk, even the way of the cross.

47 / MARK 8:27–33

Jesus and his disciples set out for the villages of Caesarea Philippi. On the way he asked his disciples, "Who do men say I am?" They answered, "Some say John the Baptist, others Elijah, others one of the prophets." "And you," he asked, "who do you say I am?" Peter replied: "You are the Messiah." Then he gave them strict orders not to tell anyone about him; and he began to teach them that the Son of Man had to undergo great sufferings, and to be rejected by the elders, chief priests, and doctors of the law; to be put to death, and to rise again three days afterwards. He spoke about it plainly. At this Peter took him by the arm and began to rebuke him. But Jesus turned round, and, looking at his disciples, rebuked Peter. "Away with you, Satan," he said; "you think as men think, not as God thinks."

As though to check on the vision of your disciples, Lord, you ask that question: "Who do you say I am?" The answers of other people are always there. We can quote the theologians, the common people, the mystics, the liberal, or what have you. Answers are everywhere, like dust, settling over our consciousness, making it difficult to shake free and offer our own word of confession. Our heads are filled with impressions, ideas, terms, and traditions. Who are you, Lord? The one whose name is used for cursing? The one pictured in Sunday school literature as a sad, sick-looking man? The one to whom we sing and in whose name we pray? The one whom scholars write about and simple people adore? That sense of presence that lurks just beyond the fringe of our conscious thoughts and fantasies? Like Peter, Lord, we know you are anointed of the Father to do his will. And like Peter we are unprepared for the Messiah to be one who suffers, is rejected, and finally killed. Power, victory, majesty—these belong to the Messiah, not weakness, death, and disgrace. We will not have it so, for look what it does to us.

Lord, free us from Satan's blinding power, even as you did Peter, so that we can perceive the real nature of your mission among us. Help us see, Lord, that a good confession leads to the way of the cross.

48 / MARK 8:34 to 9:1

Then he called the people to him, as well as his disciples, and said to them, "Anyone who wishes to be a follower of mine must leave self behind; he must take up his cross, and come with me. Whoever cares for his own safety is lost; but if a man will let himself be lost for my sake and for the Gospel, that man is safe. What does a man gain by winning the whole world at the cost of his true self? What can he give to buy that self back? If anyone is ashamed of me and mine in this wicked and godless age, the Son of Man will be ashamed of him, when he comes in the glory of his Father and of the holy angels."

He also said, "I tell you this: there are some of those

*standing here who will not taste death before they have
seen the kingdom of God already come in power."*

For those first readers, this must have been sobering,
Lord. If they were not ashamed of your name, if they openly
followed your way, not their own, then they could count on
facing physical death. The line was clearly drawn and many
who stepped across were thrown to the lions.

There have been, and maybe still are, those who seek to
leave themselves behind and follow you by denying themselves any of the luxuries of life and even some of the
necessities. But, Lord, frequently their lives are preoccupied
with themselves—always worrying and working to be sure
they deny themselves something. Their cross is their own
personhood.

Lord, if we confess your name publicly, we are not
thrown to lions, though if we seek to be obedient in all our
living, it is inevitable that we will go against the grain of the
masses. It is not popular to fight for the oppressed; basic
honesty in business and government appears to be foreign
to most; the sacredness of marriage is a joke to many; the
use of our monies is focused on us and our desires.

And yet, Lord, in each generation there are those who do
not taste of death before they experience the redeeming and
transforming power of your saving love. Give us, we pray,
the courage to take up the cross—whatever it is that needs
to be done in order that your will becomes manifestly clear
on earth—and thus follow you unashamedly.

Six days later Jesus took Peter, James, and John with him and led them up a high mountain where they were alone; and in their presence he was transfigured; his clothes became dazzling white, with a whiteness no bleacher on earth could equal. They saw Elijah appear, and Moses with him, and there they were, conversing with Jesus. Then Peter spoke: "Rabbi," he said, "how good it is that we are here! Shall we make three shelters, one for you, one for Moses, and one for Elijah?" (For he did not know what to say; they were so terrified.) Then a cloud appeared, casting its shadow over them, and out of the cloud came a voice: "This is my Son, my Beloved; listen to him." And now suddenly, when they looked around, there was nobody to be seen but Jesus alone with themselves.

Lord, your words about taking up the cross come to us with devastating seriousness. Perhaps that is the reason the apostle quickly tells us of the transfiguration. For, Lord, unless we are convinced that you are the fulfillment and completion of the Law and the Prophets, we dare not follow you. They call upon us for more than we can manage. Unless, Lord, we have some mountaintop experience which enables us to realize that there are dimensions of reality that ordinarily remain unnoticed, we dare not follow you. We need empowering beyond human limits. Unless, Lord, we hear the voice of the Father, our feeble limbs will not move.

And so you gave just these experiences to Peter, James, and John, who, in turn, followed you even unto death. This testimony you have now given to us, this witness to your mission is now ours, this glimpse of the invisible realities surrounding earthly actualities we see also. The words of the Father are addressed to us. So with grateful hearts, we live with confidence in you and your work, aware of your presence while enmeshed in the mundane realities of life, comforted and challenged by the voice of the Father.

50 / MARK 9:9–13

On their way down the mountain, he enjoined them not to tell anyone what they had seen until the Son of Man had risen from the dead. They seized upon those words, and discussed among themselves what this "rising from the dead" could mean. And they put a question to him: "Why do our teachers say that Elijah must come first?" He replied, "Yes, Elijah does come first to set everything right. Yet how is it that the scriptures say of the Son of Man that he is to endure great sufferings and to be treated with contempt? However, I tell you, Elijah has already come and they have worked their will upon him, as the scriptures say of him."

Lord, this entire section unsettles our routine version of reality. When men of old appear and the Father speaks from the clouds, our nets of human words and concepts are too full of holes to trap the reality that is here. No matter how we interpret these words, Lord, something happened, the radiance of which revealed the poverty of words and ideas. Though those early disciples had just looked upon Moses and Elijah, they still could not assimilate the meaning of rising from the dead. Lord, neither have we. Like them, we are wooden, pedantic, literalistic, unimaginative—we fail to see the Elijah whom you send. We try to force you into our mold for the Messiah. We cannot comprehend life on any other plane than the one we know now. But, Lord, since you were able to dilate the eyes of those early followers, granting them visions of the Kingdom, we are confident that you can do so even for such culturally conditioned people as we. And for this, we offer our prayers of thanksgiving.

51 / MARK 9:14–29

When they came back to the disciples they saw a large crowd surrounding them and lawyers arguing with them. As soon as they saw Jesus the whole crowd were overcome with awe, and they ran forward to welcome him. He asked them, "What is this argument about?" A man in the crowd spoke up: "Master, I brought my son to you. He is possessed by a spirit which makes him speechless. Whenever it attacks him, it dashes him to the ground, and he foams at the mouth, grinds his teeth, and goes rigid. I asked your disciples to cast it out, but they failed." Jesus answered: "What an unbelieving and perverse generation! How long shall I be with you? How long must I endure you? Bring him to me." So they brought the boy to him; and as soon as the spirit saw him it threw the boy into convulsions, and he fell on the ground and rolled about foaming at the mouth. Jesus asked his father, "How long has he been like this?" "From childhood," he replied; "often it has tried to make an end of him by throwing him into the fire or into water. But if it is at all possible for you, take pity upon us and help us." "If it is possible!" said Jesus. "Everything is possible to one who has faith." "I have faith," cried the boy's father; "help me where faith falls short." Jesus saw then that the crowd was closing in upon them, so he rebuked the unclean spirit. "Deaf and dumb spirit," he said, "I command you, come out of him and never go back!" After crying aloud and racking him fiercely, it came out; and the boy looked like a corpse; in fact, many said,

"He is dead." But Jesus took his hand and raised him to his feet, and he stood up.

Then Jesus went indoors, and his disciples asked him privately, "Why could not we cast it out?" He said, "There is no means of casting out this sort but prayer."

With these words, we reenter our frame of reference, Lord, for spirits are still clutching the throats of our children. There are countless numbers who ruin their minds with drugs, sell their bodies for the perverted pleasures of others, split their souls and smash their bones seeking a good time, following the demons of our society. We make them empty shells, robots who fit the inane round of fashionable activity: they go mad, pulled on too many sides by our inconsistencies. Yes, Lord, from childhood, we watch the spirits work on our children—and we weep.

Like the father, Lord, we turn to you, hardly knowing for what to ask. We look to you, but keep an eye on the welfare workers, the psychiatrists, and the new medications, for we know, Lord, you use many means in subduing the chaos. But through it all, help our faith as we confess its limits and weakness.

But most of all, Lord, we sympathize with those disciples. How badly your followers, including us, want to do good. People still turn to your church with their children, in their pain. And how impotent we are. The world rolls on and, so far as we can see, the church causes little or no ripple. Children around the world foam at the mouth and fall into fire and water, and we seem so helpless. Lord, help us hear your words; keep us from trying to turn prayer into a recharging apparatus that will make us strong and famous. Remind us that your prayer in the wilderness was a pitched battle with Satan and your prayer in the Garden brought drops of blood and death. Help us, Lord, to learn the mean-

71

ing of prayer so that we might become vessels of your power
for the healing of the children.

52 / MARK 9:30–37

They now left that district and made a journey through
Galilee. Jesus wished it to be kept secret; for he was teach-
ing his disciples, and telling them, "The Son of Man is now
to be given up into the power of men, and they will kill
him, and three days after being killed, he will rise again."
But they did not understand what he said, and were afraid
to ask.

So they came to Capernaum; and when he was indoors,
he asked them, "What were you arguing about on the
way?" They were silent, because on the way they had
been discussing who was the greatest. He sat down, called
the Twelve, and said to them, "If anyone wants to be first,
he must make himself last of all and servant of all." Then
he took a child, set him in front of them, and put his arm
round him. "Whoever receives one of these children in my
name," he said, "receives me; and whoever receives me,
receives not me but the One who sent me."

Again, Lord, you sound that theme—the reversal of all our
expectations as to how God's anointed ought to work. You
allude to the mystery of resurrection, and we are afraid to
ask. What does it mean when your God causes the stan-
dards, the criteria, the guidelines of the world to undergo
drastic reversals? What does it mean when being great is
defined as coming in last, of being a servant to all, of receiving the innocent and harmless? We just don't think that way,
Lord. To be last in our graduating class, lowest person in the
organizational scheme and salary scale, to be the janitor, not

the president—this is contrary to our nature. Being served is a sign of success for us, Lord, not the other way around. When people answer the phone and the door for us, drive our cars for us, make our travel plans for us, stand up for us when we enter the room—then we are somebody! Instead, Lord, you tell us to turn and care for the mentally retarded, the folks who do not know right from wrong, the innocent, the weak, the harmless, not the bank presidents, the chairmen of the boards, and the senators if we want to have fellowship with you and the Father who sent you. The ways of the world are riveted to our souls and govern our living. The way of the cross must be the way of death and resurrection, Lord, if we are to die to these and live in your light. We are afraid to ask what it all means, Lord. Give us courage, we pray.

53 / MARK 9:38–41

John said to him, "Master, we saw a man driving out devils in your name, and as he was not one of us, we tried to stop him." Jesus said, "Do not stop him; no one who does a work of divine power in my name will be able the next moment to speak evil of me. For he who is not against us is on our side. I tell you this: if anyone gives you a cup of water to drink because you are followers of the Messiah, that man assuredly will not go unrewarded.

Most of us, Lord, lack John's zeal. We see others working in your name and pay them no attention. The Pentecostals in their storefront churches, the Episcopalians in their quaint cathedrals, the solemn Romans, and the noisy Baptists—none of these folks bother us. We are proud of our tolerance, Lord, which may really be indifference. But then there

73

are others who have and even now do kill because "he was not one of us." How jealous we can be; how arrogantly we assume the rightness of our approach; how deeply suspicious are we that no one else really quite has it all together as well as we do. Resident within our hearts are the seeds of divisiveness as well as the possibility of indifference. Lord, grant us the grace to see that we do not walk alone in the way of the cross, but are accompanied by others who follow the Messiah and enable us to share with them the cup that you have provided for us.

54 / MARK 9:42–48

"As for the man who is a cause of stumbling to one of these little ones who have faith, it would be better for him to be thrown into the sea with a millstone round his neck. If your hand is your undoing, cut it off; it is better for you to enter into life maimed than to keep both hands and go to hell and the unquenchable fire. And if your foot is your undoing, cut it off; it is better to enter into life a cripple than to keep both your feet and be thrown into hell. And if it is your eye, tear it out; it is better to enter into the kingdom of God with one eye than to keep both eyes and be thrown into hell, where the devouring worm never dies and the fire is not quenched.

Lord, what does one do to cause one of your little ones to stumble, the little ones who trust in you with childlike simplicity and beauty? Do we teach them false doctrine? Should we not raise questions about the accuracy or historicity of certain portions of Scripture? Lord, we know that doctrine, even beliefs about the Bible, though important, do not open the doors to the Kingdom. Causing a little one to stumble must have to do with the breaking of trust. Something we do with our hands or our feet or our eyes—something we as persons do to or with others that shakes their confidence in your followers and thus in you—is what causes the stumbling. No wonder you advised the drastic measure of cutting off the hand or plucking out the eye, Lord, for we can become the occasion for another's straying from you. We are terrified, Lord, at the seriousness of the life to which you call us. Being a disciple in our day is more like a cultural decoration than a matter of life or death; it is more like water than blood; it is both/and, not either/or. Help us, Lord, to count the cost before setting out upon the way of the cross.

55 / MARK 9:49–50

"For everyone will be salted with fire.

"Salt is a good thing; but if the salt loses its saltness, what will you season it with?

"Have salt in yourselves; and be at peace with one another."

The life of the believer, Lord, is sprinkled with salty fire. Life in your service is not a casual matter but an earnest witness to your love. To show mercy to the poor and oppressed, to mourn with those who sorrow, to associate with the meek, to hunger and thirst to see the right prevail, to be pure in heart—this is the saltiness that adds seasoning to life. To show understanding, to share concerns of others, to go the second mile—this is the salt, Lord, that preserves and enhances the peace of your community of faith. To be salty disciples is our prayer, O Lord.

*On leaving those parts he came into the regions of Ju-
daea and Transjordan; and when a crowd gathered round
him once again, he followed his usual practice and taught
them. The question was put to him: "Is it lawful for a man
to divorce his wife?" This was to test him. He asked in
return, "What did Moses command you?" They answered,
"Moses permitted a man to divorce his wife by note of
dismissal." Jesus said to them, "It was because your minds
were closed that he made this rule for you; but in the
beginning, at the creation, God made them male and female. For this reason a man shall leave his father and
mother, and be made one with his wife; and the two shall
become one flesh. It follows that they are no longer two
individuals: they are one flesh. What God has joined together, man must not separate."*

*When they were indoors again the disciples questioned
him about this matter; he said to them, "Whoever divorces
his wife and marries another commits adultery against her:
so too, if she divorces her husband and marries another,
she commits adultery."*

Lord, how clearly you have delineated the issues: written
rules are given concerning divorce because we are so unteachable; the intent of the Father is to join man and woman
together for good. But, Lord, we do separate what God has
joined together. By the writing of many rules, we make
divorce easy and frequent. By our lack of will to love, the
absence of the courage to make love work, we break with
the pattern of creation and the Father's intention. Some,
Lord, even drift from body to body as though by a mysterious transformation they will become one with their new
partner. We are so unteachable, Lord, though your word is

clear to your disciples. Unfortunately, Lord, we also know that simply living together does not make two individuals one flesh or eliminate the possibilities of adultery. All of us, Lord, need your grace so that we can be both forgiven and taught by you. We need your mercy, Lord, lest marriage be only the first step toward divorce rather than the opportunity for joy and love.

57 / MARK 10:13–16

They brought children for him to touch. The disciples rebuked them, but when Jesus saw this he was indignant, and said to them, "Let the children come to me; do not try to stop them; for the kingdom of God belongs to such as these. I tell you, whoever does not accept the kingdom of God like a child will never enter it." And he put his arms round them, laid his hands upon them, and blessed them.

Lord, what good news is wrapped in these words about children. After stretching our souls with the rigorous demands of discipleship and the cost of following you, you make it clear that even children can enter the Kingdom. The apostles tried to drive them away, for in your day children were nobodies. They were not carried to piano lessons, ballet practice, and Little League. Youth was not idolized; children had no status. There being no welfare state, they were totally dependent upon the family, trusting those who had given them life, open to be molded and shaped, responding to touch and love. Lord, what does it mean to accept the Kingdom as a child? Is it not to love the Father; to trust without the supporting structures of reason; to be open with confidence toward the future; to respond to God's love with simple pleasure and gratitude? But, Lord, the layers of our adulthood smother our simple trust. Our hard-earned degrees, our absorption of twentieth-century culture, our dealing with the necessities of life, our preoccupation with both the serious issues of our world and the trivia we deem important—all of these make it difficult to start over again, to be reborn, to be like a child. Enable us, we pray, to trust you, to use our imaginations for the sake of the Kingdom, and grant us the ability to play. We are thankful, Lord, that what is impossible for us, is possible for you. Though we are the least, nobodies, when it comes to fulfilling the law and meeting all of the demands of the Kingdom, you put your arm around us, lay hands upon us, and bless us.

58 / MARK 10:17-22

As he was starting out on a journey, a stranger ran up, and, kneeling before him, asked, "Good Master, what must I do to win eternal life?" Jesus said to him, "Why do you call me good? No one is good except God alone. You know the commandments: 'Do not murder; do not commit adultery; do not steal; do not give false evidence; do not defraud; honour your father and mother.' " "But, Master," he replied, "I have kept all these since I was a boy." Jesus looked straight at him; his heart warmed to him, and he said, "One thing you lack; go, sell everything you have, and give to the poor, and you will have riches in heaven; and come, follow me." At these words his face fell and he went away with a heavy heart; for he was a man of great wealth.

Lord, that man who ran up to you as you were starting out on the journey was better than most of the folks you encountered then and now. Lord, he seems to have known who you were, for he knelt; he called you "Good Master." He knew and honored the commandments of the Father. Lord, you did not rebuke him for stubbornness, blindness, or hardness of heart; instead, you obviously felt affection for him and cared for him. But when you told him to become as a child—to give away his wealth, to lose his power and position, to become a nobody—he could not do it.

Lord, the truth is that none of us is able to become a child and simply follow you on the road of the cross. Our possessions, family names, goodly heritages, education, significant religious experiences, positions, and titles—we cannot give these up and merely trust in you.

We are grateful, Lord, that what is impossible for us is possible for God.

59 / MARK 10:23–27

Jesus looked round at his disciples and said to them, "How hard it will be for the wealthy to enter the kingdom of God!" They were amazed that he should say this, but Jesus insisted, "Children, how hard it is to enter the kingdom of God! It is easier for a camel to pass through the eye of a needle than for a rich man to enter the kingdom of God." They were more astonished than ever, and said to one another, "Then who can be saved?" Jesus looked at them and said, "For men it is impossible, but not for God; everything is possible for God."

As your early disciples were amazed by your words, so, Lord, are we. Maybe we are even more astonished, if the truth of the words manages to sink beneath the surface of our hearts. For most of us, Lord, are rich in some way when compared to the peoples of the earth. Being rich, we are supposed to find it difficult, yea, impossible to be a part of your Kingdom. Lord, we know a few folks who go around looking for opportunities to suffer, who are enticed by the dream of martyrdom, whose self-sacrificing makes everybody around them miserable. Lord, we do not want to live by hallucinations, but we do need a miracle—the miracle of your grace that can make rich people like us poor; a miracle that can enable us to become children in your sight. We praise you, Lord, that just such a miracle has been wrought on our behalf.

60 / MARK 10:28–31

At this Peter spoke. "We here," he said, "have left everything to become your followers." Jesus said, "I tell you this: there is no one who has given up home, brothers or sisters, mother, father or children, or land, for my sake and for the Gospel, who will not receive in this age a hundred times as much—houses, brothers and sisters, mothers and children, and land—and persecutions besides; and in the age to come eternal life. But many who are first will be last and the last first."

Because we are also disciples, Lord, these words push us to take stock. Are we those who go beyond the law to the intention of the Father? Are we like children, making no claims for ourselves? Do we hold on to our possessions and families in such a way that we are hindered in our following the Master? Can we say, "We here have left everything to become your follower"? Lord, there is no way that we can give ourselves new hearts and reverse our old natures. But neither, Lord, can we sit back and place the burden all on

you. So help us, Lord, as we join our brothers and sisters on
the pilgrim road to experience the last as first and the first
as last, to thus share in the creative purposes of our God who
is making all things new. Begin, Lord, with us.

61 / MARK 10:32–34

*They were on the road, going up to Jerusalem, Jesus
leading the way; and the disciples were filled with awe;
while those who followed behind were afraid. He took the
Twelve aside and began to tell them what was to happen
to him. "We are now going to Jerusalem," he said; "and
the Son of Man will be given up to the chief priests and
the doctors of the law; they will condemn him to death
and hand him over to the foreign power. He will be
mocked and spat upon, flogged and killed; and three days
afterwards, he will rise again."*

It is still awesome, Lord, to realize that you unflinchingly
led the way to Jerusalem, knowing, as you did, what awaited
you there. Lord, we have no way of knowing the secrets of
your inner life and, therefore, are haunted by questions: Did
you really understand that death and resurrection were
yours? Were you filled with terror and deluded by dreams?
It makes no difference now; the testimony is before us: you
were governed by the Father's will and with steadfastness
you led the way to Jerusalem. Lord, we gather to worship,
we read the Scriptures, we sing and pray as we seek to fall
into step with you who walked the way of the cross. Help
us, we pray, when we fall behind for fear; grant that we
might be filled with awe as we follow the pioneer and per-
fecter of our faith.

*James and John, the sons of Zebedee, approached him
and said, "Master, we should like you to do us a favour."
"What is it you want me to do?" he asked. They answered,
"Grant us the right to sit in state with you, one at your right
and the other at your left." Jesus said to them, "You do not
understand what you are asking. Can you drink the cup
that I drink, or be baptized with the baptism I am baptized
with?" "We can," they answered. Jesus said, "The cup
that I drink you shall drink, and the baptism I am baptized
with shall be your baptism; but to sit at my right or left is
not for me to grant; it is for those to whom it has already
been assigned."*

*When the other ten heard this, they were indignant with
James and John. Jesus called them to him and said, "You
know that in the world the recognized rulers lord it over
their subjects, and their great men make them feel the
weight of authority. That is not the way with you; among
you, whoever wants to be great must be your servant, and
whoever wants to be first must be the willing slave of all.
For even the Son of Man did not come to be served but
to serve, and to give up his life as a ransom for many."*

Lord, even as you talk about what you must endure in
fulfilling the Father's will, we who are your disciples want to
make certain that we have some position and status in the
Kingdom. There is even a scent of victory at this point in the
story and in the distance we can hear the choirs sing, "Lord
of lords and King of kings." We want to be somebody in that
Kingdom. We want to be recognized for our piety, our
knowledge of the Scriptures, our moving religious experiences, our good works, and maybe even our humility. This
will give us a little authority, the chance to lord it over

someone. We even think we have the ability to drink your cup and undergo your baptism. How subtle is the temptation for those who follow you. Lord, deliver us from the foolishness of thinking that the miseries of life are the cup we are to drink. Free us from the notion that baptism into your death is giving up something or practicing self-rejection. Remake us, Lord, so that we willingly serve all and trust the Father to make the assignments of honor.

63 / MARK 10:46–52

They came to Jericho; and as he was leaving the town, with his disciples and a large crowd, Bartimaeus son of Timaeus, a blind beggar, was seated at the roadside. Hearing that it was Jesus of Nazareth, he began to shout, "Son of David, Jesus, have pity on me!" Many of the people told him to hold his tongue; but he shouted all the more, "Son of David, have pity on me." Jesus stopped and said, "Call him"; so they called the blind man and said, "Take heart; stand up; he is calling you." At that he threw off his cloak, sprang up, and came to Jesus. Jesus said to him, "What do you want me to do for you?" "Master," the blind man answered, "I want my sight back." Jesus said to him, "Go; your faith has cured you." And at once he recovered his sight and followed him on the road.

Lord, all of us who are called by your name are like the early disciples: we find it impossible to reverse that natural pattern of life, to be like children, to leave all for you, to be the slave of all. No wonder Mark writes of Bartimaeus: the blind are not hopeless if they can cry, "Jesus, have pity on me." Though we are told that this is a sign of weakness, a refusal to take responsibility for our own lives and situations, a neurotic projection, a meaningless phrase, . . . like Bartimaeus, we shout all the more: "Son of David, have pity on us." We cry because we know you are seeking us. We take heart and turn to you, because you have called us. Renew our sight constantly, Lord, so that we may truly see and understand your call to service and join you on the road.

64 / MARK 11:1–11

They were now approaching Jerusalem, and when they reached Bethphage and Bethany, at the Mount of Olives, he sent two of his disciples with these instructions: "Go to the village opposite, and, just as you enter, you will find tethered there a colt which no one has yet ridden. Untie it and bring it here. If anyone asks, 'Why are you doing that?' say, 'Our Master needs it, and will send it back here without delay.' " So they went off, and found the colt tethered to a door outside in the street. They were untying it when some of the bystanders asked, "What are you doing, untying that colt?" They answered as Jesus had told them, and were then allowed to take it. So they brought the colt to Jesus and spread their cloaks on it, and he mounted. And people carpeted the road with their cloaks, while others spread brushwood which they had cut in the fields; and those who went ahead and the others who came behind shouted, "Hosanna! Blessings on him who comes in the name of the Lord! Blessings on the coming kingdom of our father David! Hosanna in the heavens!"

He entered Jerusalem and went into the temple, where he looked at the whole scene; but, as it was now late, he went out to Bethany with the Twelve.

Lord, when you entered the city, truly the coming of the Kingdom was at hand. God's presence would no longer be associated solely with a building or a town. Your presence, Lord, was and is to be found among the meek and your power in the humble. No wonder the priests and scholars of the Law did not come out to greet you. No wonder the gates of the city were not lifted up when the King of glory entered. You, Lord, were destroying the old and creating the new. As in Bethlehem long before, simple folk like shepherds took note of your coming and hosannas were sung by unknown choirs. Lord, forgive us when we tie your presence to some aspect of our tradition—some special place, a building or an object. Grant us the awareness of your presence at all times and in all places, even within what the world calls the meek and the humble.

65 / MARK 11:12-14, 20-25

On the following day, after they had left Bethany, he felt hungry, and, noticing in the distance a fig-tree in leaf, he went to see if he could find anything on it. But when he came there he found nothing but leaves; for it was not the season for figs. He said to the tree, "May no one ever again eat fruit from you!" And his disciples were listening.

Early next morning, as they passed by, they saw that the fig-tree had withered from the roots up; and Peter, recalling what had happened, said to him, "Rabbi, look, the fig-tree which you cursed has withered." Jesus answered them, "Have faith in God. I tell you this: if anyone says to this mountain, 'Be lifted from your place and hurled into the sea,' and has no inward doubts, but believes that what *he says is happening, it will be done for him. I tell you, then, whatever you ask for in prayer, believe that you have received it and it will be yours.*

"And when you stand praying, if you have a grievance against anyone, forgive him, so that your Father in heaven may forgive you the wrongs you have done."

The tree, Lord, was like the temple; it was without fruit. People could come and go, offer sacrifices, share in the service, but somehow the fruitful relation with the Father was no longer nurtured. The season had arrived for a new way, the way of faith and prayer. We are thankful this day, Lord, that you have bestowed on us the gift of faith, enabled us to trust and have confidence in the Father. Lord, we long to exercise the gift you have given us as we pray and forgive one another, so that our forms of worship will not be empty and our lives fruitless. And, Lord, since we acknowledge that our faith is weak and that we do have inward doubts, we are grateful that you pray in and through us by your Spirit, so that even the mountain of our sin does not prevent our being accepted by the Father and that through your faithfulness we are prompted to forgive one another even as you have forgiven us.

66 / MARK 11:15–19

So they came to Jerusalem, and he went into the temple and began driving out those who bought and sold in the temple. He upset the tables of the money-changers and the seats of the dealers in pigeons; and he would not allow anyone to use the temple court as a thoroughfare for carrying goods. Then he began to teach them, and said, "Does not Scripture say, 'My house shall be called a house of

prayer for all the nations'? But you have made it a robbers'
cave." The chief priests and the doctors of the law heard
of this and sought some means of making away with him;
for they were afraid of him, because the whole crowd was
spellbound by his teaching. And when evening came he
went out of the city.

Lord, we are still in danger of making temples, sanctuaries, or churches into robbers' caves, places where we can retreat for safety after performing all manner of evil out in the world. By your teaching, Lord, you sought to dispel this notion, change the places of worship from exclusive hideouts to occasions when people from all the nations would unite in prayer, trusting in the Father and forgiving one another. Lord, I guess we still need sanctuaries, places to remind us and others of your presence and our privilege of prayer, though we no longer need the sacrifices, for you have taken care of this. Lord, deliver us from misusing special places, else they will wither and become fruitless.

67 / MARK 11:27–33

They came once more to Jerusalem. And as he was
walking in the temple court the chief priests, lawyers, and
elders came to him and said, "By what authority are you
acting like this? Who gave you authority to act in this
way?" Jesus said to them, "I have a question to ask you
too; and if you give me an answer, I will tell you by what
authority I act. The baptism of John: was it from God, or
from men? Answer me." This set them arguing among
themselves: "What shall we say? If we say, 'from God,' he
will say, 'Then why did you not believe him?' Shall we say,
'from men'?"—but they were afraid of the people, for all

held that John was in fact a prophet. So they answered, "We do not know." And Jesus said to them, "Then neither will I tell you by what authority I act."

They had a right to ask you that question, Lord. You were tearing down the Temple, opening the door for all people to come freely to the Father and to find the power to forgive one another. By what authority were you transforming the religion of the fathers? And, Lord, your answer to them and to us still holds true. The authority of God's Messiah is recognized only by those who are willing to hear your messengers like John and obey. Your authority is not seen by timid people who fear the crowds and reject the call to repentance. Do not tell us, Lord, by what authority you have worked good for all men; let us sense it as we obey your word and follow you.

68 / MARK 12:1–12

He went on to speak to them in parables: "A man planted a vineyard and put a wall round it, hewed out a winepress, and built a watch-tower; then he let it out to vine-growers and went abroad. When the season came, he sent a servant to the tenants to collect from them his share of the produce. But they took him, thrashed him, and sent him away empty-handed. Again, he sent them another servant, whom they beat about the head and treated outrageously. So he sent another, and that one they killed; and many more besides, of whom they beat some, and killed others. He had now only one left to send, his own dear son. In the end he sent him. 'They will respect my son,' he said. But the tenants said to one another, 'This is the heir; come on, let us kill him, and the property will be ours.' So they seized him and killed him, and flung his body out of the vineyard. What will the owner of the vineyard do? He will come and put the tenants to death and give the vineyard to others.

"Can it be that you have never read this text: 'The stone which the builders rejected has become the main cornerstone. This is the Lord's doing, and it is wonderful in our eyes'?"

Then they began to look for a way to arrest him, for they saw that the parable was aimed at them; but they were afraid of the people, so they left him alone and went away.

Lord, we also must submit to your authority or be counted among those who put you to death. We either accept you as the cornerstone of God's temple, the way into the presence of the Father, or reject you as a fraud. Lord, we either acknowledge that you are the owner of the vineyard, the church which is indeed your possession, or turn away to look for another master. Lord, forgive us when we live as though the church belongs to us, as though it should satisfy our needs and serve our purposes. Help us, Lord, to submit to the authority of the one whose obedience to the Father brought goodness and life to your people. Lord, do not take the good news away from us, and thus put us to death, but grant us the ability to be faithful servants in your vineyard all the days of our lives.

69 / MARK 12:13–17

A number of Pharisees and men of Herod's party were sent to trap him with a question. They came and said, "Master, you are an honest man, we know, and truckle to no one, whoever he may be; you teach in all honesty the

way of life that God requires. Are we or are we not permit-
ted to pay taxes to the Roman Emperor? Shall we pay or
not?" He saw how crafty their question was, and said,
"Why are you trying to catch me out? Fetch me a silver
piece, and let me look at it." They brought one, and he
said to them, "Whose head is this, and whose inscription?"
"Caesar's," they replied. Then Jesus said, "Pay Caesar
what is due to Caesar, and pay God what is due to God."
And they heard him with astonishment.

Lord, they came to provoke words from you so that they
might accuse you of a crime. Those who owned the vineyard, who considered themselves the protectors of the
church and the Father's truth, were determined that you
would not tear the temple down and open the doors to all
people. Like us, Lord, they were proud of their interpretations of the Scriptures, their traditions, their patterns of worship and living. And you, Lord, then and now, make people
like us nervous. We need to neutralize you, if not get rid of
you, by becoming entangled in a debate. If you are really
spiritual and loyal to the fathers, you will not tell us to stoop
to the mundane and sordid activities of politics and tax
payments. But if on the other hand, Lord, you are against
such, you demonstrate a lack of patriotism and maybe even
treason. How nice it is to debate these matters and never
decide whom we shall obey! But you know, Lord, we carry
the coin of the realm and thus implicitly have already acknowledged the rule of Caesar. And you know also, Lord,
that if we are forced to decide the ownership of all that we
have—our churches, our homes, down to the last penny—
you know, that our duty to the state pales by comparison,
though it may not be unimportant. You know, Lord, because
you acknowledged the sovereignty of the Father and
obeyed, giving your all, even your life in obedience.

Lord, may we have the grace to obey the Father who has given us both the church and the state, and even life itself.

70 / MARK 12:18–27

Next Sadducees came to him. (It is they who say that there is no resurrection.) Their question was this: "Master, Moses laid it down for us that if there are brothers, and one dies leaving a wife but no child, then the next should marry the widow and carry on his brother's family. Now there were seven brothers. The first took a wife and died without issue. Then the second married her, and he too died without issue. So did the third. Eventually the seven of them died, all without issue. Finally the woman died. At the resurrection, when they come back to life, whose wife will she be, since all seven had married her?" Jesus said to them, "You are mistaken, and surely this is the reason: you do not know either the scriptures or the power of God. When they rise from the dead, men and women do not marry; they are like angels in heaven.

"But about the resurrection of the dead, have you never read in the Book of Moses, in the story of the burning bush, how God spoke to him and said, 'I am the God of Abraham, the God of Isaac, and the God of Jacob'? God is not God of the dead but of the living. You are greatly mistaken."

Lord, when we hear talk of the resurrection or of life after death, there are times when the drug of indifference deadens our response. We seem to care little one way or the other. But there are times when life is bitter and wearisome and we almost hope that death will in fact bring the whole venture to a grinding halt. Then again, Lord, we cannot imagine the tenderness of personal bonds ever ceasing nor dream of the love of our children evaporating. Maybe we are like the Sadducees: we think about the reality of resurrection in terms of human sentimentality or speculative logic, nor in terms of the power of the Father and the truth of the Scriptures. Lord, we too are mistaken if we miss the possibility of transformation which will lift us beyond the web of earthly marriage laws and all the rest; which will even transcend space and time to make Abraham and Jacob our contemporaries. We are grateful, Lord, that we are among those whom the living God remembers and cares for, and therefore we know that we also have life eternal.

71 / MARK 12:28–34

Then one of the lawyers, who had been listening to these discussions and had noted how well he answered, came forward and asked him, "Which commandment is first of all?" Jesus answered, "The first is, 'Hear, O Israel: the Lord our God is the only Lord; love the Lord your God with all your heart, with all your soul, with all your mind, and with all your strength.' The second is this: 'Love your neighbour as yourself.' There is no other commandment greater than these." The lawyer said to him, "Well said, Master. You are right in saying that God is one and beside him there is no other. And to love him with all your heart, all your understanding, and all your strength, and to love your neighbour as yourself—that is far more than any burnt offerings or sacrifices." When Jesus saw how sensibly he answered, he said to him, "You are not far from the kingdom of God."

Lord, how strange it is that two persons could agree on the essence of the faith and yet be found in opposing camps. You and that lawyer believed that the sum of what the God who loves us requires is that we love him with our total being and express this undivided allegiance in relationships here on earth. Both of you believed that such love and action were far superior to mere forms of worship. And still you were in separate groups, though each of you loved the other as you loved yourself and thus demonstrated that you both loved God.

Lord, give us the grace to discover even among our so-called enemies those who are seeking to respond to your love by loving you and neighbor. Give us, Lord, some breadth of meaning to the word "neighbor." And do not leave us merely not far from the Kingdom, but enable us to trust the One who has fulfilled the law and who can enable us to love aright within the Kingdom.

72 / MARK 12:35–37

After that nobody ventured to put any more questions to him; and Jesus went on to say, as he taught in the temple, "How can the teachers of the law maintain that the Messiah is 'Son of David'? David himself said, when inspired by the Holy Spirit, 'The Lord said to my Lord, "Sit at my right hand until I put your enemies under your feet." ' David himself calls him 'Lord'; how can he also be David's son?"

Lord, it is not altogether clear to me what you are saying in these words. Are you telling us that the Messiah must be the Son of God as well as the Son of David? Are you suggesting that "Son of David" may mean something other than a fleshly descendant? Whatever it is, Lord, it is clear that even those of us who rely on the Scriptures can be blind to your truth, for the Messiah was present with those early listeners, the Son of David was wrestling with his enemies and functioning as God's priest, and they did not see it. Lord, grant us the gifts of imagination and receptiveness as we read and study the Scriptures. Deliver us from the darkness and poverty that accompanies those who are convinced that their system unlocks the Scriptures. Grant, Lord, that we might be unlocked by your Word.

73 / MARK 12:38–40

There was a great crowd and they listened eagerly. He said as he taught them, "Beware of the doctors of the law, who love to walk up and down in long robes, receiving respectful greetings in the street; and to have the chief seats in synagogues, and places of honour at feasts. These are the men who eat up the property of widows, while they say long prayers for appearance' sake, and they will receive the severest sentence."

And so, Lord, you sound the warning once more against the keepers of the vineyards. It makes some of us uncomfortable, for we are leaders among your people; we wear the garments of leadership and are treated with deference as we are greeted. We are, Lord, offered seats up front both in church and on other occasions. To be appreciated and respected is not contrary to our nature, Lord. It is still true, Lord, that while we engage in ritualistic activities, even long prayers, someone acting on our behalf can be robbing the widow and taking the property of the helpless. Now as then, it can all be done legally and quietly so that we continue to look respectable and even pious. Yes, Lord, for appearance' sake, we not only dress, speak, and pray in given fashions, we even enjoy it. But now in dialogue with this word, Lord, we remember your condemnation of hypocrisy, shallowness, and lack of integrity among those who claim to be leaders of your people. You pointed your finger at this lack of obedience while you were obediently on your way to the cross. Help us, Lord, to be cross-bound followers above all else and find our strength to lead in your victory and presence.

74 / MARK 12:41–44

Once he was standing opposite the temple treasury, watching as people dropped their money into the chest. Many rich people were giving large sums. Presently there came a poor widow who dropped in two tiny coins, together worth a farthing. He called his disciples to him. "I tell you this," he said: "this poor widow has given more than any of the others; for those others who have given had more than enough, but she, with less than enough, has given all that she had to live on."

Lord, you have taught us that all that looks good and righteous on the outside may not be so on the inside. The appearance of obedience and faithful actions from the heart may be two different things. So, Lord, with money. Large offerings, if gained by robbing widows and given as an impressive show, do not amount to a hill of beans in your sight. But the smallest gift, offered in such a fashion as to leave the giver dependent upon you for life, those coins rejoice the hearts of the angels. Whether our gifts be large or small, help us to give in such fashion, Lord, that our giving becomes a symbol of our dependence upon you for life itself. This we pray in the name of the One who gave his life that we might live abundantly.

75 / MARK 13:1–8

As he was leaving the temple, one of his disciples exclaimed, "Look, Master, what huge stones! What fine buildings!" Jesus said to him, "You see these great buildings? Not one stone will be left upon another; all will be thrown down."

When he was sitting on the Mount of Olives facing the temple he was questioned privately by Peter, James, John, and Andrew. "Tell us," they said, "when will this happen? What will be the sign when the fulfilment of all this is at hand?"

Jesus began: "Take care that no one misleads you. Many will come claiming my name, and saying, 'I am he'; and many will be misled by them.

"When you hear the noise of battle near at hand and the news of battles far away, do not be alarmed. Such things are bound to happen; but the end is still to come. For nation will make war upon nation, kingdom upon kingdom; there will be earthquakes in many places; there will be famines. With these things the birth-pangs of the new age begin.

By using that fig tree, Lord, you have already pointed to the withering of the old system. With all its majesty and beauty, not one stone has been left upon another; you laid to rest that vast structure which had become a stumbling block. But, Lord, despite all you have done, we sense that the warfare is not yet over. The good and the evil still do battle in our lives and in the world. When will it happen, Lord, that this struggle will be over? When will it happen that a person can live without fighting within himself, attracted by evil one moment and lured by rightness the next? When will it happen that the demonic will no longer possess us, will cease corrupting our systems and poisoning our interpersonal relations? When will it happen, Lord?

We know you are not going to answer us, Lord, any more than you answered those four disciples long ago. We will go on with the personal, corporate, and institutional struggles that intersect in our particular life space, being cautious lest we invest too much hope in some new movement, idea, person, or group. We cannot live detached lives, Lord, so help lest we be misled and follow some new messiah.

Lord, in our time we have heard the noise of battle and witnessed the tragedy of earthquake and famine, but the signs of the end are not the important ones. You, Lord, ushered in the new age with your death and resurrection and you promised there is yet more to come. Though we cannot bring in your yet-to-be-completed work, grant that as we live in the confidence of your Lordship, our very lives may become parables and symbols of the new age as we faithfully watch and work.

76 / MARK 13:9–13

"As for you, be on your guard. You will be handed over to the courts. You will be flogged in synagogues. You will be summoned to appear before governors and kings on my account to testify in their presence. But before the end the Gospel must be proclaimed to all nations. So when you are arrested and taken away, do not worry beforehand about

what you will say, but when the time comes say whatever
is given you to say; for it is not you who will be speaking,
but the Holy Spirit. Brother will betray brother to death,
and the father his child; children will turn against their
parents and send them to their death. All will hate you for
your allegiance to me; but the man who holds out to the
end will be saved.

Even though you have not told us when your victory will
be made evident to all people, Lord, you have outlined our
calling in the meanwhile with clarity. We are to bear witness
in reliance upon the Holy Spirit before the powerful in the
religious, political, and economic realms of life. Lord, we are
to be loyal to you even though it causes divisions within the
family circle. We are thankful, Lord, for those faithful ones
who have lived before us and who bore the good testimony
in the face of the Hitlers, the unjust laws, the destructiveness
of wars, and the victimizing of the weak. In our own time,
Lord, help us as individuals and as the church to know when
to bear witness by word and deed, whether in the halls of
power or in the circle of the family. We acknowledge, Lord,
that not a one of us would have the courage to try, save for
the certainty of the testimony of the risen One, in whose
name we work and pray.

77 / MARK 13:14–23

"But when you see 'the abomination of desolation'
usurping a place which is not his (let the reader understand), then those who are in Judaea must take to the hills.
If a man is on the roof, he must not come down into the
house to fetch anything out; if in the field, he must not turn
back for his coat. Alas for women with child in those days,

and for those who have children at the breast! Pray that it may not come in winter. For those days will bring distress such as never has been until now since the beginning of the world which God created—and will never be again. If the Lord had not cut short that time of troubles, no living thing could survive. However, for the sake of his own, whom he has chosen, he has cut short the time.

"Then, if anyone says to you, 'Look, here is the Messiah,' or, 'Look, there he is,' do not believe it. Imposters will come claiming to be messiahs or prophets, and they will produce signs and wonders to mislead God's chosen, if such a thing were possible. But you be on your guard; I have forewarned you of it all.

Some of us secretly feel like those early Christians who experienced the fall of Jerusalem that we have lived through the abomination of desolation. In the short span of our lives we have seen the atom bomb used on human beings; psychological and germ warfare are part of the script; genetic manipulation, Catholic against Protestant, Christians killing Moslems, corruption in government and business—all stand as omens. We would flee, Lord, but there is no place to hide. We would claim a new savior for our insane world, but they all have clay feet.

Remind us, Lord, that the King of Peace has come and will in some fashion come yet again. The time will come because it has come—for your Kingdom is among us though not fully seen or felt. So we go on living, Lord, with hope and confidence, though we see through the maze of current chaos darkly.

"But in those days, after that distress, the sun will be darkened, the moon will not give her light; the stars will come falling from the sky, the celestial powers will be shaken. Then they will see the Son of Man coming in the clouds with great power and glory, and he will send out the angels and gather his chosen from the four winds, from the farthest bounds of earth to the farthest bounds of heaven.

For many of us, Lord, life just moves along. We get up and go to work; we enjoy a little social life; we frequent the church; we go to weddings and funerals; we eat and sleep; we worry and cry—and life moves along. Smothered beneath it all, we forget that when you died, the heavens were darkened, the fallen star Satan lost his ultimate grip on human life, and the principalities and powers—those superhuman ideologies, corporations, structures, and the like—lost their absolute claim on us and we were freed because of the power and glory embodied in you. We forget, Lord, that you have promised to come again, to gather your chosen from all levels of existence. We forget, Lord, because we daily live with it, how much of creation does not acknowledge your Lordship. Grant us this day a clearer vision of your power and a certain grasp of the fact that every knee shall bow and every tongue shall confess that you are the Christ, to the glory of the Father.

"Learn a lesson from the fig-tree. When its tender shoots appear and are breaking into leaf, you know that summer is near. In the same way, when you see all this happening, you may know that the end is near, at the very door. I tell you this: the present generation will live to see it all. Heaven and earth will pass away; my words will never pass away.

Sometimes as we share in your ministry, Lord, the realities of life around us crowd out the signs of your presence and power. Sometimes even in the church, maybe especially there, the routine and the ordinary dull our perception of the new age in our midst. So how helpful are these words—the lesson of the fig tree. The tender shoots appear in what seems to be the continuing cycle of nature, but they also point to the certainty of your victory. As generations come and go, programs emerge and subside, people cry and laugh —in all that seems so much like the regular cycle of nature —help us to internalize your words which will never pass away: you are at the door! We have lived long enough to see the Father's redemption through the crucified Christ. This has altered the scene, and given us confidence in your coming again.

So, Lord, will you this day renew our courage and hope by enabling us to perceive the signs of your redemptive presence and your final triumph?

"But about that day or that hour no one knows, not even the angels in heaven, not even the Son; only the Father.

"Be alert, be wakeful. You do not know when the moment comes. It is like a man away from home: he has left his house and put his servants in charge, each with his own work to do, and he has ordered the door-keeper to stay awake. Keep awake, then, for you do not know when the master of the house is coming. Evening or midnight, cockcrow or early dawn—if he comes suddenly, he must not find you asleep. And what I say to you, I say to everyone: Keep awake."

Waiting for you, Lord? It hardly seems so. From time to time a few nuts gather outside Chicago or on the flats of Arizona, but most of us do not look skyward for your return. We are more like those servants who, because the Master had been gone so long, assumed they owned the place and no one was coming for an accounting.

Waiting for you, Lord? Yes, maybe so. Since we all have our work to do, we are waiting for you this morning as we begin our day. We are waiting for some new glimmer of your presence, some word of direction, some confirming experience, some excitement in our work—yes, I guess we are always waiting for you to emerge from among the activities to which you have called us.

We realize we must be careful, Lord, else we fall into the trap of asking for signs and looking for words when your Word is enough. But in the time that you have given us to live, we do want to use it wisely. We want to be faithful to the work you have given us to do; and we do want to live with joy. May this be our kind of waiting.

Now the Festival of Passover and Unleavened Bread was only two days off; and the chief priests and the doctors of the law were trying to devise some cunning plan to seize him and put him to death. "It must not be during the festival," they said, "or we should have rioting among the people."

We have been reflecting on the beginning of the Gospel, Lord, and now we come to the end of the beginning, the taking up of the cross. Lord, it's your story, but it was done for us and you have told us that we also must walk in the way of the cross. And who, Lord, is cunningly devising crosses today? Could it be those same defenders of the church, the proclaimers of the Law, the protectors of the heritage? Since you, Lord, have warned us not to chase quickly after each new fad or movement as though the Messiah had come, we tend to be protective of the heritage, repeating the safe interpretations of the fathers, and defending our rituals and institutions. Can we, Lord, have become creators of crosses rather than those who bear crosses?

Lord, be the discomforting guest when we gather as the church lest we devise cunning plans that will hurt others. And give us strength to face the crosses that might be devised by others for us.

82 / MARK 14:3–9

Jesus was at Bethany, in the house of Simon the leper. As he sat at table, a woman came in carrying a small bottle of very costly perfume, pure oil of nard. She broke it open and poured the oil over his head. Some of those present said to one another angrily, "Why this waste? The perfume might have been sold for thirty pounds and the money given to the poor"; and they turned upon her with fury. But Jesus said, "Let her alone. Why must you make trouble for her? It is a fine thing she has done for me. You have the poor among you always, and you can help them whenever you like; but you will not always have me. She has done what lay in her power; she is beforehand with anointing my body for burial. I tell you this: wherever in all the world the Gospel is proclaimed, what she has done will be told as her memorial."

While the leaders plotted and Judas betrayed, this unknown woman, Lord, gracefully anointed you for burial. Your willingness to give yourself for her, caused her to give what she could. Lord, may we not spend our time bickering over church budgets, but free us as you did her to act spontaneously out of love for you. May your powerful gentleness defend us as it did her when we act in response to you, when we from time to time are freed from the necessity of calculating the cost. We know, Lord, that it cannot always be this way; most of the time we must plan carefully, count the cost, and act circumspectly. But for this memorial, this work of art wrought in a leper's home, we are thankful.

83 / MARK 14:10–11

Then Judas Iscariot, one of the Twelve, went to the chief priests to betray him to them. When they heard what he had come for, they were greatly pleased, and promised him money; and he began to look for a good opportunity to betray him.

Yes, Lord, one of the Twelve helped arrange for your death! How could that be? Had he not walked and talked with you? Had he not eaten at the same table with you? Had he not been rescued from the raging sea by you and had he not seen you feed the multitude? Yes, and we have lived to see all of these as well as twenty centuries of your grace at work in our world. And still, Lord, like Judas, we betray you. How could he do it? We know, Lord, we know how. But, unlike Judas, we have lived to hear your forgiving word.

84 / MARK 14:12–16

Now on the first day of Unleavened Bread, when the Passover lambs were being slaughtered, his disciples said to him, "Where would you like us to go and prepare for your Passover supper?" So he sent out two of his disciples with these instructions: "Go into the city, and a man will meet you carrying a jar of water. Follow him, and when he enters a house give this message to the householder: 'The Master says, "Where is the room reserved for me to eat the Passover with my disciples?"' He will show you a large room upstairs, set out in readiness. Make the preparations for us there." Then the disciples went off, and when they came into the city they found everything just as he had told them. So they prepared for Passover.

Lord, the way of obedience you have patterned for us suggests that not all the plans are made by our enemies or the spontaneous acts of friends. You, Lord, took the initiative and made some of the plans that paved the way to the cross. You, Lord, moved with decisiveness "on the first day of Unleavened Bread, when the Passover lambs were being slaughtered." You, Lord, moved within the tradition of the people, though you had in mind some new meaning.

We are grateful, Lord, that the Father knows how to weave together the acts of our enemies, extemporaneous deeds of love, and our own efforts into a tapestry that reflects his will.

85 / MARK 14:17–31

In the evening he came to the house with the Twelve. As they sat at supper Jesus said, "I tell you this: one of you will betray me—one who is eating with me." At this they were dismayed; and one by one they said to him, "Not I, surely?" "It is one of the Twelve," he said, "who is dipping into the same bowl with me. The Son of Man is going the way appointed for him in the scriptures; but alas for that man by whom the Son of Man is betrayed! It would be better for that man if he had never been born."

During supper he took bread, and having said the blessing he broke it and gave it to them, with the words: "Take this; this is my body." Then he took a cup, and having offered thanks to God he gave it to them; and they all drank from it. And he said, "This is my blood of the covenant, shed for many. I tell you this: never again shall I drink from the fruit of the vine until that day when I drink it new in the kingdom of God."

After singing the Passover Hymn, they went out to the Mount of Olives. And Jesus said, "You will all fall from your faith; for it stands written: 'I will strike the shepherd down and the sheep will be scattered.' Nevertheless, after I am raised again I will go on before you into Galilee." Peter answered, "Everyone else may fall away, but I will not." Jesus said, "I tell you this: today, this very night, before the cock crows twice, you yourself will disown me three times." But he insisted and repeated: "Even if I must die with you, I will never disown you." And they all said the same.

This passage makes us uncomfortable, Lord, for it is frightening to know that you know all of us will and do deny you. You know better than we, Lord, that each of us falls from our faith and has within us the ability to betray you. We do not want to deny you, Lord, let alone betray, but then we seem so clumsy and blind in living out the call to discipleship.

Lord, we confess that we are not as strong in our affirmations as those early disciples. We do not hear your followers talk about dying for you rather than disowning you. The world in which we live does not seem interested in forcing us to deny you, at least not verbally. There are no lions' dens waiting for us and no militant atheists or cruel churchmen threatening to put us on the rack. There is only the subtle erosion of familiarity, gentility, and apathy. I suspect, Lord, more of us die each year trying to have a good time than from almost any other cause. For that we will give our lives.

Yet, Lord, amazingly you went ahead and you go ahead even now and serve them and us the meal. You promised to lead them and us into the world even though all of us deny you. Knowing our proclivity for falling away, we live by the hope, Lord, that you will hold on to us. So grant that in our time as we celebrate the Eucharist, we may feed upon the Bread of Life and be strengthened for the pilgrimage of those who follow the way of the cross.

When they reached a place called Gethsemane, he said to his disciples, "Sit here while I pray." And he took Peter and James and John with him. Horror and dismay came over him, and he said to them, "My heart is ready to break with grief; stop here, and stay awake." Then he went forward a little, threw himself on the ground, and prayed that, if it were possible, this hour might pass him by. "Abba, Father," he said, "all things are possible to thee; take this cup away from me. Yet not what I will, but what thou wilt."

He came back and found them asleep; and he said to Peter, "Asleep, Simon? Were you not able to keep awake for one hour? Stay awake, all of you; and pray that you may be spared the test. The spirit is willing, but the flesh is weak." Once more he went away and prayed. On his return he found them asleep again, for their eyes were heavy; and they did not know how to answer him.

The third time he came and said to them, "Still sleeping? Still taking your ease? Enough! The hour has come. The Son of Man is betrayed to sinful men. Up, let us go forward! My betrayer is upon us."

After the feast, Lord, your journey was to a quiet place where alone you had to struggle. Even your closest friends did not realize the agony of your soul which was like dying while still living. They were dulled by sleep to your struggle with the cup of blood. They were resting while you were wrestling with the will of the Father and the fate of mankind. They missed the moment of the betrayal and the hatred that came from the hands of sinners. They slept during your inner battle and, therefore, later they could not understand your calmness in the face of the enemy. We live in places where the helicopter chops awkwardly above, where the sound of the jet makes muted thunder, where the steady roar of traffic never dies, where the groaning bulldozer whines as it tears down or builds up. Yet it is here that we must wrestle with life-and-death seriousness with the realities of the new covenant, with the Father's will over against our will, with the works of hate and the way of love—and do it all without resentment or fear.

Fortunately for us, Lord, you went the way of the cross before us so that our struggles in our Gethsemanes are colored by that battle which you won in the solitary acreage of your heart. Your victory makes ours a possibility. Therefore grant, Lord, that this day we may deal with the Father alone so that we might be faithful to him in the crowd.

87 / MARK 14:43–52

Suddenly, while he was still speaking, Judas, one of the Twelve, appeared, and with him was a crowd armed with swords and cudgels, sent by the chief priests, lawyers, and elders. Now the traitor had agreed with them upon a signal: "The one I kiss is your man; seize him and get him safely away." When he reached the spot, he stepped forward at once and said to Jesus, "Rabbi," and kissed him. Then they seized him and held him fast.

One of the party drew his sword, and struck at the High Priest's servant, cutting off his ear. Then Jesus spoke: "Do you take me for a bandit, that you have come out with swords and cudgels to arrest me? Day after day I was within your reach as I taught in the temple, and you did not lay hands on me. But let the scriptures be fulfilled." Then the disciples all deserted him and ran away.

Among those following was a young man with nothing

*on but a linen cloth. They tried to seize him; but he slipped
out of the linen cloth and ran away naked.*

At your moment of testing, Lord, you were prepared.
Having exposed your soul to the Father, you were now
conformed to his will. You became transparent so that the
working of the Father could become evident. We are grateful, Lord, for your obedience, through which we live.

That you did not lash out in bitterness toward Judas, nor
scold the sleepy followers, nor ridicule the one who fled
naked, gives us hope, Lord. For we are sluggish in reading
the signs of the times and are often unaware of what the
Father is doing. We occasionally swing swords and clubs on
your behalf, as though your enemies should be fought on
that level. And Lord, our commitment sometimes hangs
loosely upon us, so that the slightest tug by the enemy leaves
us retreating naked.

And so, Lord, we do not offer you our perfect lives, nor
our unshakable faith, for they are lacking. But like the early
followers, we know that your preparation, your obedience,
your life and your death were for us. You have not abandoned us, but redeemed us, and so we find courage and joy
in our efforts to serve.

88 / MARK 14:53–65

*Then they led Jesus away to the High Priest's house,
where the chief priests, elders, and doctors of the law were
all assembling. Peter followed him at a distance right into
the High Priest's courtyard; and there he remained, sitting
among the attendants, warming himself at the fire.*

*The chief priests and the whole Council tried to find
some evidence against Jesus to warrant a death-sentence,*

but failed to find any. Many gave false evidence against him, but their statements did not tally. Some stood up and gave false evidence against him to this effect: "We heard him say, 'I will pull down this temple, made with human hands, and in three days I will build another, not made with hands.'" But even on this point their evidence did not agree.

Then the High Priest stood up in his place and questioned Jesus: "Have you no answer to the charges that these witnesses bring against you?" But he kept silence; he made no reply.

Again the High Priest questioned him: "Are you the Messiah, the Son of the Blessed One?" Jesus said, "I am; and you will see the Son of Man seated at the right hand of God and coming with the clouds of heaven." Then the High Priest tore his robes and said, "Need we call further witnesses? You have heard the blasphemy. What is your opinion?" Their judgement was unanimous: that he was guilty and should be put to death.

Some began to spit on him, blindfolded him, and struck him with their fists, crying out, "Prophesy!" And the High Priest's men set upon him with blows.

Lord, you moved from the Garden and your drowsy friends to the council and your alert enemies. One wonders about those rulers of the church: Were they really jealous of your popularity? Were they frightened by your kind of obedience? Were they genuinely seeking to be loyal to the Father? We question their motives and actions, yet, Lord, you made no accusations about illegal procedures or petty purposes. In silence you listened to their frustrating efforts to manufacture charges.

And when the moment came, you yourself, Lord, gave them what they wanted. You acknowledged with clarity your identity, knowing they could not grasp the truth, but would seize upon your words. You remained faithful to the decision anguishingly wrought out in the Garden and thus brought forth their fists and spit.

As the one we are to follow, you have set the pace. Lord, help us grasp with firmness our sonship and our calling so that we might not waste words answering empty charges, but endure in the silence of inner peace. Lord, help us to realize our sonship and actualize our calling so that when the moment comes, we can also identify ourselves as children of God and face the consequences of having a part in your redemptive mission.

89 / MARK 14:66–72

Meanwhile Peter was still below in the courtyard. One of the High Priest's serving-maids came by and saw him there warming himself. She looked into his face and said, "You were there too, with this man from Nazareth, this Jesus." But he denied it: "I know nothing," he said; "I do not understand what you mean." Then he went outside into the porch; and the maid saw him there again and began to say to the bystanders, "He is one of them"; and again he denied it.

Again, a little later, the bystanders said to Peter, "Surely you are one of them. You must be; you are a Galilean." At this he broke out into curses, and with an oath he said, "I do not know this man you speak of." Then the cock crew a second time; and Peter remembered how Jesus had said to him, "Before the cock crows twice you will disown me three times." And he burst into tears.

Lord, there was a second trial under way, for while you stood before the leaders of the church, Peter was confronted by a waitress. Lord, your simple affirmation of truth brought condemnation upon you while Peter's lie got him off free. Words with clear meaning are contrasted with repeated, stormy curses. Peter did not know his place in the Father's will as you did, and so he denied you and lost his identity.

And so we ask about our own denial. In what ways and under what circumstances do we deny you? Our scenes of denial are not in the formal courtrooms, the church meetings, or even in open encounters with non-Christians. Our denials come in our daily round of life—maybe with the use of our money when we buy stocks, maybe in our social attitudes and sexist biases. We would not say, Lord, that there have not been those times when we openly denied your Lordship by some foolish act or hateful word, but most of the time our denials are linked to the small particles that compose an average day. Like dust, our denials settle over all our living—sometimes noticed and wiped clean—but mostly clinging unseen and unobserved.

Now, Lord, our knowledge of Freud and his followers bothers us. We also know the story of our Puritan heritage with its work ethics and all the rest. We know, Lord, that our unique past can shape our consciences and cause us to feel guilty about all manner of things that do not necessarily concern you. And so we wrestle, Lord, with our efforts to be obedient and our own tendencies to feel guilty.

And yet there seems to be a place for tears for those who follow the way of the cross—tears that flow not from self-pity but because we know we have denied you as we have wandered through the courtyards of our daily lives. The tears are made more bitter, Lord, because we know that by your faithfulness and consistency, our faithlessness and inconsistency can be transformed. Like Peter, we are not damned. But we weep, Lord, because we hurt the one who loves us.

90 / MARK 15:1–5

As soon as morning came, the chief priests, having made their plan with the elders and lawyers in full council, put Jesus in chains; then they led him away and handed him over to Pilate. Pilate asked him, "Are you the king of the Jews?" He replied, "The words are yours." And the chief priests brought many charges against him. Pilate questioned him again: "Have you nothing to say in your defence? You see how many charges they are bringing against you." But, to Pilate's astonishment, Jesus made no further reply.

It is an old story, Lord. We've been plagued by this uneasy alliance between state and church in every generation. The "statesman" who seeks popular support by giving the mindless crowd its way is not new. The masses chanting destructive slogans, fomented by cunning and jealous ecclesiastical leaders, is part of an ancient script. Soldiers join in the mockery to break their boredom. Lord, we are not sure whether we should despise more passionately the feebleness of the politician or the false shepherd in the church. And still the alliance continues to be formed—not openly or formally, but it is nevertheless effective and damning. The innocent are still being victimized.

Lord, it is even more painful to realize that the disciples were not there. They knew you best; they were your loyal friends. And yet the power of the alliance caused them to flee. And where were your friends in Germany when Hitler formed such an alliance? Where are your followers here in the United States when justice is flouted and children go hungry? By our actions as well as our inactivity we confess that we are often a part of the destructive mob or else in hiding.

So, Lord, it was for our sin as well as theirs that you died. And because you endured it all in imposing silence, we know we are forgiven. Like Pilate, we are amazed.

91 / MARK 15:6–15

At the festival season the Governor used to release one prisoner at the people's request. As it happened, the man known as Barabbas was then in custody with the rebels who had committed murder in the rising. When the crowd appeared asking for the usual favour, Pilate replied, "Do you wish me to release for you the king of the Jews?" For he knew it was out of malice that they had brought Jesus before him. But the chief priests incited the crowd to ask him to release Barabbas rather than Jesus. Pilate spoke to them again: "Then what shall I do with the man you call king of the Jews?" They shouted back, "Crucify him!" "Why, what harm has he done?" Pilate asked; but they shouted all the louder, "Crucify him!" So Pilate, in his desire to satisfy the mob, released Barabbas to them; and he had Jesus flogged and handed him over to be crucified.

Lord, he tried. Old Pilate made an effort three different times to declare you innocent, but the very people who claimed a special relationship with the Father, who assumed some insight into his will and ways, who longed for a Messiah—these very people, Lord, cried for your destruction. It makes us uncomfortable, for both the politicians and the churchmen were—and I fear are still—guilty; but the church persons are doubly so.

On the face of it, Lord, Barabbas seems to be the only one who profited by the spinelessness and spiritual blindness of the others. He has become a parable, Lord, reminding us that were it not for your death, we who deserve to die would surely do so.

And so we wonder about Barabbas and about us, Lord. Did he and do we realize what happened? To whom did he and do we give thanks: to the crowd or to the Father? What was life like afterward for him—and for us? Did it for him, and does it for us, make a difference? Did he and do we grow accustomed to living without the penalty of death weighing heavily upon us? Did he and do we forget that we have been redeemed by another's life?

Grant, O Lord, that sure confidence in your grace may not lead us to forgetfulness, but may we always live in remembrance of Him.

92 / MARK 15:16–20

Then the soldiers took him inside the courtyard (the Governor's headquarters) and called together the whole company. They dressed him in purple, and plaiting a crown of thorns, placed it on his head. Then they began to salute him with, "Hail, King of the Jews!" They beat him about the head with a cane and spat upon him, and then knelt and paid mock homage to him. When they had finished their mockery, they stripped him of the purple and dressed him in his own clothes.

Lord, it may be that when we read these words we should think of the hymn: "Must Jesus Bear the Cross Alone?" Or perhaps, Lord, we should recall those words of Paul's about making up in our bodies that which is lacking of your sufferings. But the truth is that our attention is arrested by your suffering, not ours. When you were in the church court before the High Priest, they blindfolded you, spat on you, struck you, and called upon you to prophesy. Then in the legal arena, Lord, you were ridiculed by soldiers who dressed you like a king, put a crown upon your head, knelt down and called you King of the Jews. They intended, Lord, to speak lies in jest; but their words bore testimony to the truth. They sought to humiliate you, not knowing that by so wounding you, we would be healed.

93 / MARK 15:21–39

Then they took him out to crucify him. A man called Simon, from Cyrene, the father of Alexander and Rufus, was passing by on his way in from the country, and they pressed him into service to carry his cross.

They brought him to the place called Golgotha, which means "Place of a skull." He was offered drugged wine, but he would not take it. Then they fastened him to the cross. They divided his clothes among them, casting lots to decide what each should have.

The hour of the crucifixion was nine in the morning, and the inscription giving the charge against him read, "The king of the Jews." Two bandits were crucified with him, one on his right and the other on his left.

The passers-by hurled abuse at him: "Aha!" they cried, wagging their heads, "you would pull the temple down, would you, and build it in three days? Come down from the cross and save yourself!" So too the chief priests and lawyers jested with one another: "He saved others," they said, "but he cannot save himself. Let the Messiah, the king of Israel, come down now from the cross. If we see that, we shall believe." Even those who were crucified with him taunted him.

At midday a darkness fell over the whole land, which lasted till three in the afternoon; and at three Jesus cried aloud, "Eli, Eli, lema sabachthani?" *which means, "My God, my God, why hast thou forsaken me?" Some of the bystanders, on hearing this, said, "Hark, he is calling Elijah." A man ran and soaked a sponge in sour wine and held it to his lips on the end of a cane. "Let us see," he said, "if Elijah will come to take him down." Then Jesus gave a loud cry and died. And the curtain of the temple was torn in two from top to bottom. And when the centurion who was standing opposite him saw how he died, he said, "Truly this man was a son of God."*

The reading of these words evokes both depression and hope in us, Lord. They show how completely and profoundly our world is twisted and bent. Blind and stupid men ridiculed the King of Heaven in a courtyard while fools and frightened men inhabited palaces. Your disciples who had vowed to die for you fled, so a passing stranger was made to carry your cross. Thieves were given to the Lord of Lords as companions in death while crude men railed and erudite churchmen mocked as their Savior silently died for them.

No wonder the Father brought darkness over the scene, Lord. It was a moment of triumph for the powers of darkness. No personal or corporate corruption was omitted as the kingdom of evil hurled its full array of forces against the King of Peace and the Lord of Light. Even unto this day,

Lord, when we use only our natural eyes, it appears that the powers of darkness still are having their way. Evil permeates us and distorts our world.

But there was more going on that day amid the darkness. The Father's will was taking place. They were not just thieves; you, Lord, were being numbered among the transgressors. You, Lord, were offered drink and the casting of lots—both fulfilled an ancient word. Even the mockery verified that the Father was in control. Dark it was, Lord, but the curtain was torn and the door opened to the Father's presence and grace. Dark it was, Lord, when you cried, "My God, why have you forsaken me?" But your crying that prayer in obedience to the Father enables us to know that you are with us always. Yes, Lord, evil is depressing, but our hope is even stronger, for we know that truly you—"this man"—were and are the Son of God.

94 / MARK 15:40 to 16:8*

A number of women were also present, watching from a distance. Among them were Mary of Magdala, Mary the mother of James the younger and of Joseph, and Salome, who had all followed him and waited on him when he was in Galilee, and there were several others who had come up to Jerusalem with him.

By this time evening had come; and as it was Preparation-day (that is, the day before the Sabbath), Joseph of Arimathaea, a respected member of the Council, a man who looked forward to the kingdom of God, bravely went in to Pilate and asked for the body of Jesus. Pilate was

*I am accepting this point as the conclusion of the Gospel, as do certain ancient texts and recent versions.

surprised to hear that he was already dead; so he sent for the centurion and asked him whether it was long since he died. And when he heard the centurion's report, he gave Joseph leave to take the dead body. So Joseph bought a linen sheet, took him down from the cross, and wrapped him in the sheet. Then he laid him in a tomb cut out of the rock, and rolled a stone against the entrance. And Mary of Magdala and Mary the mother of Joseph were watching and saw where he was laid.

When the Sabbath was over, Mary of Magdala, Mary the mother of James, and Salome bought aromatic oils intending to go and anoint him; and very early on the Sunday morning, just after sunrise, they came to the tomb. They were wondering among themselves who would roll away the stone for them from the entrance to the tomb, when they looked up and saw that the stone, huge as it was, had been rolled back already. They went into the tomb, where they saw a youth sitting on the right-hand side, wearing a white robe; and they were dumbfounded. But he said to them, "Fear nothing; you are looking for Jesus of Nazareth, who was crucified. He has been raised again; he is not here; look, there is the place where they laid him. But go and give this message to his disciples and Peter: 'He will go on before you into Galilee; there you will see him, as he told you.'" Then they went out and ran away from the tomb, beside themselves with terror. They said nothing to anybody, for they were afraid.

Lord, there is something about this ending that we like. Its authenticity strikes a chord in us. It is restrained and yet ultimately inscrutable. Those sad women in the shadows waiting to do their deeds of mercy with heavy hearts; that Jewish nobleman who stepped forward in the face of danger to do what somebody ought to have had the decency to do;

that stone which no longer blocked the entrance; that messenger with simple words—no fanfare, no trumpets, no spooks or hocus-pocus—simply the announcement that you were not in the tomb but ahead of them in the city.

Lord, I'm glad Mark was honest enough to tell us that they were afraid. Following you is fearful business, for you won't stay where we put you; you are always moving on ahead of us. You will not remain enshrined in our theological formulas or our ecclesiastical structures. What are you doing out there beyond us? We are not certain where you are in the world and precisely how we are to follow you. We grope as in the dim light of dawn as we seek to follow you. We do not actually know what you are doing in Vietnam, in Ireland, on Forty-second Street, in the ghettos of Chicago, in Underground Atlanta, in church courts and criminal courts. But we know enough to realize our own responsibilities for the world for which you died and rose again.

O Lord, the One who pushed past the forces of darkness and brought light to our world again, help us hear the call that beckons us to share in the fearful and awesome work of shaping the future into which you lead us.

"Damn it, Belinda," he said in aggravation, "what is it about you that always makes me feel like a bug on a pin?"

She smiled a little at that. "Why don't you like talking about yourself?"

"That's the pot calling the kettle black, isn't it?" he countered, glad for the opportunity to divert the conversation. "I'd wager many people wonder what's underneath your exterior. I know I do."

She looked away, staring down at her lap. "I don't know what you mean."

"No? Allow me to explain." He slid onto his knees in front of her, ignoring the way she stirred in her seat. "You are so cool, anyone would think butter couldn't melt in your mouth. But . . ."

He paused, placing his hands on either side of her hips, resting them on the roll and tuck leather. "But that's a front, isn't it?"

He leaned forward, his abdomen brushing her knees, and the contact started the slow burn of desire inside him. He was heading into dangerous territory, he knew, but just now, he didn't much care.

"I don't know much about you, Belinda Featherstone," he murmured, "but I do know one thing. I know that underneath that prim, cool exterior of

By Laura Lee Guhrke

Laura Lee Guhrke

When The
MARQUESS
Met His Match

❧ An American Heiress in London ❧

AVON

An Imprint of HarperCollinsPublishers

AVON BOOKS
An Imprint of HarperCollins*Publishers*
10 East 53rd Street
New York, New York 10022-5299

Copyright © 2013 by Laura Lee Guhrke
Excerpt from *How to Lose a Duke in Ten Days* copyright © 2014 by Laura Lee Guhrke
ISBN 978-0-06-211817-2
www.avonromance.com

First Avon Books mass market printing: November 2013

Avon Trademark Reg. U.S. Pat. Off. and in Other Countries, Marca Registrada, Hecho en U.S.A.
HarperCollins® is a registered trademark of HarperCollins Publishers.

Printed in the U.S.A.

10 9 8 7 6 5 4 3 2 1

For my friend and wonderful fellow writer
Elizabeth Boyle, who always finds a way
to inspire me, especially when she
oh-so-carelessly says things like,
"Why don't you write a matchmaker?"
This one's for you, my friend.

Chapter 1

The primary difficulty with being a matchmaker wasn't the unpredictability of human nature, or the contrariness of love, or even the interfering parents. No, for Lady Belinda Featherstone, known by wealthy American families as the finest marriage broker in England, the true difficulty of her occupation was the romantic heart of a typical eighteen-year-old girl. Rosalie Harlow was proving a perfect example.

"Sir William would make any woman a fine husband," Rosalie was saying, her voice conveying the enthusiasm one might reserve for a visit to the dentist. "But . . ." She paused and sighed.

"But you don't like him?" Belinda finished for her, and felt the inclination to sigh, too. Sir William Bevelstoke was one of many well-connected English gentlemen who had expressed a romantic interest in the pretty American heiress since her arrival in London six weeks earlier, and was not the only one to elicit a lukewarm response. To make matters worse, Belinda suspected Sir William's feelings went deeper than attraction.

"It isn't that I don't like him," Rosalie said. "It's just that . . ." She paused again, her brown eyes giving Belinda an unhappy look across the tea table. "He isn't very exciting, Auntie Belinda."

Belinda wasn't the girl's aunt, but she was as close to the Harlow family as any blood relation could be. Like her own father had been, Elijah Harlow was one of the many American millionaires who, upon striking it rich in railroads or gold mines, found the lure of Wall Street irresistible and moved their families to New York only to find the doors of social acceptance slammed in the faces of their wives and daughters.

Like the Harlows, Belinda had faced that situation when her own father had brought her to New York from Ohio the year she was fourteen. Mrs. Harlow, a kind and loving woman, had felt great compassion for her young, motherless fellow outcast and had taken the painfully shy girl under her wing, an act of kindness Belinda had never forgotten.

The summer she was seventeen, Belinda had married the dashing, handsome Earl of Featherstone after a six-week whirlwind courtship. It had proved a disastrous union, but Belinda had managed to carve out a successful place for herself in British society. Five years later, when Mrs. Harlow had desired to spare her eldest daughter Margaret the stinging snubs of a New York debut, she had asked Belinda's help to launch the girl in London. Belinda, though happy to assist, was well aware that a rushed marriage to an impoverished scoundrel could well be the consequence. She had placed the girl in the path of the amiable, warm-hearted Lord Fontaine, and as a result, Margaret had become both a social success and a happily married baroness, and Belinda's reputation as a matchmaker had been launched.

Since then, many New Money American girls, cold-shouldered by the rigid social hierarchy of Knickerbocker New York, had found their way to London and Belinda's modest house on Berkeley Street, hoping to follow in Margaret Harlow's footsteps. Rosalie, now done with French finishing school, was here to do the same, but Belinda feared she would prove more difficult to match with a good man than her sensible sister.

Belinda placed her teacup back in its saucer as she considered what her reply to Rosalie should be. Though she was a widow now and very grateful for the fact, she was also well aware that the only way for girls like Rosalie to achieve social acceptance was through matrimony. She wanted to prepare these girls for the practicalities of husband hunting without destroying any of their romantic ideals in the process, and Rosalie was a girl stuffed to the brim with romantic ideals.

"Sir William may not be the most exciting of men," she said after a moment, "but my dear Rosalie, there is so much more to a happy marriage than excitement."

"Yes, but shouldn't marriage be based on love? And,"

Rosalie rushed on as if afraid Belinda would disagree, "how can there be love if there is no excitement? To love is to burn, to feel as if one is on fire. Sir William," she added with another sigh, "does not set me on fire."

Before Belinda could point out the dangers inherent in such thinking, Jervis entered the room. "The Marquess of Trubridge has come to call, my lady," the butler informed her. "Shall I show him in?"

"Trubridge?" she echoed in astonishment. She did not know the marquess except by reputation, and that reputation hardly impelled her to make his acquaintance. Trubridge, the son of the Duke of Landsdowne, was well-known as a rakehell, a man who spent most of his time gallivanting about Paris, spending his income on drink, gaming tables, and women of low moral character. He was also a friend of her late husband's brother, Jack, and that fact gave her even less desire to make his acquaintance. Jack Featherstone was as wild as his brother had been, and both men had done plenty of carousing with Trubridge on the other side of the Channel.

Belinda wasn't surprised Trubridge would break rules of etiquette and call upon a woman with whom he was not acquainted, but she couldn't imagine his reason. Trubridge was a confirmed bachelor, and such men avoided Belinda as if she had the plague.

Still, whatever his reason for coming to see her, she had no interest in finding out what it was. "Jervis, please tell the marquess I am not at home."

"Very good, my lady." Jervis withdrew, and Belinda prepared to return to the subject at hand.

"Do not dismiss Sir William so quickly, Rosalie. He is quite well placed in Her Majesty's government. His knighthood was granted due to his excellent diplomatic skills over some tricky business in Ceylon."

"Ceylon?" Rosalie looked a bit alarmed. "If I were to marry Sir William, would I have to live in foreign places?"

The fact that she lived in a foreign place now, and a hotel at that, didn't seem to bother her, but Belinda fully understood the reasons for her concern. "Possibly," she was forced to concede, "but such posts are seldom for long, and they are an excellent opportunity for someone of your position to make an impression. A good diplomatic hostess is welcomed everywhere."

"I don't want to live in Ceylon. I want to live in England. Does Sir William have an estate?"

"Not at present, but if he were to marry, I'm sure he could be persuaded to purchase such a property. Still, it's far too early to think of that now. The point is that he is a very nice young man, well mannered and well-bred. And—"

A discreet cough interrupted her, and she found her butler once again in the doorway. "Yes, Jervis? What is it?"

The butler looked apologetic. "The Marquess of Trubridge, my lady. He has asked me to inform your ladyship that despite your words to the contrary, he knows for a fact that you are at home."

"Oh, does he?" Belinda was indignant. "What makes him presume to know anything of the sort?"

Her question was rhetorical, but Jervis supplied an answer anyway. "He pointed out that it is a dark afternoon, and your lamps are lit, but your curtains are not drawn, making him able to see you quite easily through the window from the street below. He once again requests a few moments of your time."

"Of all the high-handed arrogance!" She didn't know him, had no desire to meet him, and saw no reason to accommodate him. "When a lady says she is not at home, she may be in residence and yet not at home to *visitors*, a social custom any marquess ought to be well mannered enough to know. Be so good as to point this out to him, if you please. And also remind him that a lack of prior introduction prevents me from seeing him in any case."

"Yes, my lady."

The butler once again withdrew, and Belinda returned her attention to Rosalie. "Now, about Sir William—"

"Who is this Marquess of Trubridge?" Rosalie interrupted. "He appears most insistent upon seeing you."

"I cannot imagine why. I don't even know the man."

"Is he unmarried? If so, surely his reason for coming to you is obvious."

"Trubridge is a bachelor, yes, an adamant one. It's common knowledge he has no intention of ever marrying. He is also a man no respectable young lady ought to become acquainted with. Now about Sir William . . ."

She'd barely begun a glowing description of that worthy young man's potential future as a diplomat before a movement from the doorway caught her attention, and when she looked up, Jervis was once again standing there. "Oh, for heaven's sake!" she exclaimed. "Isn't the man gone yet?"

"I am afraid not, my lady. He said to tell you he cannot imagine what he has done to give such offense that you would cut him in this manner by pretending you have never met him before, but whatever he has done to wound you, he offers his most sincere apologies. He again requests a moment of your time."

"This is nonsense. I've never met the man in my life, and I fail to see what is of such urgency—" She broke off, struck by a thought that trumped other considerations.

Perhaps something had happened to Jack. Her brother-in-law and Trubridge did share the lease on a town house in Paris, and the marquess would be the first to know if Jack had met with an accident. Jack was known for committing the wildest, stupidest, most reckless acts imaginable, and it would not surprise her if he'd come to an untimely demise. It would also explain what had brought Trubridge here without a proper introduction.

She bit her lip, considering for a moment, then she said, "Ask Lord Trubridge if he's here because something has happened to Jack. That is, to Lord Featherstone."

"I will inquire, my lady." Jervis, who was proving himself today as the most forbearing butler in London, bowed and withdrew. During his absence, she did not return her attention to her companion. Instead, she stared at the door, waiting for the butler's return, a knot of apprehension in her stomach.

It wasn't that she was fond of Jack. She wasn't. He was too much like his brother—too inclined toward carousing with bad company, too fond of high living, and completely careless about his responsibilities at home. But though she did not approve of her late husband's brother, she sincerely hoped nothing untoward had happened to him.

"Well?" she prompted when Jervis reappeared. "What did he say? Is Jack . . . is he dead?"

"Lord Trubridge wishes to know—" Jervis hesitated, as if the message were so important as to warrant being conveyed as accurately as possible. "He has asked me to ask you if Jack's meeting with an accident would enable you to grant him an interview. If so, then yes, Jack has definitely come a cropper."

Beside her, Rosalie choked back a giggle at this absurd reply, but Belinda could not share her amusement. Like Rosalie, she suspected Trubridge's tongue was firmly in his cheek, but it was best to be sure.

"Oh, very well," she said, giving in to the inevitable. "Put him in the library, wait ten minutes, then show him up."

"Yes, my lady." The butler departed to carry out these latest instructions, and Belinda turned to her companion.

"I'm sorry to cut our visit short, dearest, but it seems I am forced to see Lord Trubridge after all, if only to confirm that my brother-in-law has not come to harm."

"But why make the marquess wait in the library? Why not simply have him come upstairs?"

The idea of that man anywhere near a sweet innocent

like Rosalie didn't bear contemplating. "I cannot allow you to meet him. Lord Trubridge is not a gentleman."

"Not a gentleman? But he is a marquess." Rosalie gave a little laugh, understandably confused. "I thought a titled British peer was always a gentleman."

"Trubridge may be a gentleman in name, but he is not one in deed. There was a scandal years ago, a girl he compromised but wouldn't marry, a young lady of good family. And . . ." She paused, striving to remember what else she'd heard about the marquess. "I believe there was another girl—Irish—who went running off to America because of him though I don't know the details, for his father managed to have it all hushed up."

"Ooh," Rosalie breathed, her eyes widening with even greater curiosity. "He sounds terribly notorious."

Belinda studied Rosalie's rapt expression and wondered, not for the first time, what it was about rakes that young girls found so captivating. By all rights, Rosalie ought to be repulsed, but no. She was all the more keen to meet him because of his wicked reputation, and Belinda wanted to bite her tongue off for having discussed the wretched fellow at all. Still, the damage was done. All she could do now was try to mitigate it and get Rosalie out of the house as quickly as possible.

"He isn't notorious enough to be interesting," she answered with a deprecating smile. "He's just an odious man with a sordid history who has no business calling on me when we've never met."

"But he says you have met."

"I'm sure he is mistaken, or he's teasing for some obscure reason of his own. Either way, I must see him, it seems." She stood up, pulling Rosalie to her feet as well. "And you, my dear, must return to your hotel."

"Oh, must I go?" She groaned. "Why can't I meet this Lord Trubridge? I am supposed to be mingling in British society. This man is a marquess, so I think I should meet him, don't you?"

Absolutely not. Still smiling, pretending a casual indifference she was far from feeling, she picked up Rosalie's gloves from the settee and handed them to her. "Another time, perhaps," she said, and began steering the girl toward the door. "But not today."

Ignoring the girl's protests, Belinda propelled her through the drawing-room doorway and down the corridor to the stairs. "Besides, I can't introduce you to a man I haven't yet met myself. That would not be proper."

She paused near the top of the stairs, casting a quick glance down to the foyer below to reassure herself that Jervis had done his job, and Lord Trubridge was safely ensconced in the library. Satisfied, she started down the stairs, pulling a reluctant Rosalie with her. "And I can assure you, Rosalie, that he's a man unworthy of your interest."

"Oh, but how could he not be interesting, with such a history? Oh, please, please, let me meet him. I've never met anyone notorious."

Belinda discerned that further excuses would be needed to make the girl lose her curiosity. "My dear girl, you expressed the wish to live in England," she reminded her, as they started down the stairs. "Trubridge lives in Paris."

"But does he have property here?"

"I believe he has a place in Kent," she answered with reluctance. "Honey-Something. But I don't believe he ever visits it. He certainly doesn't live there."

"But if he married, he might wish to."

"I doubt it. He and his father are estranged and have been for years."

"That could also change if he married, too." Rosalie stopped at the bottom of the stairs, forcing Belinda to stop as well, and as she noted the girl's mouth taking on an obstinate curve, she began to fear her own intransigence was making the marquess all the more appealing. Clearly, she needed to find something that would lessen his allure.

"I've heard . . ." Belinda paused, inventing quickly. "I've heard he's become quite fat." After all, she consoled herself, it *could* be true.

"Fat?"

"Absolutely corpulent." Belinda once again began propelling the girl toward the front door. "And I know he drinks," she added, as they crossed the foyer, "which has probably given him the gout by now. I daresay he smokes cigars as well, so his breath must be . . ." She broke off with a shudder. "Ugh."

"You make him sound dreadful."

"Well, he is getting on. Why, he must be over thirty, at least."

If she'd hoped young Rosalie would think a man of thirty too old to be attractive, she was mistaken. "Oh, Auntie Belinda, thirty's not so old. Why, you're twenty-eight, and you could easily pass for a debutante."

"What a lovely thing to say, darling. Thank you.

But my point is that Trubridge is a man of dissolute habits, and when men like that reach a certain age, they become most unattractive."

"Perhaps you're right." She looked less interested now, much to Belinda's relief. "Oh, how very disappointing."

"Well, dinner at Lord and Lady Melville's tonight ought to brighten your spirits. Their second son, Roger, is quite good-looking, and delightful company." She turned to the footman who had opened the door for them. "Samuel, please escort Miss Harlow to Thomas's Hotel and see that she arrives safely."

"Heavens," Rosalie put in, "I don't need an escort. Berkeley Square is just across the street. I don't understand all this fuss about walking everywhere with a chaperone."

"That's because you're American, darling. Things are very different here." She kissed the girl's cheek, pushed her gently out to the sidewalk, and turned to her footman. "Not just to the entrance to Berkeley Square, mind. Go with her all the way into Thomas's Hotel."

"Yes, my lady. She'll not go amiss with me."

"Thank you, Samuel."

Her footman was most reliable, but despite that, Belinda watched from the doorway as Rosalie crossed Hay Hill and entered Berkeley Square. She was fiercely protective of the young American girls who sought her help, and when it came to safeguarding their reputations, she felt it was always best to err on the side of caution. This was particularly true of the Harlow girls, who were so much like family to her.

Jervis's footsteps on the tiled floor of the foyer reminded her of her other visitor, and since Rosalie had now vanished from view, she came back inside. Meeting her butler's inquiring gaze, she nodded, then as he went down the corridor to fetch the marquess, she ran up the stairs to the drawing room. She was able to settle herself on the settee with her tea and catch her breath before Jervis came through the doorway. "The Marquess of Trubridge," he announced, and stood aside.

Another male figure appeared, moving past the butler and into the drawing room with the ease of a man who never had cause to doubt his welcome in a room where there were women. Belinda rose to her feet, studying him as he approached.

For Rosalie's benefit, she had conjured the picture of an aging roué, but that picture was shattered by the man before her. He might have all the dissolute habits she'd enumerated, but one wouldn't have known it to look at him. He was a big man, but there wasn't an ounce of superfluous flesh on him, and every line of his tall, broad-shouldered frame exuded athleticism and strength, the perfect combination to make any woman feel protected and safe in his company. But Belinda knew such an impression was nothing but illusion. Trubridge's reputation made him as safe as an untamed lion.

He had a lion's beauty as well, the tawny, windblown beauty of that splendid animal. His eyes were hazel, with lights of gold and green in their brown depths. His hair, though cut short, was thick and slightly curly, and the gold-burnished locks shimmered in the lamplight of Belinda's drawing room like the sun might shimmer on the Serengeti Plain. Suddenly, the dark, rainy English afternoon became one of exotic warmth and brilliant sunshine. Even Belinda, who knew full well how deceiving appearances could be, blinked a little in the face of such splendid masculinity.

He was clean-shaven, a rarity these days, but she could not fault the marquess for choosing to defy fashion. His lack of a beard allowed the lean planes of his face and the strong lines of his jaw to be displayed to perfect advantage. Why, she wondered in frustration, were the rakehells always so damnably handsome?

"Lady Featherstone." He bowed to her. "What a pleasure to see you again."

"Again?" Looking at him, she was more positive than ever they had never met, for as galling as it was to admit, Trubridge wasn't the sort of man a woman was likely to forget. "I don't believe we have ever been introduced, Lord Trubridge," she said, hoping her words and her withering tone might remind him that he had already broken several social rules.

"Of course you don't remember me." He smiled, a disarming smile that was boyish enough to belie his reputation and seductive enough to reinforce it. "We were introduced at the wedding breakfast following your marriage to Lord Featherstone."

Heavens, her wedding had been a decade ago. That might explain why she didn't remember him, for she'd been barely eighteen on her wedding day, navigating her first foray through the maze of British society like a moth blundering in lamplight. Horribly self-conscious, head over heels in love with her new husband, and terrified she'd make some awful faux pas that would embarrass him, she'd been too nervous to remember much of anything that day, even a man like Trubridge. How extraordinary that he should remember her, but she supposed his talent for remembering women was another reason he was so successful at seducing them. "Of course," she murmured at a loss for what else to say. "Forgive me."

"There is nothing to forgive. It was a long time ago, and we've not seen each other since, a fact which is clearly my loss. You look more radiant now than you did as a bride."

"You flatter me." *One of your greatest talents, I imagine,* she was tempted to add, but she bit back that rather acidic rejoinder. "Thank you."

His smile faded to an earnest expression that seemed thoroughly genuine. "I was sorry to hear of your husband's death. He seemed a very good chap."

All men, she supposed, would share that opinion of Charles Featherstone. He'd been a terrible husband, but from the male point of view, he'd been a very good chap indeed, able to gamble, carouse, and drink with the best of them, until the night five years ago when he'd collapsed on top of his favorite mistress and died of heart failure at the age of thirty-six.

Belinda strove to maintain a neutral expression and keep hidden her distaste of her late husband and her lack of grief over his death. In England, showing too much emotion was considered bad form. "I appreciate your condolences," she murmured. "But I take it you are not here to offer me similar sympathies about my brother-in-law?"

His mouth twitched a bit. "Fortunately not. Jack was hale and hearty the last time I saw him, which was only a few days ago at our apartments in Paris."

"Quite so. I am not surprised, sir, that a man of your reputation would use such a ruse to obtain an interview, but I am baffled as to the reason for it. What is the purpose of this visit?"

"For the same reason many bachelors visit you, of course."

"I hope you don't mean that the way it sounds."

He smiled again, a grin that was wide, rueful, and utterly devastating to the feminine heart. "Lady Featherstone, I want you to find me a wife."

Chapter 2

Nicholas's first thought upon seeing Belinda Featherstone was to curse both her husband and her father for their penchant for heavy gambling. If Charles Featherstone hadn't loved cards and racehorses to an obsessive degree, and if Jeremiah Hamilton hadn't staked and lost his entire fortune on America's Wall Street, the solution to Nicholas's problems might have been standing right in front of him, for Belinda Featherstone was one of the loveliest women he'd ever seen.

He hadn't expected that.

He'd been twenty years old when he'd attended her wedding breakfast, a decade had passed since then, and he remembered little of the event. Despite his words to the contrary this afternoon, they had never been introduced, but he hadn't wanted to waste time arranging a formal introduction. That day ten years ago, he'd only glimpsed her from across the room, and his recollection of her appearance that day was vague—a painfully thin girl swathed in too many yards of silk illusion and too many strands of diamonds. He hadn't seen her since, for he spent little time in England, and when he was here, he had never happened to run across her. Lady Featherstone's social circle was far too respectable for the likes of him.

In deciding to bring his matrimonial situation to her, Nicholas hadn't given any thought to what her appearance would be like now, but had he done so, he'd probably have envisioned nothing more than an older version of the unremarkable bride he'd glimpsed ten years earlier. Such an assumption, he saw now, would have been utterly wrong, for time had transformed the gawky girl of his memory into a beautiful woman, a fact Jack had somehow failed to mention during the past decade.

Large eyes in a heart-shaped face stared back at him, eyes of clear, sky blue surrounded by a thick fringe of sooty lashes. Irish eyes. Another thing about her he hadn't expected.

Once again, Nicholas's mind flashed backward, nine years instead of ten, to a different dark-haired, blue-eyed girl with Irish eyes, and his heart twisted, just a bit, in his chest. For a moment, he felt as if he were twenty-one again, filled with dreams and ideals and all the claptrap that only young love could inspire.

He shoved the feeling aside. This was no Irish hillside, he was no longer a callow youth, and his dreams and ideals, like his love, had turned to dust a long time ago.

Despite a superficial resemblance in coloring, this

woman was nothing like Kathleen. Her black hair was not a riot of corkscrew curls blowing loose in the wind off the Irish Sea. Instead, it was sleek and straight and caught back in an elegant, complicated chignon that had clearly been fashioned by a lady's maid. Her dress was a tea gown of soft, slate blue cashmere, not a coarse and serviceable linsey-woolsey covered by an apron. And though her house was small and modestly furnished, it was nothing like the thatched-roof cottages of County Kildare. Besides, he knew Lady Featherstone to be filled to her fingertips with scruples and rectitude, two qualities Kathleen Shaughnessy had never possessed.

In fact, Lady Featherstone had one of the most pristine reputations in London, and though that would definitely benefit him in his quest, at this moment it seemed a pity, for her mouth was full, dark pink and eminently kissable, with an unmistakable sensuality that her philandering husband had clearly not appreciated.

He took a glance down her figure, noting that the stick-thin frame of the girl swathed in tulle had given way to a figure of much more luscious proportions. Even her loosely fitted tea gown could not hide the round fullness of her breasts and the undulating curve of her hips. No, he decided, as his gaze traveled slowly back up her body, there was nothing gawky about Lady Featherstone anymore.

He paused at her throat, appreciating the bare skin exposed by the open, lace-edged vee of her gown for a moment before he returned his gaze to her face, and when he looked again into her eyes, heat flooded through his body, the unmistakable heat of desire. For him to be aroused by a woman certainly wasn't an uncommon thing, and black hair and blue eyes were a combination to which he was particularly susceptible, but given the reason he was here, any desire he might feel for Belinda Featherstone was damned inconvenient.

Not that his feelings seemed to matter much anyway, he thought in amusement, watching as those stunning blue eyes narrowed. It was clear the stirrings in his body had been perceived and were definitely not reciprocated, nor even welcomed.

Ah, well, he supposed that was for the best. There were widows happy to set aside the propriety that had been required of them during marriage, but to his knowledge, Lady Featherstone had never been one of those. Besides, he knew that these days she was a woman of modest means, and thanks to his father's latest attempts to bring him to heel, Nicholas could no longer afford to become entangled with women who didn't have money.

"This is a most unexpected surprise, Lord Trubridge."

Her voice brought him out of his reverie, and with regret, he put aside any lustful thoughts about her and reminded himself of the purpose that had brought him here. "A surprise perhaps, but a pleasant one, I hope?"

She made no reply beyond an insincere little smile that made him regret he'd asked the question. Despite her admission of surprise at his presence here, her face displayed no curiosity, and as silence once again fell between them, Nicholas began to feel deuced awkward.

Perhaps it was conceited of him to expect more favorable reactions than this from the fair sex, but if so, he was being duly punished for his conceit. The disdain that emanated from her was palpable.

But then, he didn't often encounter women like Lady Featherstone nowadays. No doubt, she felt honor-bound to disapprove of a man like him as a matter of course. The women with whom he usually associated were much more forgiving. And he supposed his rather cavalier way of gaining entrance to her drawing room hadn't helped matters, but he'd seen no other way to manage an interview after her initial refusal to see him. After all, it wasn't as if they were invited to the same parties.

Still, he was here now, she knew the purpose of his visit, and the only civil thing to do was to invite him to sit down. He waited, but she issued no such invitation, and as the silence lengthened with the only sound the tick of the clock on the wall, it became clear he would have to take the lead. He gave a slight cough. "Might we sit?"

"If we must."

Not at all an encouraging reply, but the best he was going to get, it seemed. He gestured to the celadon green settee behind her with an inquiring glance. She hesitated, as if trying to find a way to avoid settling in for a conversation, but at last, she resumed her seat, perched on the edge as if waiting for the first possible excuse to stand again and show him the door.

In light of that, Nicholas felt that a delicate, more tactful approach to his situation might do less to offend her. "Lady Featherstone," he began as he took the chintz chair opposite her, "my thirtieth birthday was four days ago."

"Congratulations."

The dryness of that perfunctory reply was not lost on him, but he persevered. "When a man turns thirty, he is often forced to consider his future in ways he would not have done earlier in life. I am at that crossroads."

"I see." She cast a pointed glance at the clock and began drumming her fingers against her knee.

"Hence my decision," he continued valiantly, "that it is time for me to marry."

She leaned back, folded her arms, and eyed him with skepticism. "From what I hear, you are not the marrying sort."

"Jack told you that, I suppose."

"No, but it would hardly be necessary for him to do so. Your reputation precedes you, sir."

Having spent a great deal of time and effort bolstering that reputation for reasons of his own, he couldn't find cause to regret it now. Still, though a few days ago Nicholas would have been happy for a matchmaker to deem him as an unsuitable candidate for matrimony, everything was different now.

"I have not been inclined to marriage, that is true," he said, "but I have come to a change of heart on the subject."

"Indeed?" One delicate black brow arched upward. "A mere birthday and a bit of circumspection have been sufficient to motivate this . . . change of heart?"

Nicholas threw tact to the winds. "Lady Featherstone, I realize custom dictates delicacy in discussions such as this, but I've never been much good at beating about the bush. Might we speak frankly?"

Without waiting for an answer, he spread his arms and admitted the truth. "Four days ago, my father, the Duke of Landsdowne, cut off my trust fund. I am forced to the marriage state by circumstance."

"How dreadful for you," she murmured. "And on your birthday, too."

"It's more than dreadful, Lady Featherstone. It's damnable. To my mind, no one should be forced to marry for material reasons. But I have no choice. My income comes from a trust bequeathed to me by the terms of my mother's will. She died when I was a boy, but unbeknownst to me, my father had somehow managed to persuade her to add a codicil just before her death that made him sole trustee of that income. I was unaware of that codicil until four days ago, when Landsdowne's attorney wrote to inform me of it and to tell me that the duke has chosen to cut me off."

"Ah, so it is a change in your pocketbook, not a change in your heart, that has brought about these reflections regarding your future?"

He stirred in his chair, feeling suddenly defensive. "The former has induced the latter," he said. "Bachelorhood is no longer an option for me, which is why I have come to you."

She frowned. "I'm not certain I comprehend your meaning. What have I to do with whom you marry?"

"Lady Featherstone, everyone in society knows you arrange these things."

She unfolded her arms and leaned forward, her gaze skewering him like an icicle. "By 'arranging things,' what you mean is that you want me to find you a wife rich enough to provide you with the income your father has cut off?"

Nicholas studied her hostile countenance, and he wondered how this woman could possibly make a living as a marriage broker when she seemed so resentful of the concept. "Well, that is what you *do*, isn't it?" he asked. "You bring wealthy girls of no background over here from America and pair them with eligible peers in need of money."

She stiffened, seeming to take offense at this assessment of her profession.

"You needn't poker up so, Lady Featherstone. You have carved out for yourself an ingenious role in society, and a very necessary one in light of our beastly agricultural depression. I would imagine many a peerage has been rescued from disaster due to your efforts."

She lifted her chin a notch. "I facilitate the introduction of various American acquaintances into British society, hoping that in my small way, I can help to smooth their path. Whether or not such introductions have the happy result of matrimony is not within my control."

"Is matrimony ever a happy result?" he quipped without thinking, but the moment the light, careless words were out of his mouth, her cool gaze became absolutely frosty, and Nicholas reminded himself that making light of marriage to a marriage broker was probably not a good idea. "I must marry. I have no other choice if I am to have an income."

"You have an estate."

"Lady Featherstone, you must know that land rents are not always enough to cover the costs of running an estate these days. Between the sale of the barley, wheat, and hops grown at Honeywood, the land rents, and the lease of the house, I am able to pay the operating expenses, but there is nothing left over for me to live on."

She shrugged, seeming wholly unsympathetic. "I don't suppose you could try earning your living?"

"Obtain employment, you mean? Careful, Lady Featherstone. You're showing your American blood when you suggest things like that. You know the son of a duke isn't supposed to peg away at a job. It's not done."

"And you care so much what people think of you."

He smiled in the face of her sarcasm. "Actually, I don't give a tinker's damn," he confessed with cheer. "And as to finding employment, I'm open to suggestions." He forced a laugh. "But what on earth would anyone hire a man like me to do?"

She tilted her head, studying him. "I can't think of a thing."

Strangely, that hurt. He didn't even know her, and yet, her words bruised him deep down inside, in that place where dreams and ideals had once existed, a place that was empty now. Still, he didn't show that her words had cut, for Landsowne had given him a lifetime of training in how not to show pain. His smile did not falter. "Quite so," he said. "And even if I were able to obtain some sort of job, it would hardly be one sufficient to support me."

"Given your hedonistic way of life, I should imagine not."

She made him sound quite depraved. "Lady Featherstone, I realize that my past is somewhat . . . checkered, but surely that alone does not make me an undesirable *parti*. I am a marquess, after all, and the only son of a duke."

"And do you not think persuading your father to reinstate your income would be a more honorable course?"

He gave a laugh. "Are you acquainted with my father, Lady Featherstone?"

"I have met him. But we are not well acquainted, no. Still, I cannot see how discussing the matter with him would be a less desirable course than marrying for money."

"I'm not the first person to seek marriage for material considerations, madam," he shot back, frustrated by her resentment toward him when surely many of her clients had sought out her help for the exact same reasons as he. "As for my father, he and I have not spoken a word to each other in person for over eight years and, let me assure you, we both prefer it that way. As for persuading him . . ." Nicholas paused and leaned forward, meeting her gaze with a hard one of his own. "I would crawl to the devil before I would ask that man for a brass farthing. I realize that a marriage based on material considerations is not ideal, but if both parties are honest about their reasons for marrying from the very start and freely choose to marry for those reasons, there is nothing dishonorable about it. Besides, as I said, I have no choice. I can live off of my credit for a while, but after that, I shall be destitute. In the normal course of events, coming to a marriage broker is not how I would go about finding a wife, but I have few options. There—"

"How would you go about it?" she interrupted. "Finding a wife, I mean? In the normal course of events?"

"Not society's way." Before she could probe further, he went on, "And I fail to see how that matters at this stage. As I said, I must marry, and as quickly as possible. I haven't the time, nor—I must confess—the inclination to engage in society's tedious rituals of proper courtship."

"And you believe that coming to me enables you to avoid those rituals?" She stared at him as if she couldn't believe what she was hearing. "You think it's as simple as that?"

"Isn't it?" Nicholas frowned in bafflement. "You are a marriage broker. I am the son of a duke. I wish to engage you in the task of finding me a suitable wife— that is, one who is rich, preferably pretty, and willing to part with some of her wealth in order to obtain a higher place in society, and later, a duchess's coronet. I will, of course, pay you a handsome commission out of the marriage portion. This seems to me a straightforward business arrangement and something you have facilitated many times before. Call me thick, but I fail to see what is complicated about it."

She made a sound of derision. "You, sir, are nothing but a fortune hunter."

"At least I am prepared to be an honest one," he countered. "I am willing to lay bare my situation for my future bride. If you can manage to find me one who is also prepared to be honest about her motives, there should be no cause for concern. And it's not as if you've shown any compunction about arranging material marriages in the past. The Duke and Duchess of Margrave, for example, or—"

"The duke and duchess made no material arrangement! And neither have any of the other couples I have brought together."

"Surely you don't believe that," he said, but she was glaring daggers at him, and he gave an incredulous laugh. "By God, perhaps you do believe it. Lady Featherstone, how can you have lived in England this long, arranged matches for countless peers, and still believe that marriage on this side of the pond is anything but a material arrangement? It's certainly not an affair of the heart. Believe me," he added, unable to stop the bitter edge that entered his voice, "I know."

"I, too, know all about marriage on this side of the pond, sir. I do not need you to explain it to me. And let me assure you that I am not in the least romantic. I am practical. I fully recognize that money plays a certain part in British matrimony, but my friends and the men they married formed unions based on far more than material considerations. Those couples had affection—"

"Affection?" he interrupted, diverted and amused by her choice of words. "Well, I daresay affection would impel any man to the altar."

She set her jaw. "Laugh if you like."

Nicholas hid his amusement at once. "No, no, your approach sounds very logical," he said, trying to sound appropriately grave. "But you do make me wonder . . ." He paused, and his gaze slid to her gorgeous mouth. "What of passion?"

A rosy tint washed into her cheeks, showing that he'd rattled her cool complacency at last. "Passion is not really relevant to matrimony."

He laughed again. Her comment was so absurd, he couldn't help it. "Since most British peers marry in the hope of producing an heir, I think passion is highly relevant."

Her expression hardened. "Passion does not last. Therefore, it makes an inadequate basis for matrimony. To those who honor me by seeking my advice, I recommend they base marriage on a solid foundation of sincere affection, shared interests, and like minds."

It was clear that teasing her was not helping his cause. "Can we at least agree that marriage should be approached sensibly?" he asked. "From that standpoint, surely you would be able to arrange several suitable introductions."

"I think not." She rose to her feet. "I do not assist fortune hunters, even supposedly honest ones. I cannot help you, Lord Trubridge. I wonder why you think I would be willing to do so."

Nicholas tilted his head back to look up at her. "And I wonder why I am summarily dismissed for desiring the same sort of arrangement aspired to by many others who have sat in this drawing room."

She did not reply, and it was clear from her stony expression that there was no chance further discussion would change her mind. A pity, for she could have smoothed his way back into society and made this whole business so much easier, but it wasn't meant to be. He'd simply have to go about finding his wife another way.

"Very well," he said, and stood up. "I shall have to conduct my search without your assistance."

"Terrible of me to expect you to find your own wife, I know," she said, her voice taking on the dulcet sweetness of sarcasm. "I fear you shall now be forced to endure those tedious, proper courtship rituals, despite your contempt for them. I must confess I shall quite enjoy observing your attempts, Lord Trubridge."

"I shall endeavor to be as entertaining as possible for you."

"Do." Now she chose to smile, and it was a smile of satisfaction, as if she'd won some sort of victory. "But I feel compelled to warn you that I shan't make your quest an easy one."

"So, if I take your meaning, you are not only refusing to help me; you intend to block my efforts?"

Her smile widened. "In every way possible."

If she hoped her words would intimidate him into giving up his quest, she was mistaken. "Are you threatening me, Lady Featherstone?" he asked, smiling back at her.

"Take it any way you like."

"Very well then, I shall take it as a challenge. And I have never been able to resist a challenge. But I'm not sure what you can do to stop me," he added, baiting her, hoping she would reveal her strategy so he would know just what he would be up against. "I appreciate that you are disinclined to help me, but I fail to see what you could do to prevent me from finding a wife by my own efforts?"

Her smile vanished, and her eyes flashed like cool, polished steel. "I shall make sure that any young lady you are considering knows just what sort of man you are, of your scandalous past, the dishonorable reasons for your courtship, the mercenary quality of your intentions, and just what a horrible husband you would make."

He was stung by this scathing and wholly unjustified summation of his character, but he didn't show it. "You must do as your honor dictates, of course," he said in his most amiable fashion, "but now that the gauntlet has been thrown, let me say that I don't think your mission will prove quite as successful as you imagine."

"No?"

"No. You are assuming I will follow society's customary courtship rituals, but I have no intention of doing so."

"What do you mean?"

"I will not be conducting a *proper* courtship at all. In fact," he added, his smile widening as he relished her shocked face, "I believe I shall conduct one that is as deliciously improper as possible." He winked. "It's more fun that way."

"Oh, you are a devil," she breathed, her hands clenching into fists at her sides, her expression one of barely controlled outrage. "A wicked, black-hearted rake."

"No point in denying it," he said with a shrug. "Many people came to that conclusion about my character long ago, including you, it seems."

"With good reason, sir!"

She knew nothing about the circumstances that had led to the tarnishing of his reputation nor his reasons for allowing the rumors to stand, and he damned well wasn't going to launch into explanations now. "Either way, it won't make a particle of difference. Women love a rake who is willing to reform. Especially if he can evoke her passion." His gaze slid to her mouth. "Mutual affection, like minds, and shared interests be damned."

With that, he turned and walked out, leaving the prim and proper Lady Featherstone spluttering behind him.

UPON BELINDA'S ARRIVAL in England a decade earlier, the Viscountess of Montcrieffe (formerly Miss Nancy Breckenridge of New York), had been kind enough to guide her through her first few precarious years in British society. She had taught Belinda the three most important precepts of a true lady, to wit: a lady never displayed shock or surprise, never gave way to fits of temper, and never, ever contradicted a gentleman before dinner.

Belinda, in those days a young, withdrawn, terribly insecure girl, hadn't had any trouble taking those precepts to heart. But now, as she stared at the empty doorway through which the Marquess of Trubridge had just departed, it occurred to her that she'd just broken all three of those rules as easily as one might break an egg.

Not that she could find cause to regret it, for his

words about conducting an improper courtship could only mean one thing: he intended to seduce and compromise a girl into marriage, and that would give any woman, lady or not, cause to lose her temper. Still, Belinda knew anger wouldn't serve her well in these circumstances. She had to think clearly, plan strategically, and find a way to stop him.

Women love a rake.

His words came back as if to mock her, and Belinda sank down onto the settee with a sigh. Trubridge was right about that, and she knew it better than anyone. Experience was a bitter teacher.

Charles had been a rake, too, handsome as sin and charming as the devil, with blood more blue than any of the New York Knickerbockers who'd looked down their noses at Miss Belinda Hamilton of Cleveland, Ohio.

Race week at Saratoga was one of the few places where a girl with no background and plenty of money might mingle with those of higher social status. For a girl like Belinda, however, such opportunities had meant little, for she'd been far too shy to take advantage of them.

When the Seventh Earl of Featherstone, on a tour of the States at the time, had singled her out for his attentions on the verandah of Saratoga's Grand Union Hotel, it had taken only one fifteen-minute conversation where he did most of the talking for her to fall head over heels in love with him.

When he'd pulled her into a darkened corner of the garden at a cotillion a scant six weeks after meeting her, his bold manner and sensuous kisses had been the headiest experience of her life. And when, after that brief but passionate courtship, he'd asked her to become the Countess of Featherstone and come live with him in an English castle, he'd presented it as such a romantic, dreamy fairy tale that she'd accepted on the spot without even noticing that his proposal had included no actual declaration of love.

But he had assured her father that his desire to marry her had nothing to do with her fortune, and her father, never good at facing unpalatable possibilities, had taken him at his word. As for herself, Belinda had been so young, so infatuated with Charles and so enamored with the British aristocracy he represented, that she'd convinced herself of all sorts of romantic tripe about what being his wife and countess would be like.

Neither she nor her father had known the precarious nature of Featherstone's finances and how dissolute his character until it was too late. Only after the wedding had she learned of her new husband's four mortgaged estates, two mistresses, and three hundred thousand pounds of debt. Left with no choice but to honor the marriage agreement, her father had paid off Featherstone's debts and handed over the rest of her dowry, which his son-in-law had thoroughly enjoyed spending.

By the time Jeremiah Hamilton lost his fortune, the money from her marriage settlement was gone. Even before then, Charles had abandoned any pretenses of gentleman-like behavior or husbandly regard toward his young American wife. He had also made clear that he had no inclination to provide her with an income of her own.

Left to her own devices, she'd managed to direct her anger and disillusionment into a very lucrative source of income for herself, but that wasn't why she'd become a marriage broker.

Fortune hunters were the bane of any heiress's existence, and it had become the mission of her life to assist as many young ladies as possible in making wiser choices than she had. She informed American mothers as to the character of young British gentlemen, she advised fathers on how to properly tie up the money, and she did her best to guide marriage-minded American heiresses toward those British gentlemen of good and moral character, the men most likely to bring them not only social acceptance, but also lasting happiness, and she was proud of the fact that nowadays any American girl determined to marry a British lord knew her first call once arriving in London was upon Lady Featherstone of Berkeley Street.

Her recollections about Featherstone led to an inevitable comparison with Trubridge, and she found their similarities a sobering reminder of her duty. She had to make good on her threat and stop that man, but when she thought of his tawny eyes and devastating smile, she knew it was not going to be easy. There were quite a few heiresses who would happily hand over their hearts and their dowries in exchange for a handsome man with a title in the euphemistic hope their love would be returned.

Jervis entered the drawing room with a stack of newspapers, but lost in thought, she barely noticed as he crossed the room to place them by her chair. It was her custom to scan the morning and evening papers, just in case any tidbits of gossip had managed to make news before she'd become aware of them, and it was a pastime in which she usually took great amusement, for the papers were so often wrong.

Today, however, she couldn't stir up much interest as the butler crossed to her side and placed a stack of scandal sheets on the table by her chair. "The evening papers, my lady."

"Thank you, Jervis." She dismissed him with a preoccupied wave of her hand and frowned at the pile of newspapers, fearing some of them had already noted Trubridge's arrival from Paris and were mad with speculation as to why he was in town.

Despite her bold words to him, Belinda knew it was unlikely she'd be able to prevent him from finding a bride, particularly if he were as desperate, as much in haste, and as willing to use dishonorable tactics as he had implied. Nonetheless, she was determined that every heiress in London and her parents, too, would at least be aware of his character and his intentions beforehand. It was up to her to warn them; but such warnings would have to be issued with subtlety, or she would appear to have a personal axe to grind, and her words would be discounted. Also, she wouldn't put it past him to sue her for slander if she went too far too fast.

Calling on the mothers, whispered consultations . . .

yes, that long-established method would work, but it would take time, and if he were truly prepared to ruin a girl to gain his objective, time was something she did not have. But other than her tongue, what other weapons could she employ?

Belinda sat up straight in her chair, inspiration striking with sudden force. There might be a way, she realized, and glanced at the clock. Yes, she had just enough time to pay a call, and that one little visit might be all she needed to do to prevent the Marquess of Trubridge from taking some innocent girl's virtue and fortune.

Chapter 3

It was a common misconception that one had to have money to stay at a luxurious London hotel, but Nicholas knew otherwise. One of the few benefits of being a titled peer was that one need not have ready money to engage a suite of rooms, and for any member of the Landsdowne family, Claridge's was the London hotel of choice. The staff, bless their trusting hearts, wouldn't dream of asking Landsdowne's son to pay in advance, and given the fact that he had a mere seventeen pounds, four shillings, and sixpence in his bank account at present, Nicholas was happy to make use of his family name to obtain accommodations, especially since it was his father's latest attempt to bring him to heel that had brought him to London in the first place.

Landsdowne's letter informing him he'd been cut

off and would remain so until he had a suitable wife had been quite a shock, but only because he hadn't known his father had that sort of power over his inheritance. But in hindsight, he supposed he should have anticipated something like this. After all, control of his money was control over him, and that had always been the old man's greatest obsession. What Landsdowne couldn't ever seem to accept was the fact that he no longer ceded the old man that sort of power. Though his father's move did force him to marry to secure his financial future, he intended to find a wife of his own choosing, not one chosen for him.

Of course, Lady Featherstone's refusal to assist him in his search did make his goal a bit trickier to achieve than he'd originally envisioned, but it didn't change it. He had to marry, and the only question now was how to set about it without her help.

The morning after his visit to Berkeley Street, he had little chance to speculate on the topic, however, for he'd barely sat down to breakfast before there was a knock on the door of his suite.

Chalmers, his valet, paused in the act of dishing up kidneys and bacon from the warming dishes that had been sent up by the hotel kitchens and gave his master an inquiring look.

He nodded in reply, and Chalmers left the sitting room for the vestibule. Moments later, the valet was ushering in a small, elderly man who carried a black leather dispatch case and whose shriveled pippin face was quite familiar to Nicholas. "That didn't take long," he murmured under his breath as he laid aside his napkin and stood up. "Mr. Freebody," he greeted in a louder voice. "How good of you to look me up."

"My lord." The older man glanced at the table. "Forgive me for disturbing your breakfast."

"Not at all. As a matter of fact, I've been expecting you."

"Have you?" The dry, precise little man who'd been in charge of legal affairs for the present Duke of Landsdowne for nearly half a century actually seemed surprised.

"Yes, indeed. I didn't know when you'd seek me out, of course, but it was bound to be soon after my arrival. Father's letter was intended to bring me scurrying home, wasn't it? So, here I am. You may tell him I arrived as anticipated." He gestured to the chair across the table. "Please sit down. Would you care for coffee? Or I can have Chalmers fetch you some tea?"

"No, no, thank you, my lord." He took the offered chair, placing his leather dispatch case beside it. "At His Grace's request, I am here to further discuss that letter."

"Of course you are." He resumed eating his breakfast. "You know, sometimes I wish Father would be less predictable. My dealings with him might be more interesting that way."

There was a rather awkward pause. Nicholas waited another ten seconds before he stopped eating and looked up. "Well?" he prompted. "You did come here to inform me of the terms under which my inheritance would be reinstated, did you not?"

Mr. Freebody smiled his dry little smile. "We don't

need to launch straight into legal matters, my lord. Do finish your breakfast. Do you plan to be in town long?"

He had no intention of giving anything away, and he kept his voice deliberately noncommittal. "I don't really know. Beyond enjoying the delights of the season, I don't have any fixed plans."

"But surely you shall at least visit Honeywood while you are here?"

"I hadn't thought that far ahead. Why do you ask?" He flashed the other man a grin. "Is Father afraid I might burn the place down for the insurance money?"

Freebody looked at him in some alarm, as if he were serious, and he reminded himself that lawyers had no sense of humor. They were rather like matchmakers in that respect.

With that thought, an image of Lady Featherstone's eyes came into his mind—beautiful blue eyes tinged with the icy frost of disdain. Glaciers were warmer than that woman; no, he revised at once, even glaciers could melt if the proper heat were applied. As to Lady Featherstone, he doubted thawing was possible. On the other hand, she did have those full pink lips and that luscious figure. A determined man could perhaps—

A slight cough drew his attention. Nicholas set aside contemplation of the various ways one might apply heat to Lady Featherstone and returned his attention to his visitor. He set down his knife and fork. "Let's cut to the heart of things, Freebody. You've known me all of my life, and there's no need to dance around, making polite conversation. Landsdowne is holding my inheritance over my head in order to force me to marry whatever woman he deems most appropriate for alliance with the great and oh-so-noble Landsdowne family. Do I have it right?"

The lawyer gave him an apologetic look. "Force is a rather harsh assessment."

"Landsdowne's a harsh man, or hadn't you noticed?"

"I'm sure His Grace's sincerest wish is for your marriage to bring you happiness."

Nicholas gave a laugh. "My dear man, spare us both the pretense that Landsdowne has ever cared about my happiness. He wants an heir, another pawn, another asset to put to use in the accumulation of his empire. That's all."

The lawyer ignored this summation of his employer's motives. "As you have already surmised, His Grace is prepared to reinstate your income from your mother's trust when you marry, if certain conditions are met. I am here to inform you of precisely what those conditions are and what else he is prepared to offer should you accept."

Nicholas raised a brow at that. "Sweetening the pot, is he?"

"He will give you a quarterly allowance—"

"No," Nicholas said, cutting off that dangling carrot at once.

"My lord, I realize you have not accepted an allowance from your father since you came into your own money, but you are entitled to his support, not only for yourself, but for your wife and children. He is willing to reinstate your allowance at double the previous amount, and by another ten percent with the birth of each of your children."

The duke was as miserly as he was ruthless, the main reason he still had so much money when peers all over England were going broke. For him to offer such a staggering sum, and without any haggling, was quite uncharacteristic of him, and Nicholas could only wonder what other shoe was about to drop. He didn't have to wonder for long.

"Your bride will one day be the Duchess of Landsdowne," Freebody went on, "and that is a position of great responsibility. To fulfill it, the woman you marry must be of the appropriate class."

Nicholas ignored the old bitterness that stirred inside him and leaned back, forcing a laugh. "There's a pretty little French dairymaid in Paris who brings the milk each morning. Perhaps I should send for her and take her up to Gretna Green. The old man might die of apoplexy, and all my problems would be solved."

These callous words made no dent in Freebody's unflappable, lawyerly reserve. "No elopements to Gretna Green, no dairymaids—French or otherwise—no shopgirls, no housemaids." There was a pause as the lawyer met his gaze across the desk. "No actresses."

So that was it. His grin widened. "Tempting as it might be to marry my most recent mistress and put the duke's knickers in a twist, Mignonette is a hardheaded Parisienne who's got far too much sense to take on marriage to me. And I do believe the little French maid's heart is already spoken for. So you may reassure my father that neither of them shall be the future Duchess of Landsdowne."

"She must be an Englishwoman of noble family, Church of England, with her father's rank no lower than that of earl. She must also have a sizable dowry."

He did not point out he was already in search of a woman who met none of those criteria except that last one. But he couldn't help being curious. "Landsdowne's rich as Croesus already. Why should he care if my wife brings a dowry into the family or not?"

The little lawyer drew himself up. "My dear Lord Trubridge, you cannot marry a girl with no dowry," he said, as if appalled by the very idea. "She could be a gold digger."

"Ah." Enlightened, he grinned. "Yes, I suppose that would make her too much like the last girl, wouldn't it?"

Freebody ignored the reference to Kathleen. "Your future bride must also have impeccable connections and an unsullied reputation."

Given this list of requirements, his father might just as well expect him to marry a mermaid. "I see. And does the duke have any idea where I might find such a woman as you describe? The aristocratic English heiress with a large dowry is a creature of a bygone era, I fear. Most men of our ranks are poor as church mice these days and in no position to provide their daughters with generous dowries."

"His Grace does have someone in mind."

"And who is this paragon of womanly virtue?"

"Lady Harriet Dalrymple."

"My God," Nicholas muttered, staring at the lawyer

in horror. "Landsdowne really does hate me. If I've ever doubted it, this gives me irrefutable proof."

"Lady Harriet is a wealthy heiress of excellent family and noble bloodlines," Mr. Freebody went on, doggedly determined to carry on with this joke of a negotiation. "She meets all your father's requirements."

"She doesn't meet mine. Lady Harriet weighs more than I do. Fifteen stone, at least, the last time I saw her. God, man, she has hair on her lip. And her voice . . ." He shuddered.

Mr. Freebody shot him a reproving glance, as if such considerations were completely irrelevant. "Lady Harriet's father is an earl, her fortune is immense, her family has no debts or mortgages, and her connections are among the best in the land. In addition, her morals are above reproach."

"Of course they are," he countered. "What chap would breach them?"

"Lady Harriet has also indicated a willingness to overlook certain . . . peccadilloes, shall we say, in your past. It's an excellent match, and your father feels that when the time comes, Lady Harriet will be an excellent duchess."

"If Landsdowne has his heart set on Lady Harriet, I advise him to marry her. I certainly shan't."

"Should you prefer another, equally suitable young lady, I'm sure your father would agree, provided she meets with his approval."

"Well, that's the sticky wicket, I fear. As you know, my father and I have such divergent opinions on the subject of suitability . . ." He paused to give the lawyer an apologetic look. "And since we've never agreed about anything else in our entire lives, it seems impossible that we should agree on my choice of bride."

"Very well. His Grace suggests that if Lady Harriet is not to your taste, you make a list of other young ladies more to your liking. He will be happy to consider them in his choice of bride for you."

Nicholas had heard enough. As a boy, his life had been controlled and manipulated by a man he barely knew, a man who had never been any sort of father to him, and he'd had little choice but to accept the situation. But he'd stopped being dictated to by Landsdowne the day Kathleen had departed for America with a sizable check from the ducal bank account, and he didn't have to listen to anything the old man might have to say.

"As much as I appreciate my father's offer to choose my wife for me," he said with a cheerful smile, "it won't be necessary. I believe I can handle that task on my own."

"Can you? Doing the season is an expensive proposition," Freebody pointed out. "You will need to lease a house, hire a carriage, and do a great deal of entertaining. With your income cut off, how will you manage?"

"Credit, of course. How else?" Nicholas shrugged and resumed eating his kidneys and bacon. "Credit is a wonderful thing, Freebody. Bankers are willing to offer it to anybody with a title."

"Quite. Have you . . ." The lawyer paused and gave a tactful little cough. "Have you visited your bankers since your arrival?"

Nicholas paused, feeling a sudden prickle of misgiving. "No," he answered, and looked up, meeting Freebody's gaze across the table. "Why?"

"They might not be as willing to extend credit as you assume."

His misgivings grew stronger, and he began to wonder if Landsdowne's latest interference in his life had only just begun. Still, it would never do to show a hint of alarm. "My bankers have never been mean about granting me credit when I have needed it."

"You do have debts at present."

"Yes, and an excellent history of paying my debts when they come due." He gave up on breakfast, set down his knife and fork with a clatter, and shoved his plate aside. "What are you driving at, Freebody? Spit it out. Is Landsdowne threatening to force my bankers to deny me credit?"

"I don't believe he shall have to take that step." The lawyer reached into the leather dispatch case beside his chair and pulled out a newspaper.

Nicholas glanced at the masthead and gave a snort of contempt. "*Talk of the Town*? I had no idea you read the scandal sheets, old boy. I am often discussed in them, I admit, but I fail to see how one more sordid, exaggerated story about me has any bearing on my credit."

"This one might." He folded the newspaper back to a particular page, leaned across the table, and placed the paper in front of Nicholas so that he could read the headline.

DUKE OF LANDSDOWNE CUTS OFF SON'S TRUST FUND!
DESTITUTE MARQUESS NOW DESPERATE
TO MARRY AN HEIRESS FOR MONEY

Nicholas stared at the article, and his apprehension gave way to something much stronger—a feeling akin to being kicked in the teeth. How had *Talk of the Town* tumbled to his straightened circumstances so quickly? Landsdowne? He knew from lifelong experience that the duke was ruthless enough to do just about anything to get his way, but not this, surely? Before he could come to any conclusions on the matter, Mr. Freebody spoke again, returning his attention to the material point.

"This story has caused your situation to be made public. Your bankers surely know of it, and it is doubtful they will offer you any additional credit, for you have no way to secure the loan's repayment."

Freebody was right, of course. Given this story, they'd want collateral. He had none. He took a deep breath and shifted his ground. "I can borrow against my expectations. As the press has already informed the world, I am in London to find a wife. Although I fear she won't come up to snuff in Landsdowne's opinion, I expect she'll bring a dowry satisfactory enough for my bankers and my pocketbook."

"To borrow against your expectations, there would need to be a wealthy fiancée waiting in the wings. Is there?" When Nicholas didn't answer, he went on, "You see? You may find your search for a suitable bride quite difficult."

Difficult? Nicholas thought of Lady Featherstone's

refusal to help him and her vow to do all she could to stand in his way, and he rubbed his forehead with an irritable sigh. Damned near impossible was quickly becoming a more apt description of his quest. He lifted his head, forcing aside his misgivings. "It won't be easy, I'm sure," he said, and took a sip of coffee. "But I shall fight the good fight, as they say."

The lawyer gave him a vinegary smile. "Forgive me for being blunt, but your blackened reputation—"

"And who was responsible for that?" he shot back, tired of having that wretched business thrown in his face, first by Lady Featherstone and now by Landsdowne's lawyer. "Did you know the duke had his fingers in that little pie? I doubt it, for you're a far straighter arrow than your employer."

A flicker of what might have been uncertainty flitted across the little lawyer's face, but it was gone before he could be sure. "Does it really matter how the incident came about? Your refusal to marry Lady Elizabeth nine years ago after the pair of you were caught in a compromising situation ruined both your reputations and will prove a serious impediment in your current search for a wife, particularly as you have made no efforts since then to regain society's good opinion."

He knew all that, but there wasn't much he could do about the past. He simply had to do his best to repair the damage now, if he could.

"Your father could be of great assistance to you," Freebody murmured as if reading his mind. "If Lady Harriet does not suit you, no matter. With his support behind you, no suitable woman would dare refuse you."

With those words, Nicholas could feel the same terrible sense of helplessness and rage he'd always felt as a boy growing up under Landsdowne's thumb. He thought he'd buried those feelings deep enough that they would never resurface, but he'd been wrong. Now, as they came welling back up inside him, he also felt a hint of despair. God, would he never be free of the damnable tyrant who had sired him?

He refused to accept that notion, and he closed his eyes, shoving all the raked-up despair back down, burying it, working until he once again didn't give a damn.

"Well," he said at last, and opened his eyes, "this has been a most fascinating conversation, Freebody. But then, it's always fascinating to see what Landsdowne's got up his sleeve. Thank you for informing me." He stood up, indicating this meeting was at an end. "I wish you good day."

The attorney also rose to his feet. "You father desires an answer to his proposition. What do you wish me to tell him?"

"Tell him . . ." Nicholas put on his most genial smile. "Tell the autocratic old bastard he can go to hell and take my trust fund with him."

Mr. Freebody did not seem surprised by his answer, but then, he was accustomed to such communications between father and son. This latest skirmish was nothing new. "Very well, my lord," he said, then he bowed and departed.

Nicholas sat back down with a sigh. As satisfying as it always was to tell the old man to go to hell, it did little to resolve his problems, which had now been made even more acute due to a sordid scandal sheet. With that thought, he snatched up the copy of *Talk of the Town* that Landsdowne's solicitor had left on the table. Just what had this damnable rag said about him?

Nicholas read the whole sordid essay, and with every word, his anger grew. Elizabeth Mayfield was mentioned, of course. And Mignonette, though the fact that he had broken with her before leaving Paris had somehow escaped their notice. Apparently the scandal-mongers at *Talk of the Town* hadn't appreciated the fact that a man with no money could no longer afford an expensive Parisian courtesan. There were also snippets about several other women he'd been involved with over the years, though thankfully, there was no mention of Kathleen.

By the time he'd finished the story, he was angry as hell, but he was also convinced beyond doubt that Landsdowne was in no way responsible. His father would never air the family's dirty laundry this way, not in a thousand years. So just how had the news of his situation fallen into the hands of the gutter press?

I'll stop you any way I can.

Lady Featherstone's voice rang in his ears as if she were sitting at his table and he had the answer to his question.

Yesterday, he'd been reasonably sure that any attempt on her part to warn young ladies away from him would fail because young ladies seldom heeded that sort of warning. But this was a different tactic, one he had not had the wits to foresee.

A man couldn't spend a season in town looking for

a bride if he had no money and no credit. And how in blazes was he to obtain said bride, with his intentions laid bare and his reputation besmirched all over again in London's most prominent scandal sheet, where every wealthy American family in London could read it?

It was an open secret that many transatlantic marriages were a trade of social position for money, but no girl wanted her social-climbing ambitions or her future husband's mercenary motives so flagrantly displayed. A public pretense of romantic love was expected on both sides, something which for him and his future bride was now off the table thanks to Belinda Featherstone. And even if some heiress were willing to ignore this bit of dirt as well as his rather notorious past, and if by chance he succeeded in obtaining her consent to wed him, what about her family? No father worth his salt would agree to the match. Eloping to Gretna Green might become his only option.

Since the incident with Lady Elizabeth, he was rather persona non grata with London society, which was why he'd gone to Belinda Featherstone in the first place. Little had he known his visit to her would have the opposite effect of the one he'd intended. In making his situation and chosen course public in so blatant a fashion, she had well and truly spiked his guns.

Devil take her. She'd not only betrayed his confidence by airing their *private* conversation in the gutter press, she'd ruined his credit and damaged his chances of marrying well. He was not about to let this move on her part go unchallenged. Taking up the paper, he rose to his feet. Lady Featherstone wanted a fight, did she? By God, he'd give her one.

Fifteen minutes later, he was on her doorstep and her butler was again expressing doubt as to whether she was home to visitors, but Nicholas had no doubt whatsoever on that score. She'd see him. How else would she have the opportunity to crow?

Nicholas was proved right when the butler returned. "If you will follow me, my lord," the servant said, and once again showed him into Lady Featherstone's drawing room.

She rose from her chair at the tea table as he entered the room, making a great show of setting aside the newspaper she'd been reading. Her expression was as cool and self-possessed as ever, but an unmistakable little smile curved her full lips. "Lord Trubridge."

"Lady Featherstone." He removed his hat and forced himself to bow.

She gestured to the silver tea service on the table. "Would you care for tea?"

"No." He strode forward, wasting no more time on banal civilities. "You went to the scandal sheets about me."

She didn't deny it nor even try to dissemble. "One scandal sheet," she corrected, and in those three words was enough relish to send Nicholas's temper up another notch.

Nonetheless, when he spoke, he kept his voice even and controlled. "The things I told you about myself and my situation were in confidence, madam."

"I deemed the hearts, virtue, and reputations of young ladies to be more important than your confidences."

"That was not your choice to make." He could feel a tiny muscle working at the corner of his jaw, and his hands were so tightly clenched around the brim of his hat, they began to ache. "You had no right."

"I had every right! The future happiness of many a young lady depends upon choosing a husband of fine and upstanding character. You, sir, are not one of those. And I fail to see why you are bothered about the story."

"Bothered? Lady Featherstone, I am more than bothered. I am outraged."

"But why should you be? According to what you told me yesterday, you are prepared to be an honest fortune hunter. If that is true, then why should it matter if the news of your financial situation comes out now rather than later?"

"Because having the news come out later would have given me the time to secure a loan from my bankers, which would have been enough to tide me over until the end of the season, by which point I had hoped to be married, or at least engaged. Now, thanks to you, I do not have even that small window of opportunity. I will be unable to secure the blunt to lease a house in town, cover the bills of tradesmen, or pay wages to a staff. How can I be expected to establish the connections I need to find a young lady to marry if I cannot even establish a household in which to entertain?"

"That is not my problem. Perhaps you should have

put by some of your income when you had it? Saved it for a rainy day?"

"Perhaps," he was forced to acknowledge. "But it's a bit late for that now."

"So it is. But for my part, I cannot feel anything but relief, knowing that no young lady shall be unknowingly beguiled and seduced by a scoundrel like you in the candlelight of your latest dinner party!"

"Dinner party?" he echoed through clenched teeth. "I doubt I could even procure the required joint of beef from the butcher, thanks to you. And as for honesty, I was prepared to be honest about my circumstances with my future wife and her family, yes, but that it is a far cry from having it bandied about in the scandal sheets! You say you care about reputations, madam, but that isn't quite true, is it? Only certain reputations matter to you. It is apparent others do not."

For a moment, a shimmer of what might have been guilt crossed her face, but it vanished before he could be sure. "You don't seem to care about your own reputation," she said after a moment. "Why should I?"

"Because not doing so makes you a humbug. You display yourself to all the world as a woman of honor and integrity, yet you do not hesitate to blacken the reputation of a man of whom you do not approve, based on no justification other than your preconceived ideas about his character."

"Your reputation was already blackened, and by your own actions. And you seem perfectly willing to blacken a young woman's reputation along with your own.

And," she added as he started to protest that unfair accusation, "your manner of living since then hardly does you credit. All of that, along with your words of yesterday, make your character quite clear."

"You know nothing about me or my character, madam. You—" Nicholas broke off, too frustrated by her reference to that episode with Elizabeth to continue. How ironic that with all the things he had done in his life, she'd chosen one of the things of which he wasn't guilty to condemn him.

"And now," she went on, "you intend to seduce another innocent girl, blacken her reputation, and force her into matrimony, so please do not pretend to take any sort of moral high ground here, sir!"

"What?" He stared at her in astonishment, but as the implications of her words sank in, his astonishment gave way to an even deeper rage. "Good God, is that what you think?"

"After you confessed your sordid intentions right to my face, what else was I to think? You said you would not be conducting a proper courtship. That you intended to conduct one that is as improper as possible."

"And you took that to mean I would ruin a girl publicly, thereby forcing her to marry me? I—" He stopped, for the notion he would do such a thing was so damned insulting that fury put him at a loss for words.

He looked down and realized he was crushing his hat. Worse, he could feel his temper giving way, and losing his temper was something no one had been able to make him do for a long, long time. Carefully, he set his mangled hat on the tea table between them, and when he spoke, he worked to keep his tone civil though it took a great deal of effort. "That you believe I would deliberately ruin a girl for money says far more about your mind than it does about my character."

"Does it? I wonder if Elizabeth Mayfield would agree."

"I doubt it," he shot back. "She's probably still cursing me for not being a more compliant potential bridegroom. After being trapped in a compromising situation that was prearranged by her, with the assistance of her mother, and conducted—I might add—under the explicit direction of my father, I was supposed to feel obligated to marry Elizabeth. I did not feel so inclined, much to my father's annoyance and Elizabeth's dismay. I realize gossip painted me the villain over it and that my reputation is still in ruins because of it, but as I told you once before, I don't give a damn what people think of me."

"You were the victim of manipulation by your own father?"

He laughed at the skepticism in her voice. "It's obvious you don't know Landsdowne, or you wouldn't be so surprised by the notion."

He leaned forward, bringing his body as close to hers as the table between them would allow, flattening his palms on the polished mahogany surface. "And it's equally obvious you don't know Elizabeth. If you did, you might not have been quite so ready to believe the worst about me. You might have paused to consider *her* character, and her mother's, too. God knows, I wish I had. I'd never intended to be alone with her at my father's house party. But when she encountered me in the library, even though it was late at night, I didn't see the harm in both of us looking for books to read at the same time. I was only twenty-one. And I was head over ears in love with someone else at the time, so amorous intrigues with Elizabeth never even entered my head. Call me a fool, but I had no idea she'd hurl herself into my arms just as her mother came through the door."

Her skeptical expression shifted to one of doubt, whether as to his actions or her own, he wasn't certain. At this point, he didn't care.

"That," he said as he straightened away from the table, "is the true version of the story, regardless of what gossip you might have heard to the contrary. I didn't know I'd be made for a mug until it was too late, but as I said, I was only twenty-one. You, however, don't have the excuse of foolish youth for your actions, madam. You could have made further inquiries into the matter, and as a result, perhaps judged me more fairly. But no, you jumped at once to the conclusion that would brand me the worst possible cad because for some reason, it's what you want to believe about me."

She bit her lip, her doubtful expression deepening, but after a moment, she rallied, shifting her ground. "Then what was your meaning yesterday when you referred to improper courtship?"

"I've no patience with the idiotic rules that govern finding a spouse. The chaperoned walks, the endless rounds of small talk where neither of us can say what we really think on any subject, dinner parties where precedent seats us at opposite ends of the table, whispered snatches of private conversation over sheets of music in the drawing room, dancing no more than twice together at balls—it's all rot. Nothing I can learn about a woman through society's stifling interactions will help me decide whether or not I want to marry her. Chaperones are a hindrance to two people getting to know each other, not a help."

"I see. So you would not compromise a girl on purpose, but you would still risk her reputation to satisfy your own ideas of courtship. And if doing so happened to result in a compromising situation that forced her to marry you, that would be quite convenient for you, wouldn't it?"

"For God's sake, I told you, I would never—" He broke off, for he was well and truly at the end of his tether. He couldn't remember the last time anyone had made him this angry. He also realized he was starting to defend himself, and he appreciated—too late—that coming here at all had been a strategic mistake.

Hadn't a lifetime as Landsdowne's son taught him anything? Defending, explaining, justifying . . . such things did nothing but make one vulnerable. And besides, his intentions, his notions of courtship, and his honor did not need defending. Not to her, and not to anyone.

"Think of me what you will," he said, and picked up his hat. "Say whatever you like. I am determined to find a wife, despite all your efforts. So do your damnedest to stop me."

"So I shall."

"Very well, then." He donned his hat. "But, by God, I hope you understand what this means?"

"No," she answered, her elegant dark brows lifting in haughty inquiry. "Enlighten me. What does this mean?"

"War, Lady Featherstone." He smiled, but as his gaze met hers, the clash of their eyes was like the clang of dueling swords. "This means war."

Chapter 4

As Belinda stared into Lord Trubridge's tawny hazel eyes, she was reminded again of a lion, one that was cornered and angry. Though there was a smile on his lips, he meant what he said about war, and she knew he would be a formidable opponent.

If his account of the Elizabeth Mayfield incident was true, and if she had indeed misunderstood his comment of yesterday, then she could not deny he had some justification for his anger. Nonetheless, he was still a fortune hunter with notions of courtship that could ruin a girl's reputation and force her to accept him. In light of that, Belinda made the only reply her conscience would allow. "War it is, then."

Before he could respond, Jervis entered the drawing room. "Miss Rosalie Harlow," he announced.

At once, Belinda's determination gave way to dismay.

She turned toward the doorway, but it was too late to stop Rosalie from entering the room. "Oh, last night was such a disaster, I just had to come and tell you— oh!"

She stopped, noticing that Belinda was not alone, and as Trubridge turned toward the door, her eyes widened, and her lips parted a little. When she lifted a fluttering hand to her throat and her parted lips formed a smile, Belinda's dismay deepened into panic. *Oh, no,* she thought, *no, no, no.*

"I didn't know that you had company," Rosalie told her without even bothering to glance in her direction. "I'm so sorry. I hope I haven't committed some awful breach of British etiquette."

Belinda could not think of a reply. She could only stare, helpless, as the girl tilted her chin down, still smiling, and lifted her gaze to Trubridge's face in a way that was openly admiring.

Belinda wanted to take her by the arm and haul her out of the room. A lamb like Rosalie in the same room with a predator like Trubridge was a disaster waiting to happen, and she cursed herself for not making that fact clear to the butler yesterday. To make matters worse, when she glanced at the marquess, his profile told her just what he was thinking.

His thick brown lashes lowered as he studied the girl, giving her the same appreciative thoroughness he'd given Belinda the day before. He bowed, and when he straightened, his mouth was curved in that devastating, deceptively boyish smile that would make any girl's heart sing.

A fierce wave of protectiveness rose up within Belinda. Her lip curled, and only just in time was she able to catch back a most unladylike snarl.

"Not at all," Trubridge answered the girl, taking advantage of Belinda's silence to step into the breach. "An interruption as charming as this is always forgivable." He turned to Belinda. "My dear Lady Featherstone, where have you been hiding this lovely creature?"

She glared at him; but, of course, he was impervious to her hostility.

"Shall you introduce me to your friend?" he asked, everything in his amused face daring her to refuse.

Insufferable man. She could not reject his request for an introduction when he was standing in her own drawing room, and both of them knew it. Left with no choice, she turned to Rosalie. "Miss Harlow, may I present the Marquess of Trubridge to you? Lord Trubridge, Miss Rosalie Harlow."

If she hoped the heavy disapproval that laced her voice would have any effect on Rosalie, she was disappointed. In fact, it was doubtful the girl even noticed.

"Lord Trubridge?" she cried with lively surprise. "Heavens, you are not at all like I pictured you." She turned to Belinda. "I don't understand. I thought you said he was—"

She stopped just in time, heeding Belinda's frantic shake of the head, and returned her attention to the man before her. "My lord," she said, remembering her manners and returning his bow with a curtsy. "How do you do?"

Trubridge, of course, couldn't let the moment pass

unremarked. "It sounds as if Lady Featherstone has been talking about me," he drawled. "How indiscreet of her. What has she been saying, Miss Harlow? Do tell me."

Rosalie laughed. "I can't. I'd be breaking a confidence."

"Ah, but confidences are made to be broken. Isn't that right, Lady Featherstone?"

Belinda tensed, but thankfully, he didn't press the point. Instead, he stepped forward, moving closer to the girl.

Belinda was quick to move with him, protective, watchful, and terribly afraid. She strove to think of a way to get Trubridge out of here before he could begin working his wiles on Rosalie, though the expression on the girl's face told her it might already be too late. Rosalie was staring up at him as if she'd just found a knight in shining armor, but Belinda knew the girl couldn't be more wrong. If he'd ever possessed a sense of chivalry, Trubridge had lost it long ago.

"I believe I detect a trace of American in your accent, Miss Harlow," he was saying. "Are you from New York? Or Philadelphia? Or perhaps you are one of those exotic creatures from the hinterlands of the Middle West?"

"Middle West?" Rosalie laughed at that very British turn of phrase. "I am from New York, my lord. Schenectady, to be exact. But I've been in France for the past year, at finishing school."

"And how do you find London?" he asked, taking

another long, appreciative glance over her person that made Belinda want to kick him.

"Quieter than I'd expected," Rosalie answered. "I thought the season here would be more exciting."

"Well, it has barely started," he told her. "Things don't really become lively until after the Royal Exhibition, and that opened yesterday. From now until August, you'll be happy to know, things will move at a pace that's absolutely frantic. You won't be able to catch your breath."

Jervis entered the drawing room before the girl could reply. "Mrs. Harlow has come in her carriage to fetch her daughter, my lady," he announced, and to Belinda, it was as if angels had begun to sing. "She apologizes most profusely for not coming up, but she's in a bit of a rush. She just remembered that she is supposed to be taking Rosalie to luncheon with the Dowager Countess of Esmonde, and she fears they will be late."

"Of course," she said at once, ignoring Rosalie's groan of dismay. "Tell Mrs. Harlow that her daughter will be down at once." She turned to Rosalie as the butler bowed and departed. "Time to be on your way, dearest."

"Must I? I was hoping to have luncheon with you."

"As Jervis just informed us, your mother had forgotten you have a prior engagement."

"Oh, but does it matter? Mama can convey my regrets to Lady Esmonde."

"That would be rude, Rosalie, and you do not want to be rude to Lady Esmonde."

"Maybe not, but I think she was quite rude to me when I was there a few days ago. She barks out questions, then answers them for you. And she makes remarks about how healthy American girls look and how nice our teeth are. It's very disconcerting. And she thinks we all live in teepees and wigwams."

Trubridge chuckled at that, causing Rosalie to laugh as well.

Belinda, the only one not amused, sent him a withering glance as she took the girl by the elbow and began pulling her toward the door. "Enough of that," she said, overriding the girl's protests. "It's nearly one o'clock, and if you linger here any longer, you'll be late. Being late to luncheon with a countess would be unthinkable."

"I don't see why. We are supposed to be late to balls. Why not lunch? And speaking of balls . . ." She stopped allowing herself to be propelled out of the room and turned toward Trubridge, yanking her arm from Belinda's grasp. "Are you attending Lady Montcrieffe's ball tonight, my lord?"

"I am, Miss Harlow," he said at once, causing Belinda to utter a sound of indignation, for she knew perfectly well Lady Montcrieffe would never invite a man like him to one of her balls. "I shall look forward to seeing you there. And I hope you will allow me the honor of claiming a dance with you?"

"Oh, that would be wonderful," she said before Belinda could think of a way to intervene. "The third waltz on my program is still open."

Belinda again reached for Rosalie's arm, but the girl

evaded the move and took a step toward Trubridge. "I've been saving the third waltz for someone special."

"I am honored," he said, taking up her hand, "that you would choose me to be your someone special."

Belinda almost gagged, but neither of the other two seemed to notice, and she could only watch as Trubridge kissed Rosalie's gloved hand. As he let it go, he gestured to the door with his hat. "I was just on my way out. May I walk you down and see you and your mother safely to your carriage?"

"Of course," she answered, and took his offered arm.

"An escort is hardly necessary," Belinda pointed out in desperation as she followed them toward the door. "The carriage is sure to be right outside."

Again, she was ignored.

"Good day, Lady Featherstone," Trubridge said, looking over his shoulder to give her a parting smile as he ushered Rosalie out of the drawing room.

In that moment, Belinda was shocked to discover the depths of rage that she was capable of feeling. No one, not even Featherstone, had ever caused the . . . the *eruption* of outrage she was feeling at this moment. Her palm itched—absolutely itched—to slap that satisfied smile off his face.

The two of them left the drawing room, but though Belinda was right behind them, she could only follow as far as the stairs, for she could not go all the way down without being forced to introduce Trubridge to Rosalie's mother. An introduction would convey her approval of him as an acquaintance to the daughter, and she most certainly did not approve. She had to content herself with hovering at the top of the stairs, watching as Rosalie performed the introduction she refused to make. When he and the ladies departed, she was racing back toward the drawing room before the door had closed behind them, and as they paused on the sidewalk outside her front door, Belinda watched from the window above.

Mrs. Harlow had indicated she was in a rush to reach Lady Esmonde's, but it was clear she seemed willing to postpone that visit for a bit. They lingered for what seemed like hours, and as she watched them through the window, as she watched Trubridge work on the girl with his charm and his smile, Belinda felt sick at heart.

Rosalie was such an innocent. If he chose, he could manipulate her into being alone with him easy as winking, subjecting her to his improper notions of courtship and leaving both of them open to scandal.

Equally awful was the possibility that Rosalie would lose her heart to him. Belinda knew how quickly girls fell in love, and Rosalie's temperament made her particularly vulnerable to the machinations of a rake. She could become infatuated with Trubridge before Belinda even had a chance to convince her of his reprobate character. Even the one dance they were to have could be enough to captivate the girl and close her ears to anything Belinda might say. In fact, the harder Belinda tried to keep her away from Trubridge, the greater her fascination with him might become. Girls could be so contrary.

She frowned, struck by a sudden thought. Just how

did he plan to attend Lord and Lady Montcrieffe's ball? Crashing it would hardly help him regain the company of good society. She couldn't imagine Nancy inviting him, but he'd seemed awfully sure of his ground.

She decided to pay a call on Nancy straightaway and clarify the matter. If he hadn't yet been given an invitation, she could at least try to prevent him from finagling one at the last minute. She might not be able to openly come out against him without hardening Rosalie's resolve, but she had to do something. The idea of her romantic, naive young friend being disillusioned, heartbroken, and chained for life to a man like Trubridge didn't bear contemplating. Somehow, this romance had to be nipped in the bud before it could flower into disaster.

IF IT WERE physically possible for a human body to burn with rage, Nicholas had no doubt Belinda Featherstone would be a smoldering mass of coals by now. He was well aware of her gaze boring into his back through the window above, and it gave him a great deal of satisfaction to know that every moment he made conversation with Miss Harlow and her mother increased her ire and her anxiety. *Good*, he thought. Now she knew what he'd felt as she had insulted his character and impugned his honor.

And it wasn't as if lingering here was a torture. Quite the contrary, for Rosalie Harlow was a pretty girl. With her honey blond hair, brown eyes, and plump cheeks, her prettiness was rather of the chocolate-box sort, and her lavish gown of pink-and-white-striped silk with its frothy white lace trimmings only served to emphasize that impression, but though she wasn't the sort of woman he usually preferred, he could not afford to be picky, and pretty was always better than plain. Nicholas began to think this visit to Lady Featherstone hadn't been a mistake after all.

He was happy to remain a few more moments, but only a few. A man who wanted to intrigue a woman never arrived too soon or stayed too long. After a few words of desultory conversation, he murmured something about another engagement, conveyed his regret that he could not remain in their company all afternoon, and expressed the hope he had not made them late to luncheon. The latter comment evoked exclamations of dismay from the two women and spurred them toward the luxurious brougham parked at the curb. He followed, assisted the ladies into the carriage, and closed the door behind them.

Rosalie immediately pulled down the window. "The third waltz, my lord?" It was meant to be a clarification, but Nicholas knew it was a hopeful reminder.

"The third, Miss Harlow." This assurance earned him a radiant smile and as he studied her happy countenance through the glass, he decided that Rosalie Harlow was a very pretty girl indeed. She was also charming, amiable, and obviously wealthy. And she seemed to like him, which was a pleasant contrast to the virago upstairs.

"Walk on," he told the driver, and he tipped his hat to Miss Harlow as the carriage pulled away from the curb. He waited on the sidewalk until the vehicle had turned the corner before he turned in the opposite direction.

He took a glance at the window as he started toward the hansom cab waiting for him, but Lady Featherstone was no longer there.

In declaring war to her this afternoon, Nicholas hadn't dreamed his first opportunity to win a battle would come so quickly. As she had introduced him to her young friend, he'd sensed a vulnerability in her that he hadn't seen before, a definite chink in her cool, polished armor that told him Rosalie Harlow wasn't just an acquaintance. She was a friend.

That thought brought with it a vague sense of disquiet, but he forced himself to shove that aside. He didn't have time for a consideration of Lady Featherstone's feelings, and truth be told, he wasn't particularly inclined to do so after what she'd done to him. It wasn't as if she'd spare him any such regard had their situations been reversed. Besides, he couldn't eliminate every woman who might be a friend of hers. No, he would have his dance with Miss Harlow, and if she proved amenable to him and he to her, there was no reason he could see not to pursue her.

A cough brought him out of his reverie, and Nicholas realized he was standing on the sidewalk with a hansom in front of him, and a driver up on the box who was no doubt charging him a fortune for each additional moment he lingered. Before he could give the driver a direction, however, he had to decide where to go from here.

His most pressing need was money, and thanks to Belinda Featherstone, his options for obtaining it had dwindled considerably, so he really had only one choice left, and that was Denys. He ordered the driver to take him to his friend's South Audley Street residence.

Denys, unlike most of their other friends, had decided to become respectable. He wasn't wealthy by any means, but like most bachelors of the aristocracy, he had a quarterly allowance, and he no longer strove to spend every cent before the next quarter's allotment came in. In addition, he had full use of his father's carriages, staff, and London house. Having mended his spendthrift ways, he'd surely be able to spare a few quid for an old friend.

Nicholas could only hope Denys had gotten over that silly business with the cancan dancer. After all, it had happened three years ago, and they'd been friends far longer than three years. Denys surely wouldn't hold a grudge.

"You son of a bitch." The fist hit him in the face before he had time to duck, sending Nicholas staggering back a step.

Damn, he thought, touching his cheek with a grimace. He'd forgotten Denys had such a smashing right hook. "Still a bit peeved about Lola, I take it?"

"Peeved? Not at all." Denys's dark eyes narrowed on Nicholas, warning him that another blow was coming.

He ducked in time. "Then why did you hit me?"

"Because you're here, and you're breathing." He swung again, but Nicholas had already jumped backward, out of reach. "Stand still, you bastard."

"I rather hoped Lola would be water under the bridge by now." Nicholas glanced around the other man's drawing room, looking for a barrier to put between them. Deciding the stout mahogany pedestal table nearby would do, he moved to stand on the other side of it. "I hoped we could let bygones be bygones."

"Did you?" Denys began circling the table, forcing Nicholas to do the same. "You were wrong."

"I can see that." He edged away as Denys came closer, but when the two men's positions were reversed, he gave it up.

"This is absurd," he said, and as the other man came the rest of the way around the table, Nicholas turned to face him, palms up in a gesture of truce. "Before you beat me to a pulp, can we take a moment to talk?"

"Talk about what? About you needing a loan?"

Nicholas sighed, lowering his arms. "I see you've read today's issue of *Talk of the Town*."

"I've no need to read it, not when everyone else already has, causing you to be the main subject being discussed at White's today. So Landsdowne's cut you off, has he? And now you need a loan, so you've come to me. Why me?"

He told the truth. "You're the only friend I've got who has any money."

Denys shook his head with a laugh. "God, you have gall, Nick, I'll say that for you."

"Well, yes," Nicholas agreed, "but in my defense, I did save your life once."

"Oh, please." Denys derided that notion with a snort. "Pongo would not have shot me."

"Only because I jumped between the pair of you and took the bullet on your behalf."

"Which was a stupid thing to do. When you came between us, it startled him, and he fired. He wouldn't have done so otherwise. He was just drunk and stirred up."

"Over a woman," Nicholas was quick to point out. "Pot," he added with a bow, "my name is Kettle."

Denys scowled at this reminder of his own past sins.

"That was different," he muttered. "Pongo didn't care tuppence for that barmaid. I loved Lola."

It was Nicholas's turn to offer a disbelieving snort. "You were in love every week."

"That's not true."

"No? Shall I take you back three years? Before Lola, there was Julianne Bardot, the opera singer. Before her, you had a passion for the Contessa Roselli. Before her, I believe it was that Scandinavian courtesan—what was her name? Anika? Angelica?"

"All right, all right, you've made your point." Denys squared his shoulders and straightened his tie with a little cough. "But I've changed since then. You haven't."

"That's absurd. Everyone changes."

"Not you, Nick. You are just the same at thirty as you were at twenty. Do you read what's said about you in the scandal sheets? I do, and your name crops up at least once a week. I vow, the London gossip columnists spend half their time across the Channel, following you and Jack around Paris, detailing your exploits. Hedonists, the pair of you. Why any woman should want you, I don't know, but odds at White's are that you'll be engaged by the end of the season, in spite of *Talk of the Town*."

"Really?" Nicholas's spirits brightened a bit. "Did you place a wager on me?"

"Only a small one. I picked Lady Idina Forsyte."

"The Earl of Forsyte's daughter?" He made a grimace. "Doesn't she have adenoids?"

"At least I didn't say Lady Harriet Dalrymple. She was one of the choices. Long odds on her, though. Most chaps think you'll do a bit better than that."

He gave the other man a wry look. "I wonder if Landsdowne placed the bet. Lady Harriet is his choice, which means that even if she were Helen of Troy, Sappho, and Aphrodite all rolled into one, I wouldn't have her."

"You really do hate Landsdowne."

"Do you blame me?"

"I suppose not. Still, Lady Harriet is horrid, and it would be no more than you deserved to end up with her."

"How vengeful you are. But, no, I can assure you that my bride will not be Lady Harriet. I'd never give Landsdowne the satisfaction. Besides, I've other, more delectable fish to fry."

"You've already set your sights on someone?"

"Perhaps. What do you know of Miss Rosalie Harlow?"

Denys whistled. "That's going for high game. She's one of the season's acknowledged beauties, and her father is one of the richest men in America. Of course, you'll have to make it past the dragon at the gates."

"Lady Featherstone being the dragon in question? She's already breathed her fire on me. I came away quite singed by the encounter."

"Good on her." Denys grinned. "That pleases me more than words can say."

Nicholas grinned back. "Pleased enough to give me a loan?"

The other man stared at him in amazement, shaking his head, laughing as if in disbelief. "How do you manage it?"

"Manage what?"

"To keep us friends."

He straightened the camellia in his buttonhole and smoothed his lapel. "My charm? My wit? My—"

"Enough," Denys cut him off. "Any more of that, and I'll be sick. How much do you need?"

"Can you spare a thousand?"

"All right, but I'm charging you interest. Four percent."

"Per annum?"

"Per month."

"That's extortion."

"No," Denys corrected, folding his arms. "It's justice."

He was in no position to negotiate. "Four percent it is. Are lodgings at your house included in this offer?"

"What? Allow you to live in my house for the foreseeable future?"

"This isn't your house. It's Earl Conyers's house. You, Viscount Somerton, live here due to your father's goodwill."

"And my mother's. She won't like it, you know, having you here with all the scandal attached to your name."

"Couldn't she see her way clear for the man who saved her son's life?" Ignoring Denys's sound of exasperation, he added, "And I won't be staying forever, just until the end of the season."

"Only if you've found a wife by then. If you don't, we shall be stuck with you for God knows how long."

"You said yourself the odds are in my favor. But if I am to find a wife, I simply must have a respectable address. And, anyway, you have a bet riding on this, so it's in your best interests to assist me as much as possible."

"Lease a house. Let a flat. Find a hotel."

"This is London, Denys, and it's the season. A house, or even a flat, is rare as hen's teeth this time of year, meaning that even if I could find one, I couldn't afford the rent. And hotels are so inconvenient if one wants to entertain."

"Is there anything else you need? Seats in my father's box at Covent Garden? An evening of cards with the Prince of Wales? Use of the carriages?"

"All those would be splendid," he said, jumping on the offer and ignoring the sarcasm. "And if you could persuade Montcrieffe to invite me to his ball tonight, I believe I'll be on my way to a smashing season."

"Lovely. I think I shall go to the country."

"Nonsense." He clapped his friend on the shoulder. "You'll enjoy yourself enormously with me for company. You always do. C'mon."

"Are we going somewhere?" Denys asked, as Nicholas began leading him toward the door.

"White's."

"But I've just come from there."

"I want to see who else has been suggested as a bride

for me besides Lady Harriet and Lady Idina. Feel free, by the way, to offer the names of any wealthy heiresses you can think of who might be open to the idea of marrying a broke, down-on-his-luck marquess."

"I thought you'd already set your sights on Miss Harlow?"

"There's no guarantee we'll suit, so I need other alternatives in case Miss Harlow doesn't pan out. I say, that's an idea." He stopped, bringing the other man to a halt as well.

"What's an idea?" Denys asked.

He turned toward his friend. "Is your sister still as pretty as I remember?"

Denys scowled. "Don't push your luck."

Chapter 5

Nicholas had the good fortune to encounter Lord Montcrieffe at White's, and with Denys's assistance, he was able to finagle an invitation to attend the ball that evening with his friend. While dressing for the event, however, a note from Lady Montcrieffe was brought to him by one of Lord Conyers's footmen, a note that told him he wasn't the only one doing a bit of finagling. "Lady Featherstone has been busy, Chalmers," he told his valet as he scanned the letter. "She has brought out the heavy guns against me."

"Indeed?" The servant's tone was polite but uninterested. Chalmers was a tall, cadaverous fellow who looked more like an undertaker than a valet and took the proper knotting of a man's tie far too seriously. It made him an excellent valet but a poor conversationalist. "If you could lift your chin a bit?"

Nicholas complied, lifting the letter as well so that he could keep reading while Conyers formed his white silk tie into a proper bow. "I'm told other members of the ball committee would be appalled if they knew Montcrieffe had issued a verbal invitation, especially at this late date. She begs that I not attend in order to spare her husband censure from the others on the committee. The implication, of course, is that if I refuse the lady's request, I am unchivalrous."

"It seems quite a conundrum, my lord." Chalmers stepped back to consider his handiwork. He tweaked the bow a bit, then brushed a speck of lint from Nicholas's black tailcoat and dressed his buttonhole with a pristine white gardenia. Satisfied at last, he reached for the ice poultice reposing in a silver bowl on the dressing table, an action Nicholas was impelled to protest.

"Good God, not again." He turned his face to the side as his valet attempted to apply the ice to his left cheek where Denys had hit him. "My face is already numb from your efforts. Surely the swelling has abated by now."

"Only for the moment. Ice must be applied for several minutes every half hour, or the swelling will return. You wouldn't wish to appear in public with a goose egg on your face. What would the ladies think?"

Desperate, he turned his face the other way to evade his valet's ministrations. "A swollen face and a black eye might be considered romantic to the ladies."

"The black eye won't appear until at least tomorrow. But though there's nothing I can do about that, it is my duty as your valet to ensure you not attend an important social event with a swollen face." He pressed the poultice gently but firmly to Nicholas's eye, seeming in no doubt that his master would attend the ball despite Lady Montcrieffe's request.

Chalmers knew him well. The letter was Lady Featherstone's doing, and Nicholas had no intention of playing along. He'd have his waltz with Miss Harlow despite that woman's machinations.

Two hours later, however, he wondered if his decision to forgo Lady Montcrieffe's goodwill had been a futile sacrifice. As all charity balls were known to be, the ballroom at Montcrieffe House was packed with people. Rosalie Harlow, however, did not seem to be among the crowd. He circled the ballroom twice, but even with only a few minutes remaining before the third waltz, he still had not found her.

He started round again, but before he could resume his search for his quarry, he came face-to-face with another woman, the one he'd thought only yesterday would be the answer to all his problems. Unfortunately, Belinda Featherstone was proving to be his nemesis.

Despite that, his gaze slid downward, and he noted with both chagrin and masculine appreciation how her ball gown of ice blue satin clung to every luscious curve of her body. The deep, square neckline emphasized the exquisite shape of her breasts. The fashionably tight skirt scattered with seed pearls sheathed her shapely hips and trailed behind her in a train edged with ivory lace. Pearls peeked from amid the tendrils of dark hair piled atop her head and wrapped her long, slender neck, pearls so well matched they couldn't possibly be real. Nicholas stared at the generous expanse of creamy skin that warmed those pearls, and his throat went dry. Only half a dozen feet away from him, and yet, she seemed as distant and untouchable as the glittering, starlit sky.

Despite that impression—or perhaps because of it—he could feel arousal flaring up within him as he looked at her. It quickened his pulses and thrummed through his veins and spread through his body before he could even think to check it.

Damnation. Of all the things he ought to be feeling at the sight of her, lust shouldn't have been one of them. He tried to gather his wits, not an easy thing to do given the sight before him, and as the seconds ticked by, he realized that while he was standing here gaping at her like a randy adolescent, she was staring back at him with all her usual polished composure.

Nicholas took a deep breath, working to tamp down desire and don the mask of indolence he'd always found so effective at hiding inconvenient vulnerabilities. It was a mask he'd had plenty of practice putting on throughout his life, but at this moment, he was finding it a rough go. He felt naked, and in a way that was not the least bit pleasant. What was it about this woman that always seemed to throw him off his trolley?

"Lady Featherstone." He gave her his deepest bow, and by the time he straightened, he was smiling, but he felt as if even the widest smile and most carefree air he could put on wouldn't convince the perceptive woman before him.

She didn't move to respond in kind, and he tensed,

wondering if she intended to give him the cut direct. With her influence in society, that would be a serious blow to his chances, but there was nothing he could do about it, so he tried to adopt a nonchalant air as he waited to be snubbed.

She was tempted, he could tell, but after a moment, she gave a quick nod of acknowledgment and a slight curtsy. It was probably the briefest, most inconsequential acknowledgment ever given by a lady to a peer, but she'd given it.

Astonished, he turned to watch her as she stepped around him and walked on, still not quite able to believe it. They were at war, weren't they? Granted, cutting him would cause gossip, but this was the perfect opportunity for her to show he was unworthy of notice by respectable society and demonstrate to any young ladies who might be watching—or at least to their mamas—that he was not a man to be trusted. So why hadn't she taken that opportunity?

As he watched her move toward the doorway, Nicholas was forced to set aside his speculations about Lady Featherstone, for the woman he'd actually come here to see had just arrived in the ballroom.

Rosalie was standing inside the doorway with her mother, greeting Lord and Lady Montcrieffe and various other members of the charity-ball committee. Dressed in blush pink silk, her blond hair a mass of soft curls and ringlets, she made quite a pretty picture— that is, he amended as his gaze strayed to the shapely backside of Lady Featherstone, if a man kept his eyes on her and not on a certain raven-haired she-dragon.

He returned his attention determinedly to the girl, but he waited until the musicians gave the cue that the third waltz was beginning before he moved toward her. Rosalie greeted his approach with a radiant smile, and he gave her an answering wink as he passed her to speak with the viscount. "Montcrieffe," he greeted for the second time this evening. "Thank you again for your kind invitation."

"Not at all," the viscount assured, though he cast an uneasy glance at his wife, just as he had upon Nicholas's arrival. For her part, the viscountess gave him the same frosty nod she'd greeted him with earlier, and when he glanced at the ladies beside her, she gestured to them with obvious reluctance. "Lord Trubridge, I believe you are already acquainted with my friends Lady Featherstone, Mrs. Harlow, and Miss Harlow?"

"I am. In fact, I believe Miss Harlow has promised me the next dance."

Rosalie's smile widened even more. "So I have, my lord."

"Then may I claim it?" He glanced at her mother. "With your permission, of course, madam?"

It was clear that Lady Montcrieffe was not the only one who had been warned about him. Mrs. Harlow's displeased toss of the head was a far cry from her friendliness earlier in the day, but she made no protest as he offered his arm to her daughter and led her to the floor.

"I was sure Mama wouldn't let me dance with you," Rosalie told him as the waltz began.

He pretended obtuseness. "Why ever not?"

"She'd been warned about you by Auntie Belinda."

"Auntie Belinda?" he echoed, surprised by the address. "I did not realize Lady Featherstone was your aunt."

"Oh, she isn't a blood relative. But she's very close to our family. I've known her since I was a little girl, and although I call her Auntie, she's more like an older sister, really."

"And did she give you the same warnings about me that she gave your mother?"

Rosalie rolled her eyes. "Heavens, yes, and before I'd even met you. I was there when you first called on her yesterday, and she sent me home at once. She didn't want to introduce us."

"So that explains why she had me cooling my heels in the library. She wanted to keep us apart."

"Yes. She told me you were an odious man." Rosalie laughed. "And that you were fat. And that you had gout from drinking and bad breath from smoking cigars."

If Belinda Featherstone was so desperate as to tell easily provable lies about him before she'd even known his purpose, she must be absolutely frantic now. He found the notion reassuring in the wake of his own tendency to let his wits go to pieces when she was anywhere near him.

"I do not smoke, Miss Harlow," he said, "and though I do drink, it is seldom to excess, for I've found it's not worth the suffering on the day after. So on those points, at least, your Auntie Belinda is quite wrong. As to the rest, well, you shall have to judge me for yourself."

The laughter left her face. She gazed up at him, her brown eyes shining. "I think you're splendid."

She hadn't meant to say that, he knew, for she blushed, biting her lip and lowering her gaze to his cravat. But though she seemed to think her comment gauche and unsophisticated, Nicholas couldn't see it in that light. He was as happy as the next man to receive such unqualified praise, especially in light of the battering he'd been receiving of late from a certain other female.

"What a beautiful compliment. Thank you." He pulled her a fraction closer. "And I think you are very pretty."

She lifted her chin, rewarding him with another smile, and yet in that moment, Nicholas was swamped by sudden doubts. This girl was so terribly young. Naive, too—far more naive than her typical British counterpart. It was also plain she'd developed an unabashed hero worship for him, and he wondered if he should disengage, now, before her heart was in play. He didn't want to hurt her, and if he kept on, he very well might. A girl like this was bound to have expectations about him, unrealistic expectations he didn't know if he could ever fulfill. Even if they wed, could he make her happy?

Nicholas had no intention of falling in love again, but a girl like this might very well fall in love with him. In such circumstances, if he married her, it was inevitable that her romantic illusions about him and about love would eventually be shattered. How ironic that the qualities that would make winning her an easier task— her youth and her artless innocence—were now the very qualities that made him hesitate. When he looked into Rosalie's big brown eyes, he received the distinct impression of a sweet little cocker spaniel gazing at its master, and he felt a twinge of something else, something that only made his doubts grow stronger.

It took him a moment to identify the feeling, and he realized in aggravation that it was *guilt*. When he thought about persuading this girl to marry him, he felt as if he was taking candy from a baby. As if he was shooting fish in a barrel. As if, somehow, he wasn't playing fair.

Irritated with himself for this inconvenient sense of fair play, he tore his gaze away from Rosalie's, but even without looking at her, he could still feel her adoring gaze on him. It made him deuced uncomfortable because he knew it was an adoration he hadn't yet earned. It wasn't real. It wasn't him she adored, but the idea of him.

That realization had barely passed through his mind before he once again caught sight of Belinda standing at the edge of the dance floor, and resentment overcame this sudden attack of conscience. It was due to her precipitate actions that his choice of candidates was so limited, and it was that thought that enabled Nicholas to return his attention to the pretty girl in his arms. He smiled into Rosalie's adoring eyes, shrugged off guilt, and reminded himself that all was fair in love and war.

BELINDA DIDN'T KNOW it was possible for a nine-minute waltz to seem like nine hours. Watching the girl fall right into his grasp like a ripe plum was infuriating, but even worse, she felt as if she were watching history repeat itself, and that was more painful than she would have thought possible.

"Penny for your thoughts."

Belinda jerked her gaze away from Trubridge and Rosalie to find Lady Montcrieffe beside her. "Oh, Nancy," she said with a sigh, "you don't want to know what I'm thinking right now."

Nancy turned her head toward the dance floor, causing her pale hair to catch the light from the ballroom's chandeliers overhead. "I think I can guess."

Belinda followed her friend's gaze. "And to think he didn't even have an invitation when he arranged this dance with her," she muttered. "How he managed to finagle one out of your husband this afternoon at White's I still don't understand. Talk about the devil's own luck. I couldn't believe it when you told me. What was Montcrieffe thinking to issue an invitation like that, on the spur of the moment?"

"You know men. They just don't understand the social implications of these things. I did try to persuade Trubridge not to come, but as you can see, I was not successful."

"Thank you for making the attempt." She lost sight of Trubridge and Rosalie amid the couples swirling across the floor, and she leaned one way and then another, trying to find them again. "I do appreciate it."

"It was the least I could do after you came to see me this afternoon." Nancy gave an unexpected chuckle. "With the temper you were in, how could I refuse? You know, in the entire ten years I've known you, I don't believe I've ever seen you like that—spitting mad and muttering about finding a pistol."

Belinda glanced at her with a smile. "And to think it was you who pressed upon me the importance of being cool and unflappable at all times when I first came to England."

"As if you ever needed that sort of instruction. Most of the time, I had to force conversation out of you, remember? It was like prying apart an oyster."

"I've opened up a bit since then, thankfully."

"Yes, but today, I saw a side of you I don't believe I've ever seen before. You were pacing back and forth across my drawing room, waving your hands in the air like an Italian and condemning all fortune hunters to perdition!"

"It's that man," she said, returning her attention to the dance floor, her gaze homing in on Trubridge almost at once. "He flicks me on the raw."

"To say the least. I thought you were going to cut him a moment ago."

She bit her lip. "I feared I would only encourage Rosalie to champion his cause if I did that. Ooh, look at him," she added, nudging Nancy with her elbow. "See how he looks at her? It's as if he's contemplating some delectable confection in a bakery-shop window."

"Well, Rosalie is rather like a confection, isn't she? Very pretty and very sweet. Trubridge isn't the only man to appreciate those qualities."

"I doubt either her beauty or her sweetness intrigue him as much as her dowry."

"Perhaps, but what else can he do but marry money? After that story in *Talk of the Town* this morning, I doubt he could even extend his credit and get a loan."

Belinda shifted her weight, feeling a nudge of guilt. "Well, yes," she mumbled, "I suppose that's true."

"Unless he marries soon or his father relents, he'll be reduced to borrowing from the more unsavory money-lenders and living off friends."

"All right, yes, so the man is without means," Belinda conceded with some irritation. "By that argument, any fortune hunter is justified in his course to marry solely for money!"

"That's not what I'm saying, but you and I both know money is a crucial consideration for most peers when choosing a bride, and for whatever reason, you are judging Trubridge rather more harshly than you have other men in his situation. I don't think you are viewing him or his actions objectively."

That was the same accusation Trubridge had thrown at her earlier today, and all of a sudden, she felt on the defensive. "You think I'm being unfair? To *Trubridge*?" She turned toward her friend in disbelief. "Nancy, of all the men whose cause you might take up, he's the least worthy of your defense!"

"There, now you've just proved my point. Why is he more unworthy than any other gentleman you've nudged toward one of our friends?"

"Because of his character, of course! He has none."

Nancy sighed. "Belinda, I've never seen a better judge of character than you. In most cases, you can glance over someone, have a few minutes conversation, and walk away with an accurate assessment of that person. It's almost uncanny."

"Thank you, but doesn't that justify my concern?"

"You didn't let me finish. You also judge people very quickly, and though your assessments are usually accurate, you can sometimes be mistaken. Remember Baron Ambridge? You had him pegged for a rascal, but Louisa Barstowe married him anyway, and she is quite happy with him. I could cite one or two other examples, if you like. And do we even need to talk about Featherstone?"

"All right, all right," Belinda said hastily, not wishing to discuss her own lapses in judgment, particularly that one. "So you think I'm wrong about Trubridge?"

"I think you *might* be wrong, and perhaps you should reserve judgment and come to know him a little better before you decide."

She didn't want to know him. She didn't want Rosalie to know him. She wanted him to go back to Paris. She started to return her attention to the dance floor, but her gaze fell upon Sir William Bevelstoke standing nearby. Like her, he was watching the dancing, and she could tell the situation was as plain to him as it was to her. The rigidity of his profile, the proud lift of his chin, and the tight press of his lips told her the acuteness of his suffering at this moment. Sir William was a good and honorable young man who genuinely cared for Rosalie and would make her a fine husband, yet the girl seemed unable to see it. Instead, she was attracted to a man who had not demonstrated any of the fine qualities Sir William possessed. Life, she thought in aggravation, was damned unfair.

"Defend him all you like, Nancy," she said, "but I doubt coming to know him any better would change my opinion of him. Will you excuse me for a moment?"

She moved past her friend to the brown-haired young man nearby. "Sir William?"

He turned. "Lady Featherstone," he said with a bow. "Are you enjoying yourself this evening?"

She made a face. "As much as you are, I would imagine."

He stiffened at once and looked away. "I don't know what you mean."

"I think you do." She watched as his gaze strayed to the dance floor, and she added, "Rosalie isn't in love with him. Not yet, not by a long way. She only just met him."

He shrugged his shoulders. "It doesn't matter."

He wasn't fooling either of them with that declaration, but she didn't point it out. This was the hellish side of matchmaking, when things didn't turn out the way they ought, and hearts were broken. In this case, however, Belinda could not simply blame the whims of fate. She feared she came in for a fair share of the blame as well. For her rash actions in going to the press had not only ignited Trubridge's temper this afternoon but had also honed his attention on her young friend. He now seemed determined to pursue Rosalie, if for no other reason than to spite her. They were, after all, at war.

She turned and put a hand on Sir William's arm.

"Fight for her. Don't stand by in typical British, stiff-upper-lip fashion. Fight for her. And I'll do whatever I can to help you."

She walked away before he could ask what she could possibly do, for she wouldn't have known how to answer. She only knew that she had to think of something fast, before Rosalie lost her heart, and possibly more, to Trubridge.

Chapter 6

Belinda hung back as the waltz came to an end, waiting just long enough for him to return Rosalie to the care of her mother before she came to his side. At once, before he could engage the girl in further conversation, she latched onto his arm.

"You haven't yet danced with me, Trubridge," she said, forcing out a laugh. "There is another waltz beginning, and I love the waltz. Shall we?"

She gave him no chance to think of an excuse to refuse. Her arm through his, she turned, pulling him with her and practically dragging him toward the dance floor. To her relief, he allowed himself to be dragged.

"Lady Featherstone, you honor me," he said as he faced her and gave a bow.

"Honoring you is not what I feel like doing at this

moment, believe me," she answered, smiling at him through clenched teeth as she sank down in a responding curtsy. "I am contemplating homicide or torture," she went on as she caught up her train and straightened with its loop around her wrist. "But I can't decide which appeals to me more."

"You can make up your mind while we dance. Speaking of which," he added as she lifted one of his gloved hands in hers and slapped the other to her waist, "do you lead when you waltz, too, or merely during the preliminaries?"

"That depends," she countered sweetly. "Can I waltz you straight to hell?"

"I'd adore it, since it's a place I've wished you to once or twice during the past two days. But if that happens," he added with an apologetic look, "you'll have to spend eternity with me."

She shuddered visibly. "Perish the thought."

The waltz began, and though it occurred to Belinda how gratifying it would be to tread on his feet in her high-heeled slippers, she resisted the temptation. Instead, she racked her brain for ideas, but she was forced to admit there was really only one option. She would have to retract her refusal and help him find a wife. If she did, some other girl's heart, fortune, and virtue might be at risk, but she'd have to worry about that later. Right now, Rosalie was her most important consideration. "All right," she said. "You win."

"I win?" he echoed. "What does that mean, exactly?"

"I mean the war is over. I . . ." She paused, hating that she had to give in. "I surrender."

"Do you, now?" His gaze roamed over her face. "And in this surrender, what shall you yield to me?"

Lord, she thought, this man could make anything sound naughty. At that thought, an inexplicable heat curled in her belly, but she dampened it at once and spoke again. "If you leave Rosalie alone, and if you swear you won't risk placing her or any other innocent girl in a compromising situation, I will use my influence to help you find someone else."

"I see." He tilted his head as if considering it, but if she'd hoped steering him away from her friend would be as easy as that, she was mistaken. "I don't see why I need your help at all, now that I've met Miss Harlow."

"It's because of me, isn't it?" She stared at him, dismayed. "You're taking revenge on me because I went to that newspaper."

His fingers tightened at her waist, pulling her an inch closer as they danced. "I have my flaws, Lady Featherstone, but exacting vengeance upon women is not one of them."

"Then why her?"

"Why not her?" he countered. "She's quite pretty, amiable—a delightful girl all around."

"And rich."

"Well, yes," he said, sounding nauseatingly agreeable. "We've already established I can't afford to marry a poor girl."

"If you want to know why Rosalie would not be the right wife for you, I can give you several reasons. The difference in your ages, for one. She is only eighteen. You're far too old for her. She's an innocent, just out of finishing school, while you are world-weary and cynical. You should soon grow tired of her, and if you were not allowing your enmity for me to cloud your judgment, you would already have come to that conclusion yourself."

"Would I? Being such a jaded—and apparently ancient—fellow, I might find Miss Harlow's youth and innocence to be charming, refreshing qualities. Why, she might even make me feel young and spry again."

Belinda made a scoffing sound at that bit of nonsense. "You know as well as I do that she's too young for you. And her youth, her background, and her temperament make her ill prepared to be a duchess."

"Ah, but she won't be a duchess yet. Plenty of time for her to learn how it's done while she's merely a marchioness."

"Is there plenty of time? Your father could die tomorrow."

"A delightful prospect, I grant you, but—alas—one unlikely to happen. I wouldn't be that lucky."

"Will you please stop making jokes?"

"What makes you think I was joking?" His voice was still lighthearted and jovial, yet even as he spoke, she watched something flicker in those warm, tawny eyes, something dangerous that reminded her of the lion about to spring, and she realized he wasn't joking at all.

Belinda wondered what could have caused the enmity that existed between him and Landsdowne even as she reminded herself that it was none of her affair. "The fact that you regard your father's death as a fortunate circumstance is something I do not wish to explore. Let's return to the point at issue, which is that Rosalie is not for you."

The dangerous glimmer vanished from his eyes, like a candle snuffed out, but she knew she had not imagined it. "Tell me, are you always this sure of yourself and your assessments?"

"Well, I do this sort of thing for my living, you know."

"Granted, and if you had pegged me accurately, I might place more value upon your opinion. But as it is . . ." He shrugged. "You'll have to do better than this if you want me to eliminate Rosalie from consideration. Aside from her youth and her inexperience with future-duchess duty, do you have any other reasons why I should not pursue her?"

"You haven't spent enough time considering other women?" She winced at her own words even before he began laughing.

"Is there no way to satisfy you, Lady Featherstone? A day ago, you accused me of having too much experience with women. Now you say I haven't enough?"

Belinda gave in to temptation and stepped on his foot.

He grimaced, but he didn't miss a step. "Careful," he warned. "Causing me pain won't help convince me."

"Then stop toying with me."

"I like Rosalie, and I see no reason why my affection for her should not continue to grow. And she seems fond of me. You said yourself that fondness and affection is a solid foundation for matrimony—"

"Yes, yes, I know what I said," she interrupted, not in any mood to have her own words used against her. "But this fondness you speak of is superficial at best. The two of you aren't well acquainted enough for anything deeper. Not yet. If you were to withdraw now, no one's feelings would be hurt. And as I said, I will help you find someone else."

"I'm still not sure why that should persuade me."

Belinda began to feel truly desperate. "For heaven's sake, what else do you want?"

His lashes lowered, and the slow gaze he ran down her body was as tangible as a caress. "What else do you have to offer?"

Her heart slammed against her ribs, and stupidly, she stumbled.

"Steady on." His hands tightened, keeping her upright until she could regain her balance. "For someone who moves in high society, you don't dance very well. You keep treading on my feet."

"Your feet aren't the only parts of your anatomy I'd like to tread on," she muttered.

That made him smile, the wretched man. "All the reasons you offer could apply just as well to every other wealthy American debutante in town. By your reckoning, I ought to steer clear of any woman who is young, sweet, rich, and who might have the slightest chance of falling in love with me."

That, she thought, would be ideal, but she refrained from saying so. "Rosalie is my main concern."

His smile faded to a serious expression and he eyed her thoughtfully. "What's really behind this?" he asked. "You hardly know me, yet you are convinced my marriage to your friend would be disastrous. What makes you so sure? If you explained your reasoning, if you told me the truth, I might be persuaded to consider someone else."

"The truth?" As she repeated those words, something inside Belinda snapped. "You really want the truth?" She jerked out of his hold, grabbed him by the arm, and started off the dance floor with him in tow.

"Leading again?" he asked, as she propelled him toward the French doors that opened onto the terrace. "I suppose next you'll be wearing trousers and petitioning Parliament for the right to vote."

Belinda didn't respond to that. She couldn't. She was in no frame of mind for his nonsense. She was having enough difficulty keeping her temper in check long enough to get him outside where they could have a flaming row without being observed by all of society. She dragged him through the open doors and out into the cool night air. Fortunately, no one else was outside at present, and she only had to pull him a few yards away from the open doors before she could let fly.

"If you want the truth, I shall be happy to give it to you." She yanked her arm out of his and faced him. "I don't want you to marry Rosalie because you'll hurt her, damn you! You're handsome, you're glib, you're witty, you can even—sometimes—be charming, and you're a man of vast experience who knows a great deal about women. Rosalie's out of her depth with a man like you. She'll fall madly in love with you, only to discover after you've married her that you never loved her."

He didn't reply. He didn't even try, and his silence only flared her temper higher.

"She'll realize you never cared for her at all and wanted her only for her money. She'll learn you never had any intention of honoring the marriage vows you took, and that the promise you made to love and cherish her was a lie. And the part about forsaking all others? When you return to whichever mistress you happen to have at the moment, she'll realize that was a lie, too."

She could hear her voice shaking, but she pressed on. "At first, she'll hope her love will change you, and when that doesn't work, she'll be heartbroken and disillusioned, with no choice but to stand by, powerless, expected to be a good and proper wife while you spend her money on your pleasures and she tries to convince herself that your behavior is just something all British lords do and she has to accept it because she's stuck with you for good. Now are my reasons clear?"

She stopped, out of breath, and they stared at each other as the lilting strains of the waltz gave way to the lively cue of a polka. It seemed an eternity before he spoke.

"I never realized Featherstone was such a bastard."

She blinked. "I beg your pardon?"

"I didn't know him all that well, granted, but I always thought him an amusing, delightful fellow. I knew about his women, of course, but I didn't know you, or why the two of you were estranged, and I didn't really dwell on Featherstone's qualities as a husband. If someone had asked me to consider him in that light, I daresay I'd have offered a different opinion of the man."

Belinda lifted her chin a notch. "Leave my late husband out of this. He has nothing to do with it."

"He has everything to do with it when I'm being tarred with the same brush. You don't know me well enough to judge what sort of man I am or what sort of husband I would be, but you've formed a very definite opinion on the subject. You think I'm like him."

"Are you saying you would be any different?"

"Damned right I'd be different. As I told you, I'm prepared to make any woman I'm considering fully aware of my situation and the financial aspects of our union beforehand. And I would never expect fidelity from my wife without offering it in return. And when a man has a beautiful woman who adores him waiting at home, he's not only a prize bastard for going elsewhere, he's also a fool."

"Oh." Belinda didn't know what else to say. She'd probably said far too much already. She bit her lip, assailed by sudden doubt, something she didn't often have cause to feel, and she looked away.

"You sized me up before I'd even set foot inside your drawing room," he went on, "and I'll wager that not once since then have you wondered if your assessment might be inflexible, unfair, or just plain wrong."

His words echoed Nancy's from earlier in the evening, but this time, she could not dismiss the notion so easily. Was she being unfair? There was only one way to find out. "You think I'm wrong about you? Then prove it. Agree to my proposition and show me you're not the man I've pegged you to be."

"Is that even possible? You've buried your knife so deep in my back, I'm not sure I can get it out again."

"Take it as a challenge. You said yourself you can never resist a challenge."

A wry smile curved his mouth at having his own words used against him. "So I did. Very well, I'll veer off Rosalie if you agree to help me find someone more suitable."

"And will you promise not to place any young woman at risk to be compromised?"

The smile widened into a grin. "I promise no one will catch us."

"That's not the same thing!"

"That's the most I'm willing to offer." He stuck out his hand. "Take it or leave it."

"I shall take it." As she put her gloved hand in his, she met his amused gaze with a meaningful one of her own. "But whenever I introduce you to a young lady, I'm not letting either of you out of my sight."

He chuckled. "Fair enough. How do we begin this sort of thing?"

She pulled her gloved hand from his. "Call upon me tomorrow at two o'clock, and I shall interview you as I would any potential client."

"Interview me?" He seemed surprised. "What on earth for? You know quite a bit about me already."

"As you've pointed out, a lot of what I know doesn't seem to be accurate. And I don't know what sort of woman you would wish to marry. Do you prefer a quiet woman, or one who carries the conversation? Do you find women with brains attractive? Or does an intelligent woman intimidate you?"

That made him laugh. "I've only been intimidated by one woman in my life."

"What woman is that? Your mother?"

"No. I don't remember my mother. She died when I was a small boy. The only woman who has ever been able to intimidate me was Nana."

"Nana?"

"My nanny. She weighed probably eighteen stone, could wield a knitting needle like a weapon, and always managed to know when I was lying. She was the kindest, most wonderful woman I've ever known."

"Was?" Belinda echoed. "What happened to her?"

Not a muscle of his face moved, he continued to smile, but something she couldn't quite pinpoint changed in his expression. It was as if he'd just donned a mask. "My father sacked her when I was eight."

"Why?"

"I don't know. But if I were to guess—" He broke off and looked away. "I think it was because I loved her too much."

"But that's ridiculous."

"Is it?" He looked at her again, his smile still in place.

She frowned, uneasy, not liking the strange, mask-like quality of his smile. She wasn't sure she wanted to pull back the mask and find the real man beneath.

"I already told you what I'm looking for," he went on, and she forced herself to stop speculating about his deeper qualities. "It isn't complicated. I need a wife with a dowry, I'd like one who is pleasant company, and I'd prefer one who is pretty."

"And that's all you require?"

He considered. "If she were American, or any other nationality than English, that would be good, too."

"Other than English?" she echoed, not certain she'd heard him right.

He nodded, confirming that there was nothing wrong with her hearing. "And if she's Roman Catholic, or Jewish, or Methodist, all the better. Any religion but Church of England."

Belinda was beginning to feel as if she'd stepped through Alice's looking glass, for there were things here she simply did not understand. "But your family is Church of England."

"Yes," he agreed with a chuckle. "Exactly so."

She made a sound of impatience. "I am trying to determine what sort of woman would be the best match for you. Must you be so flippant?"

"Sorry." He gave her a penitent look, but she greatly feared he wasn't the least bit chastened. "But do you seriously think interviewing me will accomplish that objective?"

"I do have some degree of success at this," she pointed out. "To assist you in finding the right spouse, I need to know more about you and what you enjoy. Do you like breeding roses, for example? Or composing poetry? Or hunting?"

"Are those the interests a gentleman of my position ought to pursue? If so, I fear mine shall not quite come up to snuff. Grafting roses takes far more patience than I possess, I think worrying about tercets and quatrains is just plain silly, and I hate riding to hounds. Why, the fox has almost no chance of getting away, which I've always found terribly unfair. There's a requirement, if you like: a wife who doesn't care for foxhunting."

She shook her head, staring at him in disbelief. "You must expect very little from married life if you don't even require some mutual interests with your spouse."

"I try not to have expectations about anything, to be honest." His amusement vanished, his expression hardened. "Nothing causes more pain, frustration, and disappointment than unfulfilled expectations."

"That may be so, but it's hardly helpful here," she grumbled. "I need guidelines. What about her appearance? Are there certain physical traits you prefer? If you don't like gardening or hunting, what are your interests and pastimes? What about your politics? What?" she added as he gave an unexpected laugh. "What is so amusing?"

"You make finding a wife sound like visiting the tailor. No, not this fabric. The wool's a bit too coarse. No, that one's too light and flimsy. And that one's a horrid pattern. My politics, my pastimes . . . are any of those things important?"

Belinda decided at that moment that her task would be easier if she accepted that everything about this man was going to confound her notions and defy her conventions. "I take it you think these things are not important?"

He shrugged. "Not really, no. Until I've met her, any considerations other than the ones I've given you don't matter."

"How can you say that? Why would a potential

bride's personal attributes, interests, and character not matter?"

"I said they don't matter *until I've met her*," he corrected. "You could find dozens of women who meet all the qualifications I could possibly require and who possess all the attributes I would most prefer, but if I don't feel something passionate when I look at her, if I don't want to yank her into my arms and kiss her breathless and pull her clothes off, none of those requirements will mean a thing."

Belinda stared at him, an image flashing across her mind of him with his face buried against some woman's neck, his arms around her, and his hands unlacing the stays at her back.

Her throat went dry.

"Is something wrong, Lady Featherstone? You look quite flushed all of a sudden."

The amusement in his voice shattered the picture in her mind like a rock thrown at a mirror, and she strove to recover her poise. "I'm quite well. I'm still a bit warm from the dancing, that's all. And if I am to assist you," she added with some asperity, "I would ask you to refrain from these lurid descriptions of your animal passions. It's most unseemly."

That got a genuine smile from him. "I already told you passion was important to me. Call it a pastime if it makes you feel better."

"Such a criterion is hardly help—"

She stopped, for the perfect way to handle this entire situation suddenly entered her head, a way that would not only give him what he wanted and get him out of her hair, and at the same time save the worthy young ladies of London from life with a fortune-hunting rakehell.

"Lady Featherstone?" he prompted in the wake of her sudden silence. "Is something wrong? Have I shocked you beyond speech?"

Belinda gave up on discerning his preferences. "Not at all," she said, returning her attention to him even as her brain worked furiously. "Far be it from me to make my task more difficult than it needs to be."

She watched his eyes narrow a fraction in suspicion, and it took everything she had to keep her expression bland and innocent. "You are prepared to be so open-minded," she said with a shrug, "this ought to be the easiest match I've ever brought about. Meet me at Claridge's on Friday at five o'clock for tea. There, I shall introduce you to a girl I believe just might meet your exact requirements."

With that, she decided to depart before he could ask any questions, and she turned to walk back toward the ballroom, but his voice stopped her before she'd taken three steps.

"Belinda?"

She turned and looked at him over her shoulder. "Yes?"

"There is one thing I'd like to clarify." He paused a moment, then went on, "Despite what's been said of me, and what you think of me, I am not like Charles Featherstone. I wish you could believe that."

"I'm not the one you have to convince, Lord Trubridge. And you'll have every chance to demonstrate to your future wife that I've been mistaken about your character. That's what those tedious courtship rituals are for."

He groaned in protest, and Belinda smiled as she walked away. Now that Rosalie was safe, she was going to enjoy this.

Chapter 7

"Why, I think England is just the greatest country in the world. Daddy insisted on seeing Parliament, and Big Ben, and the Tower of London, and the British Museum. I thought all of that was a *teeny* bit dull, of course, but the shopping has been heavenly. Daddy's bought me so many pretty things in Bond Street, I don't see how I'll ever get to wear them all."

Nicholas sat in the tearoom of Claridge's Hotel, staring into the stunning face of Miss Carlotta Jackson of Baltimore, and all he could conclude was that God had a perverse sense of humor to fashion such a lovely shell for such an empty interior. Her conversation, unceasing, inane, and wholly self-absorbed, had been flowing over him for half an hour now. He was quite dazed in consequence.

"The ladies here are so elegant," she went on. "A bit

standoffish, but that's just the way it is here, isn't it? But everyone's been so kind to me. Lady Montcrieffe having me at her ball, and Lady Featherstone inviting me to tea today. It's so much better here than it was in New York. It was awful there. I was so unhappy." She sighed. "I do hate being unhappy."

The fact that everyone hated that didn't seem to have ever entered her head. She smiled at him, a very pretty smile that didn't stir anything in him except the desire to run for his life. "You'd want me to be happy, wouldn't you, my lord?"

He refrained from asking if she could be happy somewhere out of his earshot. "In a perfect world," he said instead, "everyone would be happy."

Those lovely, cornflower blue eyes opened wide. "Oh, but I wasn't thinking of everyone. I was thinking of me."

"I daresay," he murmured. "What a surprise."

That little jibe sailed right over her empty head. "Living in England would make me happy." She blinked at him, her dark brown lashes fluttering like butterfly wings, and he wondered why some women thought such a talent made them more attractive. "Why, I should just adore living here forever, my lord. Don't you think I would?"

"Absolutely," he said with fervor. "No doubt, you'll love England as much as I love Paris."

She blinked again, this time in discomfiture. "Oh," she said, and a blissful silence followed. Unfortunately, it didn't last.

"Of course, Paris is lovely, too," she said. "We went

there over the winter. That's where Worth is, you know. And it was so exciting. He sure does know everything about clothes, and he was so nice to me that I bought tons of dresses from him. He's just the cat's whiskers, isn't he?"

Nicholas didn't answer, she didn't notice, and as she twittered on happily about herself and her clothes and her jewels and her pet canary, Bibi, he ate cucumber sandwiches and drank tea and murmured something every once in a while in response to the unceasing monologue, and all he could think was that if he were to live with a woman as vacuous as this for more than half a day, he'd have to shoot himself in the head. What could Belinda have been thinking?

He glanced sideways to where she was sitting across the tea table. Though she was turned toward the girl's mother—who seemed to have the same predisposition as her daughter to rattle on endlessly about nothing—Belinda was also looking sideways, watching him from beneath the brim of an absurdly plumed straw bonnet. The moment their eyes met, she pressed her lips together to hide a smile and returned her attention to the mother, giving him the answer to his question. She forced him to endure another half hour, however, before she reminded Miss Jackson and her mother of a dressmaking appointment in New Bond Street, causing the two Americans to depart in a rush and leaving him able to confront Belinda on the subject of his first potential bride to be.

"You chose that girl on purpose."

Her eyes, the color of sky rather than cornflowers, opened wide. "Why, my lord," she chirped, pressing a hand innocently to the ruffled jabot of her bodice, "I don't know what on earth you mean. It would make me so happy to find you a wife. Don't you want me to be happy?"

"For God's sake, Belinda, don't imitate Miss Jackson, not even in fun. That girl has the brains of a gnat."

"She isn't the most intelligent heiress in London, that's true, but what difference does that make to you?"

"What difference does it make?" he echoed. "What sort of question is that?"

"A perfectly valid one." She opened the handbag on her lap and pulled out a pocket-sized black notebook. "Since you were so opposed to meeting with me for a thorough interview, I was forced to make do with the preferences you did give me."

She opened the book and flipped through several pages before she found the one she wanted. "Rich and pretty," she read. "Must be willing to accept marriage based on material considerations. Sizable marriage settlement is required. Love is not. American preferred . . . no Church of England, no foxhunting . . . hmm . . ."

She paused a moment, studying the page, then looked up. "I didn't note that intelligence was a consideration for you. Did I miss it in our conversation the other night?"

"I didn't think I had to specify that my future wife have a brain," he muttered, chagrined that he hadn't seen this coming. "I thought it would be obvious. What man wants a stupid wife?"

"Many men do," she assured him. "An intelligent girl upsets their vanity."

"Perhaps, but I'm not one of those men. I could never spend the rest of my life with a mindless chatterbox like Carlotta Jackson or I should go mad as a hatter. But then, you knew that already, I suspect." He paused to tug at his cuffs and straighten his tie. "Now I hope you will stop wasting my time and yours by introducing me to henwits and find me some suitable candidates."

"I don't see how I was supposed to know intelligence was so important to you," she grumbled as she set the little notebook on the table, reached into her handbag again, and retrieved a pencil. "Intelligence required," she murmured, scribbling as she spoke. "No chatterboxes or henwits."

She stopped writing and looked up, frowning at him. "You might have told me this at the ball. It would have spared Miss Jackson any false hopes."

"If Miss Jackson harbors any hope after only one hour of tea, then she has a vivid imagination. I did nothing to encourage her. A man can hardly encourage a girl's hopes when he can't get a word in."

She sighed as she tucked her notebook and pencil back in her handbag and pulled out her gloves. "I fear that you encourage women simply by looking at them."

"I shall take that as a compliment."

She gave him a wry look as she began to put on her gloves. "I must have said it wrong."

He leaned closer, unable to resist flirting with her.

"What about you?" he asked, smiling. "Do I encourage you when I look at you?"

"Be still, my fluttering heart," she said in a dull monotone. "Oh, Nicholas. Oh, Nicholas."

"You're cruel, Belinda. So cruel and so lovely." He propped his elbow on the table and his chin in his hand. "Is it really true you've no money?"

She frowned, staring down at her hand and studying her glove as if she feared there might be a spot on the pristine white kid. "Jack told you about my finances, I suppose?"

"That there was none of your dowry left? Yes. When Featherstone died, the attorney had to tell Jack there was no money to support the estate. Deuced frustrating since Jack had no say in how the money was spent."

Apparently satisfied she'd been mistaken about her glove, she looked up, but her face was devoid of expression. "Am I supposed to feel sorry for Jack?"

"No." He straightened with a sigh. "Belinda, that's not what I meant. I appreciate that if anyone knows what it's like to feel helpless while your inheritance is spent heedlessly into oblivion, it's you. I only meant that it's a pity when a man has inherited the title and the estate, but has not inherited the income to keep it up."

"Knowing Jack, do you think that would have made any difference?"

"Probably not," he was forced to concede. "But it will make a difference with me."

"Will it?" She studied him for a moment, her head tilted a bit to one side. "What happened to your face?"

"My face?" The abrupt change of subject took him back a bit. But then he remembered Denys's fist slamming into his cheek, and he laughed. "Oh, that. It's nothing."

"I'd hardly call a black eye nothing. Did you engage in a tavern brawl? Or a dispute over cards, perhaps?"

"Neither, actually," he said with breezy disregard. "It was a fight over a woman, if you must know. A cancan dancer. I only mention her occupation," he added as she gave a disapproving sniff, "in case you were wondering who she was."

"I wasn't, but I should advise you to invent a more tactful way of fielding any questions from ladies on the subject. A fight over a cancan dancer would hardly commend you as a possible husband."

"It won't matter if you keep introducing me to women as dim-witted as Carlotta Jackson. I doubt she even noticed my black eye, much less spared a moment to contemplate how I got it."

Her lips curved up a bit at the corners. "That's probably true, I admit. But as I said, you didn't tell me you wanted an intelligent woman. And, my point—if we can return to it—is that even as you speak of how you would be more responsible than Jack, I am looking at evidence to the contrary on your own face. It's hard to believe that a man is sincere about changing his life and being a better man when only a few days before he'd engaged in fisticuffs over a cancan dancer."

"Belinda, the two are hardly the same thing!"

"No? I don't see much difference."

"Well, the business with the dancer actually happened three years ago, and the man who hit me the other day was Lord Somerton, one of my best friends."

One of her black brows lifted in skepticism. "Your best friend struck you because of something that happened three years ago?"

Nicholas decided not to explain since his only defense was that at the time he'd spirited off Denys's cancan dancer, he'd been in an advanced state of intoxication. That was not the sort of explanation likely to raise him in Belinda's estimation, so it was best to keep mum.

"Never mind," she said in the wake of his silence. "I don't want to know anything about it. But I warn you that whomever you marry, you won't be allowed to spend her money on cancan dancers, and you will be forced to spend a good portion of it on your estate."

"If that's what she wants, it's quite all right with me," he said agreeably. "Though any girl with sense won't want us to live at Honeywood, I won't cut up rough about improving the place."

"Just so you understand it won't be all beer and skittles for you just because you're marrying a girl with money. I intend to tie your future wife's dowry up as tightly as possible in the marriage settlement."

"But you and I could negotiate the terms," he murmured, and leaned over the table, giving her what he hoped was his most charming smile. "Couldn't we?"

She didn't seem impressed. "If you've got any absurd notions going on in your head that you can wheedle me into letting you off the hook, rid yourself of them at once. I intend to make sure you'll be on a strict allowance."

"I've no doubt of it, but that doesn't stop me from having notions." He slid his gaze down over what he could see of her luscious body. The tea table prevented him from seeing the rest, but his imagination was happy to complete the picture. Just that, just one moment of letting his imaginings about her take hold, and arousal began flowing through his body. "At least," he added, as his gaze moved back up to her face, "not about you."

She looked away, a hint of pink washing into her cheeks, and he felt a spark of hope that she wasn't as indifferent to him as she might wish to pretend, but when she looked at him again, her expression was as cool as ever. "Are you, or are you not, trying to improve my opinion of you?"

"I am, but not if that means I can't think delicious things about you. Perhaps it makes me a cad, Belinda, but I'm not willing to make that particular sacrifice."

The color in her cheeks deepened, and she stirred in her chair. "Really, Trubridge," she said, frowning with disapproval even as her fingers lifted to touch the side of her neck, "this sort of flirtation is quite inappropriate."

Her attempt to chastise him was utterly ruined by the breathless quality of her voice, but he decided not to push his luck by pointing that out. It was satisfaction enough to know she felt at least a little of what he was feeling. "I know," he answered her with a sigh of mock regret. "But I can't help myself."

"Try." She snapped her handbag shut, shoved back her chair, and stood up. "Now that I know you want an intelligent girl, we can get on. Come to the National Gallery on Wednesday afternoon at two o'clock. The

Dutch painters' exhibit. There, I shall introduce you to Miss Geraldine Hunt, a girl who is as pretty as Carlotta Jackson and of far greater intelligence."

"Oh, very well," he said as he also rose to his feet, "but it's a bit of a burn to my masculine pride that you can push me into the arms of other women without even a smidgen of regret." He bowed and started to turn away, but her voice stopped him.

"Trubridge? You can't leave yet."

He turned, hopeful she was asking him to linger. "Why not? Do you want me to stay?"

"Just long enough to pay for tea." She thrust a bill of fare into his hand and smiled. "Clients pay all expenses."

She turned away, hooked her handbag over her arm, and started out of the tearoom.

"You really enjoyed yourself this afternoon, didn't you?" he called after her, and her laughter rang out as she walked away, proving him right.

Forced to wait for the maître d'hôtel, he sat back down and contented himself with admiring Belinda's shapely, bustled backside as she departed, and he couldn't help imagining things that didn't stand a chance of becoming reality.

IT WAS SILLY, Rosalie told herself, to be disappointed. After all, she barely knew the Marquess of Trubridge. They'd had two conversations and one dance, and yet, she feared she was already falling in love with him because the sight of him sitting with Carlotta Jackson tore at her heart and made her want to cry. When she'd seen him walk by, her heart had given a leap of joy, only to sink again in dismay at the sight of him stopping by Auntie Belinda's table.

She'd watched in disbelief from her own seat on the other side of Claridge's tearooms as Belinda had introduced Trubridge to Carlotta and Mrs. Jackson, and it had been almost more than she could bear. She hadn't known Belinda and Carlotta even knew each other, much less that they were on intimate enough terms to have tea together. Not that she expected to know Auntie Belinda's plans every moment of the day or that she was in any way bothered by which other girls Auntie Belinda might be sponsoring, but still . . . *Carlotta Jackson*? That girl was denser than packed sand.

What made Carlotta better suited to have tea with Lord Trubridge than she was? Rosalie wondered, resentful and baffled. And why was Belinda having tea with him and introducing him to other girls if he was the scoundrel she'd claimed him to be? And why had she lied about his appearance? The more she thought about it, the more confused, and hurt, and downright mad she became.

But after the others had gone, when she saw him sitting alone, she couldn't help harboring a tiny speck of hope. He had to come back toward this side of the tearoom in order to leave it, and though her table was stuck back in a corner, maybe he would see her.

She watched him sign his bill with the waiter and stand up. Her heart began to pound hard in her chest. Maybe, she thought as he started in her direction, if he saw her as he passed, he would stop to talk with her.

And maybe she could invite him to sit with them. She bit her lip, waiting.

He walked right by without even glancing in her direction, and Rosalie's momentary hope came crashing down.

"Don't you think so, Miss Harlow?"

Sir William's voice interrupted this wretched state of mind, and she tore her eyes from the marquess's splendid back and shoulders. She returned her attention to the brown-haired young man on the other side of the tea table, striving to conceal the disappointment she felt.

"Of course, Sir William," she answered although she didn't know what on earth she was agreeing with since she hadn't paid a bit of attention to the conversation. She forced herself to smile, vowed to pay more attention to her companions, and tried very hard not to wish that Lord Trubridge was sitting across from her instead of Sir William Bevelstoke.

Chapter 8

Miss Geraldine Hunt proved to be every bit as pretty and intelligent as Belinda had claimed. Alas, she was also dull as paint, a fact Belinda had somehow failed to mention.

She was one of those earnest girls who read Marx and Dostoyevsky, and Nicholas suspected that he fell at once in her estimation by confessing that nowadays he only read novels. "Oxford," he explained, straight-faced, "cured me of serious reading."

In consequence, he was given a stern lecture on his derivative reading habits.

When she asked him about the state of the world, his comment that as far as he knew it was still turning did not elicit so much as a smile, and he was treated to a dissertation on the inevitable disastrous future that awaited them all.

As they moved through the exhibit, she probed him for opinions on the significance of the paintings, and after an hour of trying to offer a deeper significance for every portrait, landscape, or vase of flowers, Nicholas couldn't help just stating the obvious.

"I don't suppose," he offered, as they stood in front of an image of a country house with lawn and trees, "this could just be the artist's home, and he painted it because he liked living there?"

"Nonsense," she scoffed. "No great artist would paint a picture for such mundane reasons."

"Quite," Nicholas agreed. Having decidedly been put in his place, he moved on to the next picture, and though he strove to find some hidden deeper meaning, a still life of flowers in a glass vase didn't give him much to go on. "The tulips aren't a surprise, I suppose, since it's a Dutch exhibit. But there are roses, too. How . . . umm . . . extraordinary." He peered closer and grasped at the only thing he could think of. "The petals of the roses are falling off. Symbolism in that, do you think?"

"Oh, rose," she murmured in answer, staring at the picture, "thou art sick."

Surprised by the sudden thrust of Blake into the conversation, he looked at her. "I beg your pardon?"

She turned toward him. "The sick rose," she prompted, but when he continued to stare at her, she gave a heavy sigh that implied he was the most hopeless pudding head alive and proceeded to explain, "The poem by William Blake, from *Songs of Innocence and Experience.* Do you know it?"

Oh, God. She wanted to talk about poetry. It wasn't

that he disliked poetry. Quite the contrary. But academic discussions on the topic bored him to death. Remembrances of school went through his mind, where he'd listened to dry-as-dust lectures on quatrains and iambic tetrameter and the most ridiculous interpretations of Shakespearean sonnets. He suspected a lecture on Blake by Miss Hunt would be far worse than those of the dons at Oxford, and desperate, he tried to veer her off the topic. "Sorry, no," he lied. "I've never read Blake."

" 'Oh, rose, thou art sick,' " she repeated, her voice rising to an oratory level. " 'The invisible worm that flies in the night, in the howling storm, has found out thy bed of crimson joy.' "

A choked sound came from somewhere nearby, and he glanced sideways to find Belinda a few feet away. He glared daggers at her, but that did him no good since she wasn't looking at him. She was pretending vast interest in a Vermeer, one gloved hand pressed over her mouth.

Miss Hunt stirred, moving closer to him, and he was forced to return his attention to her. He watched in some alarm as her eyes widened with lurid excitement, and speculations as to her sanity began running through his head. " 'And his dark, secret love,' " she hissed, " 'does thy life destroy.' "

She stopped, waiting, as if he were expected to now impart an opinion, whether on the poem or her recitation of it he wasn't sure. "Lovely, quite lovely," he said with an emphasis he hoped was convincing enough not to hurt her feelings, and he moved on to the Vermeer. "I quite like this picture, Miss Hunt. Don't you?"

Before the girl could reach his side to study the painting, he leaned closer to Belinda and muttered, "I am going to wring your neck."

As Trubridge walked with Miss Hunt through the elegant rooms of the National Gallery, Belinda followed at the discreet distance appropriate to a chaperone, delighted with how this afternoon was living up to all her expectations.

Ever since last Friday, she'd been savoring that episode at Claridge's. Every time she'd thought of Carlotta's unceasing, self-absorbed chatter and Trubridge's dazed expression, she'd laughed all over again. Today, she was happy to know that her second attempt to present the marquess with an heiress who met his stated requirements was proving just as enjoyable as the first.

Unfortunately, her entertainment was not destined to last long. To his credit, Trubridge did his best to respond to Geraldine's pretentious topics of conversation and her outbursts of poetry, but after ninety minutes, his patience ran out, conversation between the pair lapsed into an uncomfortable silence, and Belinda knew it was time to bring this meeting to an end.

"What an enjoyable afternoon this has been," she said, breaking the silence. "But I fear Miss Hunt and I must be going. You're ready to depart, Geraldine, are you not?"

The girl gave a toss of her head. "Quite ready," she

said with an emphasis that made it clear she was as unimpressed with Trubridge as he with her, and as they made their way out of the building, she recited no more poetry, a fact for which Trubridge was no doubt grateful.

"I didn't bring my carriage," Belinda told him, and when he'd managed to wave down a hansom for them, she started to follow Geraldine immediately into the vehicle, but of course, he was not about to let her escape that easily.

"A moment, Lady Featherstone, if you please," he said, catching her by the arm. "You don't mind, do you, Miss Hunt?"

Without waiting for an answer, he turned away, pulling Belinda with him until they were out of earshot before he stopped, then he turned to face her. "Having fun?" he asked, and though he was smiling, she wasn't certain if it was for Geraldine's benefit or if he was genuinely amused by her little joke.

"Yes," she answered, giving him a wide smile in return. "I confess I am."

"Enjoy it now, because if you keep wasting my time this way, I will be forced to reconsider Rosalie Harlow."

She sobered at once. "We had an agreement."

"One which will be void if you don't start living up to it."

"I don't know what you mean. I am living up to it, given the vague preferences you imparted to me."

He stirred, leaning closer. "Then it's clear I must explain my requirements in more detail."

Given that she had asked for those details, she could

hardly protest. "That would be helpful, of course," she said with dignity.

"Good. I shall pay a call on you in an hour, and we will discuss the matter more fully."

"One hour? That's not possible, Trubridge. I have an engagement with the Duchess of Margrave."

"I don't care if you have an appointment with the Queen. I shall see you in one hour."

"But I told you, I don't have time today—"

"Very well." He gave a shrug and put on his hat. "I'm sure Miss Harlow will be happy to make time for me since you are unable to do so."

"All right, all right, we'll meet in an hour. But I hope you are prepared to be more clear about your requirements now?"

"Oh, don't worry. I'll be clear as glass." With that, he turned toward the hansom and tipped his hat to Geraldine, then walked away down the street without a backward glance. Belinda watched him go, rather let down at having her fun cut off so soon, but she hoped she had succeeded in making her point. Finding a spouse was serious business, requiring considerable thought, attention, and effort. If he was going to marry money, by heaven, she intended to make sure he earned it first.

She returned to the cab, requested the driver to take them to Geraldine's hotel, and stepped inside the vehicle. "What did you think of Lord Trubridge?" she asked as she settled herself opposite the girl.

"He's very good-looking," Geraldine said, making handsomeness sound rather like a disease. "But appearance is meaningless. The inner person," she added, pressing a hand to her heart, "is what matters."

"I see," Belinda murmured, wishing the marquess was able to overhear this conversation. "And you did not find Lord Trubridge's . . . umm . . . inner person satisfactory?"

"I did not! He isn't serious, Lady Featherstone. He cares nothing for the things that matter. I tried to discuss the news of the day with him, and the state of the world, and all he did was make flippant remarks. The only books he reads are novels, and even there, he seemed not to care in the least about discussing current literary themes and allusions. And," she added with an injured sniff, "it's obvious he has no appreciation of poetry!"

"It seems not," Belinda agreed, keeping her voice appropriately grave. She leaned forward and patted the girl's gloved hand with her own in an encouraging fashion. "We shall have to keep looking, my dear."

BY THE TIME Belinda returned home to face Trubridge, she had decided her best defense was a good offense, so when he arrived, she waited just until he'd stepped through the door of her drawing room before she spoke.

"I can allow you fifteen minutes, Lord Trubridge," she said the moment he came in. "After that, I must rush off, for as I told you, I am expected at the Duchess of Margrave's house in Grosvenor Square for an Afternoon-At-Home. I cannot be late, and you wouldn't want me to be, for there are several young ladies attending who might be possibilities for you."

"That," he said dryly, "doesn't inspire my confidence."

She strove for an air of innocent bewilderment. "You didn't like Miss Hunt? But you insisted that intelligence was important to you, and there's no doubt Miss Hunt is intelligent. Quite well educated for a woman. She went to Radcliffe College. Graduated *summa cum laude*, I believe."

"And if I wanted to discuss the dismal state of things over breakfast each morning, Miss Hunt might do. But I don't."

"Still, Geraldine is pretty, don't you think?"

"I suppose she is, but—"

"And she's quite rich, too—richer than Carlotta, or even Rosalie. And she's willing to make a material marriage. She can't inherit until she marries, you see, and she has great plans for what to do with her fortune."

He held up a hand. "Don't tell me. No doubt she has grand, sweeping ideas of how her money can be used to improve the world, but—"

"Don't you care about improving the world?" Belinda asked, momentarily diverted.

"Would it matter if I did? In case you hadn't noticed, the world is quite resistant to change. Rather inconvenient, that, for people like Miss Hunt, but there it is."

"And you don't think things can be improved?"

"Not by talking about how awful they are all the time, no. And I told you already, I don't expect all that much from life. I'll grant you that, day by day, a little bit at a time, one can make things better within one's own circle. There are things one can do in one's own village, perhaps, or—"

"And what are you doing in that regard?" she cut in. "How are you improving things in the village of . . . where is your estate in Kent?"

"Near Maidstone. And if you could stop questioning my every word and listen, I'm fully aware that if I had the funds to make Honeywood a grand estate, it would make a vast difference in the lives of the people of the county, but I don't have those funds. That's rather the point. And no, before you even ask, my trust income isn't enough to make much difference. The place is leased, and that enables it to keep going, and if I chose to live there myself, I could do the same with my trust income—if I still had it, of course. But beyond that, not much can be done to improve the lot of the people there, not with crop sales and land rents so low. A great influx of cash is the only thing that would make any difference."

"But Landsdowne is enormously wealthy. He could help you—"

"No."

"But if he knew you needed it, not to spend on yourself, but for your estate . . ." She paused as she watched his jaw set. His massive frame stiffened to the rigidity of a wall. She sensed she was skating onto thin ice, but if she were going to find him a wife that suited him, she had to know more about him, so she persevered. "If you asked him for the money—"

"No. I already told you, I will never ask Landsdowne for anything. I hope that's now understood."

She could see the anger in his expression, but whatever it was about his father that flicked him on the raw, she'd not learn it by further pressing him. "All right, then. Shall we return to the topic at hand?"

His body relaxed. The tension in his shoulders eased, and the anger vanished from his expression. "Gladly. I'd rather talk about the state of the world, contemplate marriage to Geraldine Hunt, or be stuffed with nails and rolled down a hillside than discuss Landsdowne."

"Well, there's no need to contemplate marriage to Geraldine," she said with a sigh, "since you're not the least bit interested in her. She feels the same about you, by the way," she couldn't help adding.

"Thank God," he muttered. "I am saved from spontaneous eruptions of poetry in public places, then."

This reminder of Geraldine's reciting Blake in the National Gallery was too much, and Belinda burst into laughter. "You should have seen your face," she said. "It was beyond description."

Trubridge's lips twitched, but he didn't laugh with her. Instead, he folded his arms and waited for her to stop laughing.

"Oh, come now, Trubridge," she choked at last, "you must admit that today was amusing."

"I can see that you think so, especially when your amusement is at my expense."

"Well, yes," she confessed, unashamed. "Especially then."

"Still, this isn't bringing you any closer to fulfilling the terms of our agreement."

She tried her best to seem bewildered. "I don't know what you mean. Matchmaking isn't an exact science. It's a matter of try, try, and try again. There's no way to predict the results of these encounters ahead of time." She shot him a meaningful look. "Especially when a client refuses to provide any specific information."

"On the contrary," he said as he unfolded his arms and began walking toward her, "I think you predicted the results of today's events with perfect accuracy, and last Friday's as well. And I can't help wondering why you are presenting me with choices you know will not appeal to me."

Belinda lifted her chin to meet his gaze as he halted in front of her. "If you won't allow me to conduct my customary interview, how can I determine what sort of women appeals to you?"

"Oh, I don't know," he answered in his careless, off-hand way. "Look in a mirror perhaps?"

Shocked, she could only stare at him, and he made a rueful grimace in the wake of her silence. "Hard to believe, I know, since you despise me, but there it is."

"I—" She broke off, forgetting what she'd intended to say. It seemed incredible that she should be the sort of woman he fancied—ludicrous, in fact.

He closed the last bit of distance between them, making her aware of things she'd never noticed about him before. She could see the dark brown ring around each of his irises and the blunt straightness of his eyelashes. She could smell the fresh, light spiciness of bay rum and feel the warmth that emanated from his body.

His gaze roamed openly over her face, but though she found the scrutiny unnerving, she couldn't look away. "You seem to want jokes at my expense, after all," he went on, "and that's a good one, you must admit. Laugh if you like." He lifted his hand to touch her face. "I don't mind."

At the touch of his fingers, warmth pooled in her midsection. Her toes curled in her shoes. Her wits began slipping, and laughter was the furthest thing from her mind as his fingertips grazed lightly across her cheek to her ear.

"You see," he went on as he curled a loosened tendril of her hair around one finger, "I've always been partial to women with black hair and blue eyes. It's a particular weakness of mine."

His hand opened, his palm cupped her cheek, his fingers slid to the nape of her neck, and desire washed over her like a wave, bringing a flood of sensations she hadn't felt for years. Tingles raced up her spine, her pulses quickened, inner muscles flexed and tightened.

Desperate, she tried to find safer ground. "M . . . many clients are attracted to . . . to certain physical traits. I'll be sure to take that information into consideration."

"That's all very well." His breath was warm on her face. "But I'm still not sure you understand what I'm looking for."

She knew she should stop him, shove him back, duck past him, do . . . something. Yet even as her mind willed her to act on any one of those options, she couldn't seem to move. "What is there to understand?" she asked, fighting hard to regain her scattered wits. "I'm giving you what you said you wanted."

"I beg to differ." His palm caressed her cheek, and though it seemed scorching hot, the caress made her shiver. "You're not giving me what I want at all."

Heavens, what was wrong with her? She was no innocent. Men had made advances upon her person before, and she'd never had trouble giving a firm rebuff. But this man, a man she didn't even like, was making her melt like butter.

She strove to regain control of herself and of the situation. "I am operating on the criteria you gave me: rich, pretty, willing to make a material match. Your preferences in looks aside, what else is there?"

"You forgot one." He was so close now that as he spoke, his lips brushed hers. "The most important one, in fact."

She couldn't think well enough to determine what she'd left out. "Which one is that?"

He wrapped his free arm around her waist and pulled her hard against him. "This one," he said, and kissed her.

The touch of his lips sent a flood of pleasure through her entire body, pleasure so unexpected that she cried out against his mouth. The desire he'd stirred to life opened within her, blossoming into pure carnality, spreading heat through every cell of her body.

I don't want this, she thought wildly. *I don't want it.*

Even as repudiation and denial passed through her mind, she gripped the lapels of his jacket in her fists and pulled him closer, hungry for things she thought she'd never want again. The lush openness of a man's mouth on hers, the thrill of his arms around her, the hard strength of his body . . . these were things she thought she'd left behind long ago, but this man was proving her wrong. At this moment, in his arms, her body had a will of its own, reason was forgotten, and painful lessons of the past floated away like so much flotsam, vanishing on the wind.

Her lips parted, and at once, he deepened the kiss, caressing her tongue with his own, inflaming her desire even further. She let go of his lapels and rose on her toes, wrapping her arms around his neck to bring him even closer, needing more.

He made a rough sound against her mouth. His hands cupped her buttocks and lifted her off the ground, pressing her hips to his. In a position of such intimacy, there was no mistaking his arousal, and that enabled Belinda to regain a vestige of sanity.

She turned her face, breaking the kiss, and she could hear her own panting frantic breaths as she rested her forehead on his shoulder. His breathing was as ragged as hers, and she wondered if his heart was thudding in his chest with the same painful force.

He eased her down, lowering her to the ground, but when she pressed her palms against his shoulders, he did not let her go. Keeping one arm around her waist, his free hand glided up and down her spine, and he pressed a kiss to her hair.

Reality began to set in. Not only had she allowed a man she hardly knew to commit a violation of her person, she had welcomed it, even relished it. Trubridge had no doubt done this many times before with many other women, but she was not like him. She did not do this sort of thing. She did not feel these exciting, wanton things anymore. And to make things even worse, this man was a client.

She pushed harder against his shoulders, but when

he still seemed reluctant to let her go, she leaned back to meet his gaze. "Release me," she said, trying to put some dampening scorn into her voice. Her words, however, came out in breathless rush.

Nonetheless, he complied, easing his hold until, at last, his arms slid away and he stepped back. "There now," he said, his voice a bit unsteady. "I hope I've clarified what I'm looking for?"

With that, he turned and walked out, leaving a stunned, chagrined, thoroughly mortified Belinda staring after him.

Chapter 9

Nicholas strode out of Belinda's house into the cool spring air, his body burning, his brains—obviously—missing. He wasn't quite up to snuff on matters of etiquette, but he'd wager a hefty sum that kissing the woman who was trying to find you a wife was not *comme il faut*. Not that he cared much about things like that, but she did. Hell, she already considered him an inch or two below pond muck, and hauling off and kissing her wasn't likely to raise him in her estimation.

He paused in front of Conyers's carriage. The driver was holding the door open for him, but after a moment of consideration, he shook his head. "I think I'll walk, Smythe. You go on ahead."

"Very good, my lord, if you're certain," the driver

said, and closed the carriage door. "But it's a bit chilly to be walking."

"All the better," Nicholas muttered under his breath as he turned away. "I could do with some chilling just now."

After her insistence on entertaining herself at his expense, all he'd intended to do was turn the tables, and yet, somehow, he'd ended up confessing an attraction he'd had no intention of ever revealing.

How idiotic was that? He'd left himself open and vulnerable to a woman who despised him. He was surprised she hadn't slapped his face and sent him packing then and there.

But she hadn't. Nicholas stopped on the sidewalk. He'd just kissed Belinda Featherstone, London's most proper widow, a woman filled to her fingertips with rectitude, moral sensibility, and nothing but contempt for men with rakish tendencies. But instead of giving him a stinging slap across the face for the liberties he'd taken, she'd kissed him back. She'd wrapped her arms around his neck and parted her lips and kissed him back.

A grin of pure manly satisfaction spread across his face, but that momentary good humor was checked at once by the thought that he'd probably be receiving a letter in the morning post terminating their agreement. Without her support, he might not be able to find a wife. On the other hand, if she did continue to work with him, that would probably be worse. A man just couldn't go lusting after his matchmaker, but he suspected that whenever he was in proximity to Belinda, lust would be the inevitable consequence. And that put him squarely between the devil and the deep blue sea.

THE DUCHESS OF Margrave's At-Home parties were among the most anticipated delights of the season. Any hostess worth her salt could manage to fill her drawing room with plenty of women on a given afternoon, but persuading the men to come was a trickier business. An Afternoon-At-Home not only competed with race meetings, cards at the club, and riding the Row as diversions for London's bachelors, but these events were also designed for the purpose of making them acquainted with marriage-minded young ladies, and in consequence, many hostesses found only the most desperate and unattractive bachelors at their Afternoon-At-Homes.

The Duchess of Margrave, however, was far more subtle than most London hostesses, and also more sensible. She always made sure there was plenty of meat and cheese on hand, provided good, strong claret cups as well as champagne ones, and took pains to invite only those young women who were clever and delightful company as well as pretty to look at. The men came in droves.

Belinda was always invited to these At-Homes, for the duchess was a personal friend and these parties a perfect foil for her profession. Today, however, she could take little interest in just who she ought to match up with whom. Only one client dominated her thoughts, and as she looked around the duchess's dining room, she found little hope of pairing him with anybody. How could she, after what had happened less than an hour ago? Her lips still burned from his kiss.

Even now, she could still taste his mouth on hers and feel the heat of his palms cupping her buttocks and the hardness of his arousal pressed against her body. She could still feel her own desires flaring up out of nowhere and making her as indifferent to propriety as he. She winced, remembering with painful clarity how she'd flung her arms around his neck and returned his kiss.

She didn't understand what on earth had come over her. How? she wondered in abject bewilderment. How could she have participated in that kiss with such wantonness? With all she knew, with all the pain and humiliation she'd experienced at Featherstone's hands, she'd willingly accepted the advances of a man who seemed—despite his denials—to be just like her late husband. She'd not only accepted Trubridge's kiss, she'd reveled in it with an abandonment she hadn't felt since she was a lovesick girl of seventeen. And now she was supposed to find Trubridge a wife? It was hypocritical. It was ludicrous. It was awful.

She wished she could terminate their agreement, but she had no doubt he'd go straight back to Rosalie. After this afternoon's events, it was more clear than ever that a romantic girl like Rosalie would find no lasting happiness with a man like Trubridge. Belinda knew her only choice was to steer him toward a woman who would suit him better.

But who would that be? As she looked around

the room, she tried to envision one of these charming, lovely young ladies with Trubridge, and she just couldn't form the picture. How could she recommend him to any girl when he wasn't likely to be an attentive or faithful husband? Hadn't that kiss today proved as much?

The Duchess of Margrave came into view, her tall, slender figure moving with easy grace amid the guests. The duchess was not a beautiful woman—in fact, there were many who called her plain—but at this moment, her titian hair shining in the afternoon sunlight that poured through the windows, her pale skin gleaming like porcelain, she looked lovely. She'd come a long way since her debut four years earlier. The first time New Money heiress Edith Ann Jewell had sat in Belinda's Berkeley Street drawing room, she'd been a truculent, awkward girl, with a defensive glint in her eyes and an unmistakable chip on her shoulder. Now, she was a graceful, confident woman, an excellent hostess, and devoted friend.

If only Margrave could see her now, Belinda thought with a hint of bitterness. But that wasn't possible, for the Duke of Margrave was in Kenya.

Edie turned her head to smile at one of her guests as she walked through the crowded dining room, and the sight of that smile hurt Belinda's heart and smote her conscience, for the duchess's marriage to Margrave was her most colossal failure.

She had brought the pair together four years ago, and she'd been sure they would make a good and happy marriage. The duke had assured her quite convincingly of his deep and abiding affection for Edie, he had promised to give the girl everything to make her happy, and yet, after his enormous debts had been settled by Edie's even more enormous dowry, only a month after the vows had been said, Margrave had deserted his wife and departed for Africa. He had not been back once in the four years since, seeming quite content to leave his wife childless and alone, and wholly indifferent to the humiliating social limbo in which he'd placed her.

In introducing Edie to Margrave and encouraging a match between them, she'd never dreamed the marriage would fall apart in such short order. She'd had no doubts, no misgivings. She'd been absolutely sure Edie and Margrave would be happy. Too sure.

Sometimes, Belinda, you can be wrong.

Nancy's words from the ball echoed back to her, and she sighed, for though she might have been wrong about the Margraves, she feared she was anything but wrong about Trubridge. That kiss rather proved it. She glanced down at the tea dregs in her cup, wishing she could read in the wet leaves the name of a girl who would not be made unhappy by marrying him. She didn't want another girl to make her own mistake, and she didn't want another Edie on her conscience.

Suddenly, Belinda felt swamped by doubts—doubts about her judgment, her abilities, and even the rightness of her profession. Not all the marriages she'd helped bring to fruition turned out well, of course. That was too much to hope for. But never before, not even after the Margrave debacle, had she questioned the rightness of what she did. Now she was doubting even that, thanks to one man and one electrifying kiss.

"Is something wrong, Belinda?"

She looked up with a start to find the duchess standing beside her. "Edie," she greeted, ignoring the question. "Lovely party."

"Thank you, but if you mean what you say, then why are you standing here in a corner alone, looking gloomy as an undertaker?"

"Was I? How rude of me. But I'm quite preoccupied today."

"I can see that, darling. What's troubling you?"

The kisses of a rake. She wondered what the duchess's reaction would be if she said that aloud. "I'm dealing with a difficult client," she said instead. "One I'm finding hard to steer toward a girl who would suit him."

"Ah. Would we be talking of Lord Trubridge? What?" she added, laughing at Belinda's surprised expression. "You think people aren't buzzing like bees about who was sitting with whom in Claridge's tearoom last Friday? But really, Belinda! Carlotta Jackson?"

Belinda laughed, too, her mood lightening a bit at the memory of the previous Friday. "I thought Carlotta a fitting match for him."

"Why? Do you hate him that much?"

That kiss flashed through Belinda's mind again, underscoring the fact that hate was not quite what she felt about Lord Trubridge. "I shouldn't wish to place him with a nice, sweet girl, Edie. The man's notorious."

Edie made a face, her freckled nose wrinkling up. "Even a notorious man doesn't deserve Carlotta."

"I'm not sure I agree with you there," Belinda countered with some asperity. "His father's cut off his trust fund, you know, and he's only looking to marry because he has to."

"Yes, I read about it in *Talk of the Town*. So did everyone else, if the gossip that's going round is any indication. But I am rather surprised that you agreed to help him. You've always had such a low opinion of fortune hunters."

Belinda sighed as she handed off her teacup to a passing footman. "I didn't have much choice. It's a long story," she added as Edie looked ready to ask for details. "I shan't bore you with it. Suffice it to say, I decided to take Trubridge on, thinking it would be just what he deserved if he ended up with someone awful."

Edie laughed. "So that explains Carlotta."

"Yes, well, it wasn't to be. He didn't come away from tea with a favorable impression of her, I'm sorry to say."

"So the man has brains and good judgment! That makes your task harder, I suppose, but it's early days yet. Plenty of time to find him someone before the season's over."

"The sooner the better, as far as I'm concerned," she said with feeling. "And that would suit Trubridge's book, for he wants to be married as quickly as possible. The question is who might do for him."

"Why don't you bring him to Highclyffe for my house party? It begins sixteen days hence, the week before Whitsuntide. The party's sure to be a large one, forty people or so, including quite a few pretty girls with fat dowries. One of them," she added with a wink, "might be awful enough to pass muster."

She sighed. "You never invite anyone that awful to your parties."

"My, my. Is he as bad as that?"

"He's a rake." Perhaps if she repeated those words often enough, his kiss would stop burning her lips.

"Perhaps, but I'd still adore it if you'd bring him along. There never seem to be enough single men to balance the numbers at a large house party. And despite your scruples about material marriages, they suit some people down to the ground." The duchess paused, turning to study the crowd milling about her dining room. "Mine certainly suits me."

"What?" Taken aback, Belinda stared at her friend's profile, noting in disbelief the little smile that curved Edie's mouth. "You can't possibly be content this way, with Margrave in Africa and you here."

"Can't I?" Edie turned to her and laughed. "Dearest Belinda, you look so shocked. Did it never occur to you that I wanted just the sort of marriage I have?"

"No," Belinda confessed, still trying to wrap her mind around the idea. "It certainly did not. I suppose . . . I suppose because you seemed so genuinely happy during your engagement. I know it was a short one, but both of you assured me—not only me, but your father, too—that you adored each other. Not madly in love, you said, but deeply fond—"

"What else could we say? Daddy would never have allowed me to marry Margrave if we'd told the truth.

And if we'd tried to act as if we were madly in love, you'd never have believed it. And even if you had, you'd have insisted we have a long engagement so we could be sure, and you'd have convinced Daddy to make us wait. But that didn't suit us at all, so we decided fondness and affection was the way to play it."

"Wait." Belinda held up one hand, palm toward her friend to halt the flow of words. "You mean you and Margrave prearranged this marriage? You planned it all out?"

"Yes." The duchess glanced down at the champagne cup in her hand, swirled the contents, and took a swallow before she looked up again to meet Belinda's gaze. "I'd met him at the Hanford ball before you introduced us, and we discovered that our requirements for matrimony coincided exactly. So, we made the deal, the mercenary marriage you abhor. The terms were the usual ones; I'd be a duchess, he'd receive my dowry, we'd live together a few weeks for show, then we'd go our separate ways."

"So when he asked me for an introduction to you, he already knew you. The scoundrel!"

"Don't blame him, Belinda. The whole thing was my idea, not his."

Belinda stared at her friend in complete astonishment, and as she did, Trubridge's words echoed through her mind.

It's not as if you've shown any compunction about arranging material marriages in the past. The Duke and Duchess of Margrave, for example.

How had Trubridge known about the Margrave arrangement, and she had not? Had he simply made a shrewd guess? Or was she so blind to the results of her profession that she couldn't see the obvious?

"But why, Edie?" she asked after a moment. "Why would you marry a man you don't love? Why would you settle for that?"

She shrugged slim shoulders. "It was almost the end of the season, and you know I hadn't exactly bowled London over with my dazzling beauty and charm during my debut." Belinda started to protest this self-disparagement, but Edie interrupted her. "It's all right. I know I wasn't the prettiest heiress, and I was certainly not the sweetest." She paused for a grin. "Although I was definitely the tallest. Anyway, Daddy wanted to go back to New York, and I . . ." She paused, a glimmer of pain crossing her face. "I did not."

"I know." Belinda put a hand on her arm. "It would have been dreadful to go back. But still, to make a loveless marriage . . ." She sighed and let her hand fall. "Oh, Edie."

"Don't you dare feel sorry for me!" The duchess shook her head, the shadow passed, and her radiant smile returned. "I was damaged goods back home, but here, I'm a shining social success. "

"I know, but I wish you had told me this before now. I've been wrecked with guilt, thinking how miserable you must be."

"Oh, no, you mustn't feel that way!" Edie looked at her in dismay, conscience-stricken. "I didn't tell you because I was afraid you'd hate me for deceiving you and for selecting my husband in such a calculated fashion. So I kept putting it off, and the more time that passed, the less important it seemed to tell you the truth. I didn't realize I was a blight on your conscience. If I had known that, I'd have told you much sooner." Edie bit her lip, her green eyes regarding Belinda with some uncertainty. "Are you terribly angry?"

"Angry? No, I'm too shocked to be angry. I'm . . . I'm . . . oh, hell, I don't know what I am." She sighed and rubbed a hand over her forehead. "I think I'm in need of a drink."

Edie laughed. "But you don't even like spirits."

"I'm making an exception." She lifted her head and glanced around. Spying a footman with champagne cups, she waved him over and pulled one of the cocktails from his tray. "After the day I've had, anyone would take to drink."

She took a swallow of the cocktail and grimaced, making Edie laugh.

"You always look like you're taking cod liver oil when you drink. So if it isn't me, what's troubling you enough to make you imbibe?"

She sighed and lowered the cup, staring into the milling crowd. "I've come to be so sure of myself," she murmured, "but I am beginning to appreciate that I don't really understand anything about myself or anyone else."

"That doesn't sound at all like you."

She made a face. "It doesn't, does it?" She took another swallow of her cocktail and made another grimace. "To think that all this time, ever since Margrave went to Africa, I've been thinking you were secretly miserable and just putting on a good front for society."

"Yes, well, no one seems to believe me when I say otherwise. It never occurs to anyone that a woman can be perfectly happy without a man."

"And you are happy?"

"Of course I am! Who wouldn't be, with an enormous income, complete social acceptance, a luxurious house in Grosvenor Square, several lavish country estates, and the freedom to manage it all myself without a husband messing about getting in my way?"

"And the duke? Is he equally content?"

"I expect so." Edie gave her an impish grin. "We don't correspond. But if he wasn't content mucking about in Africa, his mother would be sure to tell me so—in her subtle, well-bred British way, of course. No, Margrave and I are both happy as clams in the mud. For us, separate continents has proved to be the perfect recipe for marital bliss."

"Oh, Edie, that's not at all what I wanted for you."

"You're a darling." The duchess put an arm around her shoulders for a quick hug. "But it's what I wanted. And you, of all people, should understand how wonderful it is to be an independent woman of means."

"It can be," she admitted. "But I never chose it."

"I did." Edie grinned and took another swallow of her champagne cup. "There, now. See how simple I've made things for you? All you have to do is find Trubridge a woman like me."

"The situation isn't quite that simple."

"Dearest Belinda, that's because you know the deal's what Trubridge wants, and you don't like that because you're a romantic at heart."

She felt compelled to protest. "I am not in the least romantic!"

"Nonsense! Of course you are! You adore romance. Why do you think you became a matchmaker? Even more telling, why do you think you became infatuated with a charming, handsome devil like Featherstone, then expected him to reform?"

"Well, yes, but I was a silly girl when I married Featherstone. I've changed since then—"

She broke off as the memory of Trubridge's kisses came back as if to taunt her. Her lips began to tingle, and her cheeks flushed with heat, making a mockery of any notion that she was wiser than the girl who'd married Charles Featherstone. Belinda hid her hot face behind her free hand with a groan of dismay.

"Are you all right?" Edie asked. "What's wrong?"

She merely shook her head in answer. She didn't look up, for she knew she must be pink as a peony, and she cursed Trubridge for reawakening physical desires and romantic notions she thought she'd left behind ages ago.

She didn't want to feel these things, for they were as insubstantial as cobwebs. Trubridge was a man she didn't like and didn't respect, and she knew it was crazy, self-punishing, and just plain stupid to feel anything for a man like that.

BELINDA WAITED TEN days before she sent word to Trubridge suggesting another meeting. During those ten days, she strove to suppress memories of his mouth on hers and the thrill of desire she'd felt at his touch, but though she didn't quite succeed in that endeavor, she knew she could not put him off forever.

The fact that she had dismissed him as unworthy of most of her clients and yet had found his kiss so intoxicating herself was a nauseating irony Belinda preferred not to dwell on. It was clear that scoundrels still held an inexplicable fascination for her, but she did her best to quell it.

She redoubled her efforts to find suitable candidates for him, and the more awful they were, the more suitable she liked to think they were. She prepared a social calendar for him that would put him in the path of as many of those young ladies as possible. She repeated to herself the various things he'd said that she found most infuriating. She refrained from considering any of his good points. And every time she remembered his kiss and felt again that warm, intoxicating wave of desire, she immediately suppressed it. By the time ten days had passed, she felt sufficiently in command of herself and the situation to invite him to call, and by the time he arrived, she was confident she would be as indifferent to his charms as she'd been during their very first meeting.

But then he walked through her door and ruined all her efforts.

His wide-shouldered frame in the doorway reminded her of the strength of his arms wrapped around her. A glance at his mouth burned her lips and curled tongues of fire in her belly. He'd already given over his gloves, and the sight of his bare hands evoked memories of how he'd cupped her buttocks in his hands, lifted her up, and pressed her hips against—

"You wished to see me?"

The sound of his voice jerked her out of these most unhelpful contemplations, and Belinda took a steadying breath.

"Yes, I did." She glanced at the butler, who was still standing by the door. "Tea, Jervis, if you please," she said, feeling in need of the bracing fortification of a cuppa.

After the butler had departed, she returned her attention to Trubridge. "Shall we sit down?"

She gestured to the large round tea table where her appointment book, her client book, and her inkstand were already laid out, relieved that the table was large enough to provide a substantial barrier between them, but the fact that she felt the need for barriers proved that ten days had not been enough time.

It would tickle his vanity, no doubt, to discover that humiliating fact, but a quick glance at the mirror on the wall showed that she looked just as usual, and as she sat down, she could only thank heaven that what she felt wasn't plainly written on her face. Gesturing for him to take the chair directly opposite, she pulled her pen out of its holder and opened her appointment book.

"My friend, the Duchess of Margrave, is having a house party at her home in Norfolk. She was kind enough to invite me, and she suggested I bring you along. The party begins six days hence, and concludes on the following Thursday. It will be a large party, and the duchess assures me there will be several young ladies there who might be suitable for you."

"Suitable to my way of thinking?" he asked wryly. "Or yours?"

At this point, she was desperate enough to get him married off that she wasn't sure she cared either way. "The more young ladies you meet, the better your chance of finding someone who . . ." She paused, feeling her skin flush with heat, but she forced herself to carry on. "Someone who attracts you."

He didn't reply, and she forced herself to look at him. But she only got as far as his mouth, which was curved in a hint of a smile, before she lowered her gaze again at once. She could not be indifferent if she looked at his mouth. No woman could, not after being kissed the way he had kissed her.

"Since you've never met the duchess," she continued, desperate to keep her mind on her job, "I think it would be best if we travel to Norfolk ahead of the rest of the party. That way, I can introduce you to her before everyone else arrives. I shall look up the schedule for trains to Clyffeton, consult with the duchess, and inform you of which train we shall be taking. I hope that suits you?"

Without waiting for a reply, she made a notation in her book as if he had answered in the affirmative. "In the meantime, the theater and the opera might be good places for you to be seen. You are staying at Lord Conyers's home, if I'm not mistaken?"

"I am, yes."

"Excellent. Lord Conyers is very highly regarded in

society, and he has a box at Covent Garden. If you are seen with him there, that will help bolster your image in the eyes of the *ton*. The more you are seen in respectable places, and in the company of respectable people, the more society's judgment about the episode with Elizabeth Mayfield will soften. Do you think you can arrange to attend a performance during the coming week?"

"That depends. Will you be able to attend as well?"

Belinda froze, her pen poised above her inkwell. "That would not be wise."

"Probably not, but I would enjoy the opera much more if you were there."

Pleasure bloomed in her at those words, and it suddenly seemed vital to appear preoccupied and busy. She dipped her pen in ink, tapped the nib, and wrote notes in her book—notes that were absolute nonsense—and she could only hope he did not possess the talent of reading handwriting upside down.

"You might enjoy it more, too, if I were with you," he said, undeterred by her silence. "I'm vastly more entertaining than Wagner's Valkyries or Rossini's Figaro."

"It would not be wise," she repeated, scribbling away. But she didn't know if she was reiterating the point for him or for herself, and she decided it was best to shift the topic. "We should also talk about Ascot. As you know, Race Week begins shortly after we return from Norfolk, and it is a very important week in the social calendar. Because most of the American young ladies aren't fortunate enough to receive an invitation to the Royal Enclosure, I offer a luncheon, as a sort of consolation to them. I hope you would be amenable to attending?"

"Since I assume you have to attend your own luncheons, then, yes. I'll come."

"Excellent," she said, and ignored the rest of his comment. "Now, in the interval between the duchess's house party and Ascot, there is Lady Wetherford's ball to consider. I believe you are well acquainted with her son, James?"

"Pongo? Yes, we were at school together. But—"

"Good. I believe I can persuade her to send you an invitation." She inked her pen again, but before she could make an affirmative note about the ball, he leaned forward, placing his hand over hers to stop her. His palm felt hot, and her hand tightened around her pen. "Lord Trubridge," she began, but he cut her off.

"Before we talk any further about my social calendar," he said, "I think I should point something out to you."

She pulled her hand free and forced herself to look at him. "Yes, what is it?"

He leaned closer as if to impart a vitally important secret, and she caught the scent of bay rum. "There's an elephant in your drawing room," he whispered.

That was so absurd and so appropriate to the situation that she almost laughed, but she caught it back in time, pressing her lips together. She didn't want him to make her laugh. She didn't want him to be absurd or charming, or so terribly attractive. She wanted to keep her mind on all his faults, damn it all, or she would start to remember how susceptible she was to men who could charm her and make her laugh.

"I thought perhaps I ought to mention it," he went on, leaning back in his chair and straightening his cuffs. "Just in case you hadn't noticed. Although how someone fails to notice an elephant, I can't think."

She strove to maintain an air of indifference. "I don't wish to discuss elephants, thank you. Lady Wetherford's ball is on the tenth of June—"

"But Belinda, it's rumbling about, getting in the way. How can we possibly carry on as if it isn't here? Wouldn't it be best to talk about it?"

The last thing she wanted to do was talk about that kiss. Steeling herself, she looked up, trying to remember her cold regard for him during their first meeting. It was difficult, for she felt anything but cold right now. "Lord Trubridge, the metaphorical elephant to which you refer was a most unfortunate experience, and I feel it is best if we both forget it ever happened."

God, how prim she sounded. Like someone's maiden aunt.

"I don't think I can forget about it." His lashes lowered, and it was his turn to study her mouth. "As kisses go," he murmured, "it was quite unforgettable."

The arousal he'd awakened ten days earlier, arousal she'd worked so hard to snuff out, flooded through her like a wave. Desperate, she fought back. "Unforgettable?" she echoed with a laugh meant to make light of his declaration. "Was it, indeed?"

He looked up, meeting her gaze. "It was for me, Belinda."

The pleasure in her deepened and spread, radiating outward to the very tips of her fingers and toes, the first stirrings of arousal. "I said I don't wish to discuss it," she said, somehow managing to make her voice hard as stone even though she felt soft as butter. "And a true gentleman," she added, glaring at him across the table, "would not keep bringing it up."

That made him grin. "A true gentleman wouldn't have done it in the first place."

"Quite. Now that we've agreed that you are not a gentleman, can we carry on? After all, it's clear you didn't broach the topic in order to offer an apology."

"An apology?" His grin widened. "No man is ever sorry for kissing a woman, so if he apologizes for it afterward, he's a liar. I'm not a liar, and I'm not sorry, and I haven't the least intention of apologizing, so put that in your pipe, my beautiful Belinda, and smoke it. And," he added before she could reply, "in my defense, allow me to point out that you weren't precisely fighting me off."

Inwardly, she grimaced, well aware that fighting him off was the exact opposite of what she'd done. "I shouldn't have had to," she pointed out. "If you were any other client, I would terminate our agreement, but since I do not wish you to renege on your promise to me, I cannot in good conscience renege upon mine to you. Therefore, it's best if we carry on as if that . . . that elephant had never occurred."

He shook his head as if bemused. "You really think that's possible?"

"What would you have me do?" she cried, unable to keep up any pretenses of indifference. "Engage in a torrid affair with you while I help you find a wife?"

He tilted his head, taking another lingering glance at her lips, still smiling faintly. "Give me a moment," he murmured, "while I remind myself of all the reasons why that would be wrong."

With a sound of exasperation, Belinda tossed down her pen, rose from the table, and walked away. "The fact that you need time to give yourself such reminders speaks volumes," she said over her shoulder.

He didn't reply, and when she glanced back over her shoulder, she found to her dismay that he had moved from the table and was standing right behind her. She looked away again at once, stiffening when he curled his hands around her upper arms. But when he turned her around, and she looked into his face, she saw something there that she hadn't seen before. She saw tenderness, and it seemed so genuine that it threatened to crumble her already fragile resolve.

"I was teasing, Belinda." He leaned down until his forehead almost touched hers, still smiling a little as he looked into her eyes. "Don't you know by now that I always make jokes when I'm feeling particularly vulnerable?"

"Don't!" she cried, feeling rather vulnerable herself. She wrenched free and stepped back, out of his reach, shoring up her defenses. "Don't make me like you. Don't make me want you. Don't charm me or tempt me or try to beguile me or make advances toward me. There's no future in any of it. Not for you, and certainly not for me."

"I know that." He raked a hand through his hair. "God, don't you think I know that?"

She didn't answer, and, after a moment, he gave a deep sigh. "I won't bring up the subject again, and I won't make any more advances toward you, tempting as it may be. All right?"

His promise left her feeling strangely flat and a bit dismal, but she made the only answer possible. "Yes. Thank you."

"But if you throw yourself into my arms and beg me to make love to you," he added irrepressibly, "I'll fall like a ninepin. What can I say? I'm weak."

Thankfully, the door opened just then, and Jervis entered with the tea tray. "I'll keep what you say in mind, Lord Trubridge," she said, and returned to the tea table, reminding herself that it would be best all around if she got him married him off as quickly as possible.

Chapter 10

Nicholas didn't stay to tea. He'd already arranged to meet Denys at White's, and he was glad of it, for that engagement gave him the perfect excuse to refuse tea and make a quick exit. Desire for Belinda was flowing like hot lava through his body, and sitting across from her through something as sedate and proper as tea while she discussed various possible brides for him would not only have been ludicrous, it would have been impossible.

Lusting after her was a delicious exercise and one he'd engaged in quite often during the past ten days, but it was also pointless. The carnal imaginings that had been haunting him ever since that kiss could never be fulfilled.

Despite her response to his kiss—which had been wildly, blissfully beyond any expectations he might have had, Nicholas had no illusions regarding her opinion of him. Either way, it hardly mattered. He couldn't marry her. Not only because he couldn't afford to support a woman who didn't have a dowry but also because she'd never marry him in a thousand years. To her mind, he was and always would be that most loathsome of creatures: a fortune hunter. And as she had pointed out, an affair while she helped him find a wife was also out of the question. Even his somewhat flexible sense of morality wouldn't stretch that far.

No, his only option was to put any carnal imaginings about Belinda out of his head. Nicholas leaned back against the leather seat of Conyers's carriage and closed his eyes, resolved to work on that particular task. But a picture of her came immediately into his mind—an image of her sitting naked across the tea table from him, her full breasts partially concealed by waves of long black hair that spilled around her bare white shoulders, and a teapot in her hands. Curiously, the teapot made the image all the more erotic, and he knew without a doubt he was going off his chump.

The carriage jerked to a stop, bringing him out of this lustful reverie and making him grateful the journey from Belinda's house to White's was only two blocks.

He took a deep breath and rubbed his hands over his face, working to regain his equilibrium. By the time the driver opened the door for him, he felt he was once again master of his own body, at least master enough to convey himself from the street to one of the club's dressing rooms, where he intended to order an ice-cold bath. He needed it.

An hour later, his arousal abated by a dousing of cold water, his clothes freshly pressed by a member of White's staff, and his face freshly shaved by the club barber, he felt considerably better. All he needed to feel completely restored to a sensible state was a stiff drink. Nicholas went downstairs to the bar of the club, where he had arranged to meet Denys.

He found the viscount just inside the entrance, waiting for him with a whiskey in one hand and a small, sealed envelope in the other.

"This note came for you a few minutes ago, just as I was leaving the house," Denys said as he held out the envelope. "So I thought I'd just bring it along."

Nicholas took it in some surprise. "I can't imagine who would be writing me a letter so urgent that it needed to be hand-delivered," he said, and turned the missive over. The small round seal with a feather pressed into the red wax hinted at the identity of the sender, and when he opened it, his guess was confirmed by the delicate, elusive scent of Belinda's perfume.

Desire flickered up dangerously inside him, threatening to send his efforts of the past hour straight to perdition, and Nicholas tamped those feelings down at once, striving to concentrate on the note itself rather than the provoking, impossible woman who had written it.

On Friday, the best train for Clyffeton departs from Victoria at half past one. This puts our arrival at Highclyffe just before tea time, and the duchess has assured me that our arrival at that time would be satisfactory since most of the other

*guests appear to be taking the four o'clock train.
If this plan is equally satisfactory to you, you
need not reply.*

Lady Featherstone

Satisfactory? The word almost made Nicholas want
to laugh. A week of being near her without being able
to be alone with her, touch her, or kiss her, while she
shoved him at other women was the most unsatisfac-
tory thing he could imagine. And yet, he had to go
through with it. He couldn't afford not to.

"Not bad news, I hope?"

Denys's voice intruded on his thoughts, and he
looked up to find his friend watching him. "Not bad
news at all," he answered, trying to believe his own
words. "Quite the contrary, in fact."

"That's a good thing," Denys said, glancing past him
toward the door, "because I fear that some very bad
news is headed your way as we speak."

Nicholas turned to look over his shoulder and found
Landsdowne coming through the doorway right behind
him. The duke saw him at the same moment and stopped.

My God, he's grown old, was Nicholas's first thought.
It took him back, rather, to see the other man's sunken
cheeks, gray complexion, and gaunt frame, for to everyone who knew him, Landsdowne had always been
an overpowering presence, striving to dominate everything and everyone in his vicinity, and to see him like
this was a startling revelation. In some ways, however,
he hadn't changed at all. The bitterness of his mouth,

the calculating gleam in his green eyes, the arrogant tilt of his head—those things, Nicholas knew, would never change.

"Trubridge." The old man glanced over his face, no doubt noting the now greenish yellow bruise beneath his eye, but he made no reference to it. In fact, he said nothing more at all giving only a brief nod. When addressing a mere marquess, nothing more was required of a duke, and Landsdowne never did more than what was required. That, of course, impelled Nicholas to adopt the opposite demeanor.

"Papa!" he cried, loudly enough for those around them to hear. "My dear, dear papa!"

He wrapped his arms around his father in an exaggerated display of affection before the old cod could slip away. He patted the duke's back with a bit too much heartiness, then drew back just far enough to plant a kiss on each of the old man's cheeks, and he thoroughly enjoyed Landsdowne's grimace of distaste at that French custom.

"Sorry, old man," he apologized at once, making no effort to look regretful. "I know how you hate displays of affection, but it's been so long since I've seen you, I got carried away. And living in Paris, one is so apt to take on Continental habits."

He drew back. "I didn't know you were in town, Papa, or I'd have called." A lie, that, but he didn't care. The pang of alarm in Landsdowne's eye at the idea of his dropping by almost made the idea a tempting one. "I could come by sometime this week," he offered, "and we could settle in for a nice, long visit."

"I've only just arrived, and I'm quite busy, I fear." The duke shifted his weight and glanced past him, clearly wishing to move on, but Nicholas couldn't let him go, not quite yet.

"Oh dear," he said, bending a bit to peer at the white carnation adorning the lapel of Landsdowne's morning coat. "I've set your buttonhole askew. Allow me to adjust it."

He made a great show of tweaking the smashed flower, and he succeeded in mangling the petals even further before Landsdowne shoved his wrist aside, and hissed, "For God's sake, must you embarrass me by your conduct at every opportunity?"

"Oh, yes, Father," he answered, his voice low and fervent. "I absolutely must. It's what I live for. Did you see that tidbit about us in *Talk of the Town*?" he added, raising his voice on the last question so others could hear. "I fear the world thinks we've had a row. Silly of them, isn't it? We've always rubbed along so well."

Landsdowne cast an uneasy glance around, observing that the bar had gone from subdued to silent, and that all the other gentlemen there were watching them while striving to seem as if they weren't.

Nicholas pretended to be oblivious to both his father's hostility and the curious crowd. "Heavens, how rude I'm being," he exclaimed, and gestured to the man beside him. "Do you know Viscount Somerton?"

"Of course. Good evening, Somerton." The duke gave another short nod and started to step around them, but Nicholas moved just enough to keep him from going quite yet.

"Why don't you join us, Papa?" he suggested, his voice filled with joviality and friendliness. "After all, it's been ages since I've seen you. Is it seven years, or is it eight? I forget."

The bitter mouth turned down further. "Eight."

"My, how time does fly. In town for the season, are you? So am I," he went on before the duke could answer. "And I don't know about you, but I'm having a ripping good time. Did Freebody tell you I'm looking to marry? I must say, this business of finding a wife is proving to be much more enjoyable than I'd first thought it would be. Of course, Lady Featherstone's assistance has been invaluable."

The duke's face didn't change, but his eyelids flickered a bit. He was rattled and no mistake. "Lady Featherstone?"

"Why, yes." He tapped the letter from her against his palm, smiling. "Delightful woman. Do you know her?"

His father gave a cough of discomfiture he found quite gratifying. "I believe I have met her. American."

He said the last word just as Mrs. Beeton might have said, "Mice," or as Gladstone might have said, "Disraeli," with just the same inflection of disdain the other two might have used.

"It's not surprising that you know her, however," the duke went on, "You are acquainted with all manner of people."

The way he said it, Lady Featherstone might have been a convicted criminal. "I didn't," he answered. "But one's always apt to make new acquaintances during the course of the season, particularly Americans. Lady Featherstone has so many American friends, and they all seem to have heaps of money. I really can't understand why you dislike Americans, Father. The girls are so pretty and so charming. I've met quite a few already, thanks to Lady Featherstone."

Landsdowne's lip curled with distaste. "Sunk that low, have you?" he muttered. "Hiring someone to find you a wife? Trading on your title for money? You must be desperate."

"On the contrary, I think hiring a matchmaker is a practical and efficient course. You taught me well, Papa. One can have anything one wants if one is willing to pay for it. I'm willing to pay with my title." He clicked his teeth and gave his father a wink. "I've finally found a good use for it."

Landsdowne pressed his lips together, bowed, and turned away, leaving Nicholas laughing after him as he walked out of the bar.

"He's in high dungeon now, Nick," Denys murmured. "You really shouldn't antagonize him, you know."

"You're right, of course." Spying a waiter, Nicholas gestured for the fellow to bring him a drink. "But whenever I see Landsdowne, I just can't help myself."

"It always gets you into trouble."

"That's why I spend most of my time on a different continent, old chap." He gestured to an empty table. "Shall we sit down?"

"You didn't tell me you'd brought in Lady Featherstone to assist you," Denys said, and laughed as they took seats.

"You devil. Now I understand why you're going after Rosalie Harlow and you weren't worried about the dragon at the gates. You managed to get the dragon on your side."

"I've veered off Miss Harlow, for I don't think we'd suit. But yes, Lady Featherstone is assisting me."

As he spoke, he realized Belinda's letter was still in his hand. Resisting the impulse to inhale the scent of her that clung to the paper, he shoved the letter into the breast pocket of his jacket. This conversation with his father was a forcible reminder of the course he'd chosen and why he'd chosen it, and that he couldn't afford to be diverted from it by one luscious, unobtainable woman.

"I wonder, Nick . . ." Denys's musing voice intruded on his thoughts. "Was it wise to tip your hand to your father about your plans? He'll use the knowledge against you somehow."

"I don't see how he can." Nicholas leaned back as the waiter placed a tumbler of whiskey in front of him. "It's already public knowledge that I need a wife for financial reasons, and he'd have learned about Lady Featherstone eventually anyway."

"I suppose that's true."

"Besides," Nicholas added as he picked up his glass, "there isn't a thing he can do to me that he hasn't already done or tried to do at some point in my life." He downed the whiskey in one swallow and grimaced, relishing the burn. "Trust me on that."

DURING THE NEXT few days, Belinda made no effort to introduce him to prospective brides, and to Nicholas's way of thinking, that was just as well. The more time that passed before he saw her again, he felt, the more he would be able to put his priorities back in order.

Not that it was easy. Although his encounter with his father served to renew his determination, it did not lessen his desire for Belinda. In addition, the various distractions a man might employ to forget about a particular woman were unavailable to him.

He was in the process of salvaging his shredded reputation, and he could not risk anyone respectable seeing him doing anything that might tarnish the image of a man sincerely looking to marry, so bawdy houses were out of the question. Nor was Mignonette a possibility, for though she was discreet, a Parisian mistress was a luxury he could no longer afford, and they had mutually agreed to end their liaison upon his departure for England. He'd never found streetwalkers appealing in any circumstances. All of which made the distraction of another woman unfeasible.

And even if he had access to the physical relief another woman might provide, it wouldn't have mattered, for he didn't want any other woman. Perverse fellow that he was, he wanted Belinda, a woman he not only could not afford but whose opinion of him could not be considered by even the most self-deceptive fellow to be much above an ant's knees.

During the six days that followed, he attended race meetings, called on old friends, played staid rounds of whist at White's, and tried his best to forget about her and about that kiss. By the time he arrived at Victoria Station on Friday, he felt he was reasonably back in control of his mind, his heart, and his body.

And then he saw her standing on the platform, and he knew he'd spent the past week fooling himself. When she turned at the sound of his calling her name, he felt the world tilt a little sideways, and he knew that even if a decade passed before he saw her again, he would still remember every detail of her face—the exact blue of her eyes and the luminous glow of her skin and the delicate arch of her brow. Worse, he suspected he'd still feel the same sensations a decade from now—a dry throat, a pounding heart, and an inability to say a single word. And when he found himself alone with her in a first-class compartment, it didn't take long for his imagination to set to work and put him right back in the suds, and he feared that if things kept on this way, by the end of the house party, he'd be well and truly mad.

Desperate, he cleared his throat. "It seems we shall have fine weather for the journey."

Before he'd even finished the sentence, he was grimacing at his own inanity. The weather? Really? That was the best he could do?

"Yes," she agreed, turned her head, and looked out the window. She said nothing more.

In the silence, he tried to think of what to say next as he studied her profile. She wore a traveling hat of cream-colored straw topped by a massive quantity of ostrich plumes in various shades of blue, with a brim that curled down on one side of her head and up on the other. The upside faced him as she stared through the glass, and the light washed over the pale, translucent skin of her cheek, her impudent nose, and the finely cut lines of her chin and jaw. He could read nothing in her profile of what she might be thinking or feeling; indeed, she seemed precisely the same as the woman he'd first met—cool, polished, and wholly indifferent to him. Yet he knew how much fire lay beneath her smooth surface.

It was probably best not to think about that.

He took a deep breath and tried again. "It seems a bit stuffy in here. Since it's so fine today, and we're now outside the city, perhaps I should open the window a bit? Bring in some fresh air?"

"If you like." She leaned back as he rose to slide down the window sash, but she didn't look at him. Instead, she continued to gaze outside.

It was clear he needed a topic that would require more from her than these brief, uncommunicative replies, but he was rather at a loss. He'd never been so ill at ease around a woman, but knocking him off his trolley seemed to be Belinda's special gift. Women often found his lighthearted wit and offhand charm quite likeable, but those particular talents never seemed to cut any ice with Belinda. She seldom laughed at his jokes, and she didn't usually find him either witty or charming. And, most aggravating of all, he'd had the idiocy to admit to her that using humor was his favorite way of hiding his weaknesses.

"Tell me about our hostess," he said at last, settling back against his seat. "What's Margrave's duchess like?"

"Edie?" She looked at him, pulled away at last from her seeming fascination with the view. "That reminds me of something I wanted to ask you. How did you know she and Margrave had made a marriage solely based on material considerations? I didn't even know that fact until very recently, and I helped bring them together."

"Margrave is a friend of mine. We were at school together. He's usually off in Africa somewhere, but he does come to the Continent occasionally, and whenever he is in Paris, he looks me up."

"I see. And was it Margrave's marriage that led you to decide on the same course?"

"Not really, no. I knew Margrave and his wife had agreed to marry for material considerations. But at that time, the thought of marrying anyone myself never even entered my head. In fact, I was determined not to marry at all."

"Until your father cut you off?"

"Yes." He met her cool gaze with a hint of defiance. "Just so."

"And you require a wife with a dowry because his decision is irrevocable? Could he not be persuaded to relent once you are married?"

He shrugged. "I've been told he is quite willing to do so, but only if certain requirements are met, and I have no intention of meeting those requirements."

"And what are these requirements?"

"Given our conversations regarding my preferences, can't you guess? Allow me to offer a hint," he added before she could answer. "Landsdowne loves imposing his will on all and sundry, moving people about like chess pieces on a board. I, being a contrary sort of fellow, don't care to oblige him by being one of those chess pieces."

She frowned, thinking it out. "So you are choosing to marry, but you intend to deliberately choose the sort of woman he would disapprove of. A Roman Catholic girl, for example, or an American. And she has to be rich, because if she's the sort he won't approve, he won't reinstate your income."

That wasn't the entire reason, of course, but he thought of Kathleen and decided it was best to leave it at that. "Yes."

She tilted her head, studying him thoughtfully. "Do you do everything in life in opposition to what your father wants?"

"As often as I can. You find that appalling, I daresay."

"No," she said quietly. "I find it sad."

There was a hint of compassion in her eyes, and he didn't like it. It hurt, deep down, in places he didn't want anyone to know about. "Sad?" he echoed, and gave her his most provoking smile. "On the contrary, aggravating Landsdowne provides me with a great deal of entertainment."

"Yes, I suppose it does," she agreed, not seeming the least bit surprised.

He wriggled on his seat. "Damn it, Belinda," he said in aggravation, "what is it about you that always makes me feel like a bug on a pin?"

She smiled a little at that. "Why don't you like talking about yourself?"

"That's the pot calling the kettle black, isn't it?" he

countered, glad for the opportunity to divert the conversation. "I'd wager many people wonder what's underneath your exterior. I know I do."

She looked away, staring down at her lap. "I don't know what you mean."

"No? Allow me to explain." He slid onto his knees in front of her, ignoring the way she stirred in her seat. "You are so cool, one would think butter couldn't melt in your mouth. But . . ."

He paused, placing his hands on either side of her hips, resting them on the roll and tuck leather. "But that's a front, isn't it?"

He leaned forward, his abdomen brushing her knees, and the contact started the slow burn of desire inside him. He was heading into dangerous territory, he knew, but just now, he didn't much care. "I don't know much about you, Belinda Featherstone," he murmured, "but I do know one thing. I know that underneath that prim, cool exterior of yours, you are hotter than hellfire."

One of her black brows rose in a gesture he guessed was supposed to intimidate him. "I believe any woman, prim or not, hot or not, would consider your proximity at this moment as an advance upon her person, which means you are breaking the promise you made to me less than a week ago. Do you break all your promises to women so easily?"

That defeated him, and they both knew it. He sat back, cursing himself for ever making such a ridiculous promise, and he could only watch as she reached into her morocco traveling case and pulled out a book, opened it on her lap, and began to read. Conversation, clearly, was no longer an option, and he was right back where he'd started upon boarding the train—with the delectable Belinda right across from him and not a distraction to be found.

Not having not had the foresight to bring a book, he gazed out the window, but even the prettiest English countryside was no match for the view opposite him, and it wasn't more than five minutes before he was giving in to the inevitable.

He started at her high, cameo-pinned collar, and as he began working his way down, it occurred to him that it was a fortunate thing her navy-and-cream traveling gown was so elaborate. With its countless ruffles and flounces, its dozens of buttons and ribbons, and undergarments that were no doubt equally complicated, he was hopeful that undoing the whole ensemble in his imagination would take longer than their train ride. Because if she was naked before they reached Norfolk, and he had to sit here with that sort of view in his head, blocked from touching her by his idiotic promise, he would have to walk to the back of the moving train and hurl himself onto the tracks.

Chapter 11

He was still watching her. Belinda didn't look up from her book, but she didn't have to, for she could feel his gaze on her like the blazing sun. Her knees still burned where they'd been pressed against his body, and his words seemed like a brand on her brain.

Under that prim, cool exterior, you are hotter than hellfire.

She was now, and it was all his fault.

Belinda tried to concentrate on her book, but that proved an impossible task with him watching her. He knew it, too, the wretched man.

"You know, if you're pretending to read," he murmured, "you probably ought to turn a page every once in a while. It's more convincing that way."

She looked at him over the top of her book and found

that he was lounging back in his seat in an indolent pose, one shoulder propped against the window, a slight smile curving his mouth.

She frowned. "Didn't anyone ever tell you staring is rude?"

"I know, but I can't help myself. I'd rather look at you than the view outside. Much prettier."

"Such lavish compliments," she said as she turned a page. "But they're wasted on me."

"Don't I know it?" he said with a rueful look. "Still, that doesn't make them any less true."

She sniffed. "I daresay you'd deem any young woman preferable to a view out a window."

"Well, yes," he acknowledged, his smile widening. "I am a man, after all. Besides," he added, straightening in his seat with a glance at the window, "Cambridgeshire isn't precisely my favorite part of England. Bad memories."

"Oh?" Intrigued, she lowered her book to her lap. "How so?"

His smile faded, and he was silent so long, she thought he wasn't going to answer her question. "Does it matter?" he asked after a moment.

Belinda studied his profile, the sudden rigidity in his shoulders, the press of his lips. "Yes," she said softly. "I think it does."

"I can't imagine why it should. The past never matters." He fell silent, and he seemed to find the view through the window much more fascinating now than he had before.

He was not a man who cared to talk about himself,

and this was a rare opportunity to learn more about him. She had no intention of letting it pass. "You may not think it matters, but it does. I realize you hate answering questions of a personal nature, but you shall have to overcome your reluctance. Any woman who would consider marrying you will want to know more about you."

"You're right, of course," he said with a sigh, and turned to face her. "As a boy, I'd hoped to go to Cambridge, for I'd always been fascinated by chemistry and science. I was forever asking questions, pestering anyone and everyone who had any scientific knowledge—my tutor, the brewing master at Honeywood, the local doctor, the owner of the chemist's shop. I collected butterflies, bugs, and tadpoles. I even—" He broke off and smiled at a past memory. "I even set up a laboratory at Honeywood once. I had to smuggle in the apparatus, and Mr. Hathaway and I had to keep it a secret, of course, but we did some smashing experiments." He paused, his smile fading. "For a while."

Belinda frowned. "But I don't understand. Why should you have had to smuggle in equipment and keep it a secret?"

He shot her a rueful look. "If you knew my father, you wouldn't even have to ask that. Anyway," he went on before she could probe further, "some of my experiments were very successful, particularly those I did on the use of chloride of lime for hygienic purposes. When I was at Eton, I wrote a paper proposing the addition of chloride of lime to public water supplies to curtail the spread of typhoid, and my professor sent it on to Cambridge with a recommendation of my abilities. I was invited to submit my application and come to be interviewed. I did, and I was accepted."

Belinda frowned in puzzlement, thinking of the comment he'd made to Geraldine that day in the National Gallery. "But I don't understand. Didn't you attend Oxford?"

"Of course." He smiled again, but this time, the smile did not reach his eyes. "All Landsdowne men go to Oxford."

"But if you wanted to study the sciences, surely Cambridge would have been better. And if you were accepted, then why didn't you go?"

"A Landsdowne go to Cambridge?" The lightness of his voice could not quite conceal the pain beneath it. "That would be absurd, Belinda. No Landsdowne has ever attended Cambridge." He swallowed and looked away. "I was reminded of that axiom when my father forwarded the retraction of their acceptance on to me. They'd sent it to him . . . by mistake, he said."

Belinda pressed her fingertips to her lips, feeling slightly sick. "He forced them to withdraw their acceptance."

"Of course. There's a reason Oxford has Landsdowne College, you know. As I said, all Landsdowne men go to Oxford. For a short time in my life, I forgot that fact."

He stood up abruptly. "I believe I'll walk the carriage and stretch my legs. Excuse me."

He departed without another word, and as she watched him go, Belinda suddenly understood the meaning of his offhand comments at the ball.

"No wonder you have no expectations about life," she murmured, as he walked away. "Why should you if they'll only be snatched away?"

SHE DIDN'T SEE Nicholas again until just before the train pulled into the station at Clyffeton. He made no reference to their earlier conversation, and neither did she, but when their eyes met, she felt as if a barrier between them had broken down. Odd, she reflected, that a ten-minute conversation could provide a sense of intimacy that even that scorching kiss hadn't achieved. Very few people, she suspected, knew about Cambridge.

She didn't have much time to dwell on it, however. Upon their arrival, they found Edie's driver waiting for them with one of the ducal carriages, and with the help of Trubridge's valet, the porter secured the luggage, and they were soon on their way to Highclyffe.

Margrave's estate was a sprawling Italianate structure of limestone and granite, with a dome at the center and wings on either side that seemed to stretch out endlessly into the distance. The grounds consisted mainly of boxwood hedges formed into elaborate, geometric designs, spires of yew meant to resemble the cedars of central Italy, and more fountains, temples, and statues than the palace of a Roman emperor.

"Are we still in England?" Nicholas asked, as they started up the long drive lined with chestnut trees.

"Or have we somehow been magically transported to Tuscany?"

Belinda laughed at that, welcoming his propensity for humor at this moment. "Yes, the third duke—or the fourth—I forget which—fell in love with Italy while he was on his Grand Tour. He razed the previous house to the ground and built this."

"The opposite of Landsdowne, then." He turned from the window to look at her. "Landsdowne Abbey still has its castle keep, and some of the original fortifications are still in place. It sprawls, like this house, but it wasn't designed that way. It's simply been added onto with each generation, and my father, being all about family traditions, has never pulled any of it down, even the parts that are crumbling."

"And Honeywood?" she asked. "Isn't that your estate? What's it like?"

"Ghastly."

"I don't believe you. What does it look like?"

"Tudor. It's all white plaster and red brick, with diamond-paned windows and dark oak half-timbering."

"But that sounds charming."

"The outside's all right. But the interiors are simply awful. You see, upon my parents' marriage, Honeywood became the depository for all the worst pieces of Landsdowne art and furniture. My father, unlike most of our ancestors, happens to have a certain amount of taste, and since Honeywood was entailed to me through my mother in their marriage settlement, Landsdowne had no compunction about culling the most hideous paintings, sculptures, and furnishings from the other estates and using them to furnish Honeywood. It's a mishmash of all the worst examples of art from every period since Queen Elizabeth."

"You're exaggerating."

"I'm not." He laughed, shaking back his hair. "If you don't believe me, ask Chalmers here. He's seen the place. Or better yet," he added, saving the valet from having to express an opinion, "come down to Kent with me and see for yourself."

Before she could assure him such an invitation could merit only a refusal, and before she could ask any more questions about his estate, the carriage turned into the wide, graveled drive of Highclyffe and came to a halt. Edie was standing with a row of servants in front of the wide stone steps that led to the immense front doors, waiting to greet them. With characteristically American abandon, the duchess came running to envelop Belinda in a hug the moment she was out of the carriage.

"Oh, I'm so glad you could come," she said laughing, as they pulled apart. "It's been far too long since you last came to Highclyffe, and I do want you to enjoy yourself."

"I'm sure I shall." She gestured to the man beside her. "Edie, may I present the Marquess of Trubridge? Lord Trubridge, the Duchess of Margrave."

"Duchess," he greeted her. "Thank you for your kind invitation."

He bowed over her offered hand, and she gave Belinda a meaningful glance over his head. When he straightened, she bestowed on him her most radiant smile. "Not at all, Trubridge. I'm happy to have any acquaintance of Belinda's down for one of my parties. Especially a man as handsome as you."

He laughed, accepting her words with an ease that said he was quite accustomed to such compliments. "You flatter me, Duchess. You've some lovely grounds," he added, successfully diverting the subject. "I hope you don't mind if I do some exploring while I'm here?"

"Not at all. Go anywhere you like." She paused and glanced at Belinda. "Would you care for refreshment, or would you prefer to be shown your room?"

"My room first, if you please. Perhaps tea afterward?"

"Of course." She turned to the servants standing nearby. "This is Wellesley, the butler at Highclyffe. And Mrs. Gates, the housekeeper. I see you've brought your valet with you."

"Yes."

"Excellent." She beckoned the butler forward. "Wellesley, will you show Lord Trubridge to his rooms? And Mrs. Gates, take His Lordship's valet along to his room, if you please. Oh, and have Molly take up her ladyship's maid? I," she added, hooking her arm through Belinda's, "will show Lady Featherstone her room myself."

"Very good, ma'am." Wellesley turned to Nicholas. "If you will follow me, my lord?"

The two men turned toward the house, but as Belinda and Edie followed, the duchess slowed their pace.

"Darling," she murmured once the others were out of earshot, "you've been holding out on me."

"Holding out? I'm not sure I understand your meaning." But she had a reasonably good idea.

"You told me Trubridge was a rake, but you didn't tell me he was such a treat to look at."

Belinda gave her friend a reproving look. "Handsome is as handsome does."

"Oh, I do hate it when you sound like a minister's daughter. And given that your own father is such a scapegrace, I can't imagine where you get it from. Where is the old rascal these days, by the way?"

"Somewhere in Nevada. Silver mines or something." She waved a hand. "I confess, I stopped listening to his schemes years ago. I've seen him make a fortune only to lose it so many times, I've lost count."

"But for all that, you still love him."

"I know." Belinda sighed, fearing she had an incurable weakness for the scoundrels of the world. "Inexplicable, but true."

"Speaking of scapegraces, I expect Trubridge to be quite a success with the ladies this week. I have nine single women coming, and you'll surely find one to suit. All of them have heaps of money."

"Who are they?"

"Well, there's Rosalie Harlow, but I know you won't want her for Trubridge since Sir William—"

"What?" Belinda stopped so abruptly that she caused Edie to skid on the gravel before she was able to stop as well. "Rosalie's here?"

"Yes. She and her mother arrived on the morning train. Is that a problem?" she asked in surprise as Belinda groaned.

"It's not a problem, it's a disaster! Oh, Edie, why didn't you tell me you'd invited Rosalie and her mother? You know the girl is one of my clients!"

"Of course I know. As I started to say, I was aware that you're trying to pair her with Sir William Bevelstoke, which is why I invited him, too."

"That's lovely, but it won't matter. Don't you see?"

"Sorry, no. I'm utterly fogged. I thought I was being so clever by bringing her and Sir William together this week, and that you would be pleased. And as for not telling you, I simply forgot. What with packing to come down and all that, sending you a note before I left London completely slipped my mind. But why should it be a problem? Mrs. Harlow assured me you had arranged no fixed engagements for them during Whitsuntide, and I added them to the guest list on the spur of the moment. After all," she added with a laugh, spreading her arms wide "when you have a house with fifty bedrooms and forty people already coming, what's a few more?"

Belinda waved aside her discussion of bedrooms. "You're missing the point. I'm trying to keep Rosalie away from Trubridge. I fear she's become infatuated with him."

"Oh! Still, if she prefers him to Sir William, is that really a problem? I mean, Trubridge does need a rich wife, and Rosalie's certainly rich. And if she likes him better than Sir William, why should you be opposed?"

"I *told* you, he's looking to marry only because he needs money. I don't want that sort of man for Rosalie."

"Oh, yes, that's right." Edie laughed. "You're trying

to match him up with someone awful. Still, I do believe a few of the young ladies coming might be so described. And the county girls are coming for the parties, too, and the fete. Some of them have dowries, I expect."

Belinda didn't find any of that very comforting. "Oh, I can't believe I didn't write ahead and verify the final guest list with you before we came down! How stupid of me to make such a mistake." She pressed the heel of her hand to her forehead. "Where are my brains? Ever since I met that man, they seem to have deserted me completely."

"Indeed?"

She scarcely noticed the duchess's thoughtful murmur. "Trubridge can't stay here now, not with Rosalie here, too. He'll have to leave in the morning. He can surely think of some sort of excuse. A business matter in town? Or sudden illness, perhaps? Food poisoning over the tea cakes?"

"At my house party?" Edie cried. "Absolutely not!"

"Well, whatever the excuse, he has to leave first thing in the morning. As long as Trubridge is around, Rosalie won't even notice poor Sir William."

"Having met both of them, I rather agree with you there. Sir William is a nice young man, but compared to Trubridge, he could seem rather dull to a girl."

"Exactly."

"But I don't see why he has to go. As the hostess, I arrange all the amusements, and I can easily send Rosalie off with Sir William to events and games where Trubridge won't be, so she has little opportunity to speak with him. At dinner, given precedence, they won't be anywhere near at each other at the table. And if you don't see any suitable young lady among the other guests to divert him, I'd be happy to step in. It won't be a hardship for me, I assure you," she added, fanning herself with one hand.

"Not you, too?" Belinda made a sound of complete exasperation and started toward the house. "Why is it that so many women seem to go all silly and weak-kneed over him?" she asked, hating herself at that moment because she'd done exactly that less than a week ago.

"And that bothers you?" Edie asked, falling in step beside her and once again slipping an arm through hers. "That makes no sense, darling. Surely his good looks make your task easier. You are trying to marry him off." She paused. "Aren't you?"

"Of course I am! It's just that—" She broke off, realizing that her plan to find Nicholas the sort of wife she thought he deserved was falling apart. He was proving to be not quite the villain she'd first thought, and yet, despite his assurances to the contrary, she wasn't convinced that he would be a good and faithful husband for a worthy girl. "It's difficult to explain. I just—" She paused and bit her lip, thinking of that kiss. "I just don't want one of my girls to marry him, then end up heartbroken, that's all."

"Well, if money is the only reason he's marrying," Edie responded as they entered the house, "perhaps he could be persuaded to a different course."

Belinda frowned. "I'm not sure I understand you. He's quite determined."

"If all Trubridge needs is a woman with money to support him, I'd be happy to step in."

"Edie!" Shocked, Belinda stopped in the center of the wide, tiled foyer, bringing her hostess to a halt as well.

"What?" The duchess turned toward her, looking surprised. "It makes perfect sense. I'm rich. He's lovely. This could be the perfect solution all around, and," she added with a grin, "he wouldn't even have to marry me."

"That's because you're already married!" Aware she'd raised her voice, she cast an uneasy glance around, but Trubridge must have already gone up, for he was nowhere in sight. Nonetheless, when she spoke, it was in a much lower voice. "I can't believe I'm hearing you say such things."

Edie rolled her eyes. "Oh, don't be such a puritan!" She resumed walking, pulling Belinda with her across the foyer toward the stairs. "What does it matter if I'm married or not?"

"There are so many reason I can't even list them all!"

"Goodness knows, if Trubridge needs money," she went on with breezy indifference to Belinda's words, "I have the means to provide it. I could afford to keep that man in high style."

Belinda shook her head, striving to find a way to make Edie see how wrong this was. "But if you took a lover . . . you might . . . there could be . . . you could become with child, and you couldn't even pretend it was Margrave's. And—" She stopped, feeling her face growing hot. "And I can't even believe we are having this conversation!"

"Really, Belinda, sometimes you can be such a prude."

"I am not a prude!"

"Still," she went on, sailing right past Belinda's denial, "you do have a point. If I took Trubridge as a lover, and I did become pregnant, I should have to go to Kenya and see Margrave, and finding him could take a bit of work. Lord, I might have to go into the bush, face snakes, spiders, leopards, my husband . . . all manner of wild creatures. And when I find him, he'd have to agree to acknowledge the child—oh, it sounds terribly complicated, doesn't it? On the other hand . . ." She paused as if considering the matter. "Bedding Trubridge might be worth it."

"You're talking nonsense!"

"Heavens, don't look so stricken, darling! It's not as if *you* want him." She paused, tilting her head, her green eyes sparkling with mischief. "Or do you?"

"No, of course I don't!" Memories of that kiss rose up, making her lips tingle and her cheeks grow hot, proving her a liar. "I told you before, he's a client. He's also an irresponsible ne'er-do-well with a notorious reputation where women are concerned."

"Perfect for me," the duchess said, her voice still inexplicably indifferent to any moral considerations. "He won't break my heart, so you needn't worry about that. And the bank accounts and hearts of London's debutantes would be saved from his fortune-hunting clutches. What's the problem?"

"I—I—" She broke off, just too flabbergasted to continue, and as she met her friend's gaze, she saw the knowing gleam there, and the truth came to her in a flash. "You don't want him yourself," she said accusingly. "You're just teasing me."

"Indeed?" A slight smile curved Edie's mouth, confirming Belinda's guess. "What makes you say that?"

"Because in all the time I've known you, I have never seen you display an interest in any man but Margrave."

"First time for everything," she said with a shrug and looked away, running one finger lightly along the bannister of the staircase. "But if you want him, of course, I'll bow out."

"I don't want him!" Belinda could hear for herself how unconvincing she sounded, and it dismayed her to know that despite her resolve to be cool as a cucumber where Trubridge was concerned, she was failing dismally. Unable to tolerate any more of this ridiculous conversation, Belinda yanked her arm free of her friend's. "More guests will be arriving soon, so you'd best see to them. I can find my own way up. I'm in the Willow Room as usual, I presume?"

"Oh, now don't go off in a huff," Edie said, laughing as Belinda turned away and started up the curving staircase of stone and wrought iron. "If you want him, Belinda, why not just admit it?"

"Want him?" Belinda muttered as she stomped up the stairs. "I don't even like him!"

"My, my," Edie drawled behind her. "That sounds like famous last words."

Belinda did not bother to reply but continued up the stairs. After all, with Nicholas's kiss still burning her lips, what could she say?

THOUGH IT HAD been relatively easy for Belinda to escape Edie's teasing, it wasn't so easy to escape what her friend had said.

As her maid flitted about, putting her things away, Belinda washed the travel dust from her face, then sat down with her book. Again, she tried to read, but as on the train, she found one flesh-and-blood man far more fascinating than all the characters in her novel, and she couldn't read long enough to turn a single page. All she could seem to think of was him, and whenever she did, her lips tingled and her insides quivered. Yes, there was desire there. She couldn't deny it, but she didn't understand it. How could she want a man she didn't respect? A man she wasn't sure she even liked?

Perhaps this was Fate's way of testing her character and her fortitude. Belinda heaved a rueful sigh. Or perhaps Fate just had a perverse sense of humor.

"I'm finished unpacking everything, my lady."

"Hmm?" She gave a start at the sound of Molly's voice and looked up to find the rotund little maid standing by her chair. "I beg your pardon?"

"I've finished the unpacking, ma'am. Would you like anything else? A cup of tea brought up, or some biscuits?"

What she really wanted was to be alone. "No, Molly, thank you. I believe I shall take a nap. Why don't you go down to the servants' hall and have your tea?"

"Very well." Molly gave a bobbing curtsy. "If there's anything you need, just ring for me. Otherwise, I'll wake you at the dressing gong."

The maid went out, closing the door behind her, and Belinda moved from her seat by the window to her dressing table, pulled out the vanity stool, and sat down. She stared at her reflection, dismayed by the flush in her cheeks brought back by memories of Nicholas's kiss.

What on earth was wrong with her? She'd always been a reserved, self-contained sort of person, and life with Featherstone had exacerbated that trait in her, until forever holding in what she felt was as natural as breathing. No other way to be with a man who could bed another woman without a pang of conscience or drop ten thousand pounds on a racehorse without a thought where it had come from. She'd pushed passionate, intemperate feelings like love and desire down a little deeper with each disappointment Charles had given her, smothering them a little more with each thoughtless act he'd committed, until she'd thought she'd snuffed them out completely.

Where was the cool, proud, implacable Lady Featherstone now? she wondered, staring in misery at her reflection. Where was the sensible woman she thought she'd trained herself to be? The woman to whom fondness and affection meant more than passion?

Edie was right about her. She did want Trubridge herself, wanted him just as much as the shy, reserved Miss Belinda Hamilton had wanted Charles Featherstone. The reasons why were beyond any understanding, and the fact that she seemed to have learned nothing from her previous experience only made her feel more wretched and muddled up than before.

Belinda looked away from her flushed face and reached for the soothing mint face cream on her dressing table, but her hand stilled over the jar, her attention caught by the aubergine handbag also on the table.

She'd had that bag with her that afternoon at Claridge's, and as she stared at the dark purple leather, Nicholas's words from that day echoed through her mind.

Is it really true you've no money?

How startled she'd been to discover he didn't know anything about her money. But then, why should he? It was her own private fortune, one she'd amassed all by herself, one client at a time.

Nicholas didn't know about her wealth, and yet, he still wanted her. That thought brought a tiny, absurd burst of joy, until she remembered that he wasn't supposed to want her at all. He was supposed to be finding a wife, and any momentary joy she felt was replaced at once by hard realities.

Yes, for some inexplicable reason, she wanted him. Here, alone, in the privacy of her room, she could admit it. And Nicholas wanted her. But what difference did any of that make?

All very well for Edie to talk of affairs and lovers. She wasn't serious, but if she were, if she wanted an affair, she could have one because she was married. Though it was considered morally wrong to commit infidelity, it was tolerated in society, as long as one's husband claimed any children that resulted. But for unmarried women, even for a widow such as herself, the risks that came with love affairs were enormous. She wasn't the sort of person who took risks like that.

Her problem, she realized wryly, was that she knew too much about desire. She knew it was really nothing much at all. Oh, it was glorious while it lasted, but it didn't last long. When there was nothing deeper, when there was no mutual respect or liking to turn desire into love, desire faded and died, and—for an unwed woman, at least—there was nothing much to show for it afterward except a broken heart, a ruined reputation, a baby, or possibly all three.

What she'd felt when Nicholas kissed her was as insubstantial as the wind. Featherstone had taught her well. Desire wasn't love, and if she ever made the mistake of confusing the two a second time, she'd deserve the painful consequences because this time around, she didn't have the excuse of youth and naiveté.

Slowly, with sheer force of will, Belinda pushed desire back down into the deep, dark pit where she'd first buried it years ago, and this time, she could only hope it stayed there.

Chapter 12

It was nearing twilight, but even though the light was dimming, making it more and more difficult to read, Rosalie could not bear to give up her book and go back to the house. Not yet.

Instead, she turned a page of her well-worn copy of *Pride and Prejudice* and continued to read. Around her, bees were giving up on the flowers of the garden and returning to their hives, and the finches were no longer squabbling around the birdbath, but that was all right with her. She wasn't out here to admire the beauty of the duchess's gardens.

She'd come out here to enjoy a few minutes of her favorite pastime. Odd how she had longed for the balls and parties of the London season, but now that she was in the midst of it, she was beginning to appreciate how tiring it was. She'd had little time for reading, and given the lavish entertainments planned for the house party, she doubted she'd have much time for it during the week ahead, so she was stealing some time for it now, before the house party really began.

Ah, she was coming to the best part. Rosalie settled back more comfortably on the garden bench, smiling in anticipation as she turned another page. Though she'd read this book dozens of times, she still delighted in Darcy's confession of love to Elizabeth as much as she had the first time she'd read the book.

The dressing gong sounded through the window of the nearby library, and she looked up with a frown. Was it seven o'clock already? Oh, Lord, she was out of time.

Rosalie stood up and started toward the house, but she kept her book open. With an occasional glance to direct her way, she continued reading as she mounted the flagstone steps and started down the long terrace.

I must tell you how ardently I admire and love you.

Rosalie gave a pleasurable sigh, turned another page, and went around the corner, but before she could read another word, she ran smack-dab into what seemed to be a solid wall.

"Oh!" she cried, as the impact of the collision sent her stumbling backward, and she stepped on the hem of her skirt as she tried to regain her balance. Her book went flying out of her hands, and she would have fallen to the hard, tiled granite of the terrace if a pair of hands had not caught her by the arms and kept her upright.

She blinked, drawing a shaky breath as she stared into the black-and-white obstacle she'd cannoned into.

She realized at once that what she was looking at was a man's chest sheathed in evening dress, and the hands holding her upright were strong, manly hands.

"Are you all right?" a deep voice asked, an unmistakable voice that caused her gaze to fly up in disbelief, and when she saw that it was indeed Lord Trubridge standing before her, happiness welled up within her, pressing against her chest and making it impossible to breathe.

"Miss Harlow?" Lord Trubridge said, his surprise seeming as great as hers. Instantly, his hands released her, and he stepped back with a bow. "How do you do?"

She opened her mouth to reply, but her heart was hammering against her ribs with such force, she couldn't seem to speak. He was here, he was really here, right in front of her.

"I didn't realize you were coming for the house party," he went on.

This confirmation of her thoughts made it seem as if the two of them were in perfect mental harmony. What bliss.

I didn't realize you were coming either.

She tried to force the words out, but they remained stuck in her throat, unsaid, and she wanted to kick herself. The handsomest man in the world was standing right in front of her, the man she'd been thinking and dreaming about for weeks, her very own hero, and she could not manage to say a single word. She was completely tongue-tied. Even worse, she could feel a hot blush washing over her face, and she always looked awful when she blushed, a bit like a scarlet ranunculus.

He glanced at the ground around them and spied her book splayed out on top of a terra-cotta pot filled with flowering thyme. He retrieved it, glancing at the title as he did so. "You're reading Austen, I see," he murmured.

She wanted to ask if he liked Austen, but she simply couldn't do it. She could only stand there in mute, ecstatic agony.

He started to hand the book back to her, but then he stopped. "We've killed a bee, I fear," he said, and pulled his handkerchief from his breast pocket to wipe away the remains of the unfortunate insect before he held the book out to her.

Rosalie stared up at him as she took the book, and the only coherent thought that passed through her mind was that he had beautiful eyes. When he smiled at her, the sweetness of it pierced her heart like an arrow.

"If you will pardon me, Miss Harlow?" He didn't wait for a reply—not that she could blame him for that, when she was standing here speechless. Instead, he simply offered her another bow, stepped around her, and continued on his way.

Dismayed, desperate, she turned around. "Thank you," she managed to call to his splendid but retreating back.

"You're welcome," he replied over his shoulder, but he did not turn around. He didn't even stop walking, and as she watched him descend the steps to the south lawns and enter the boxwood maze, the joy in her heart twisted into disappointment. Wretched, she ducked back around the corner and pressed her flushed face against the cool stone of the house.

"Thank you?" she muttered to herself in a paroxysm of disbelief and self-recrimination. Weeks of imagining a moment such as this, and when it had finally come, all she'd been able to say to him was thank you?

Rosalie tapped her forehead three times against the wall, grinding her teeth in frustration, and she vowed that before the week was out, she would work up the courage to speak with him. After all, no self-respecting heroine could allow herself to be tongue-tied in the presence of her hero. What kind of romance would that be?

DINNER WAS AGONY.

Nicholas sat beside the duchess, who had declared upon walking in with him that she'd heard he was full of wit and that she expected scintillating conversation at dinner in consequence. That declaration forced him to pay attention to those around him so that he could insert the proper clever rejoinder now and again, and this was no easy task. In addition, there was a bishop on his other side, and the man had given him a most disapproving frown upon their introduction, showing that Nicholas's tarnished reputation preceded him even in ecclesiastical circles.

To make matters worse, Lord and Lady Wetherford were directly across the table, and both of them seemed to squirm in their seats every time he so much as looked at them, and they winced every time he opened his mouth. He could only guess that they were so embarrassed their son had shot him while in a state of intoxication and terrified he might tell everyone in earshot all about it that they couldn't seem to string together coherent replies to any of his questions. An inquiry about Pongo's health and well-being probably would have sent both of them sinking beneath the table in a paroxysm of embarrassment.

Belinda was so far down the dining table—twelve people away, at least—that it was impossible for him to talk with her. But he could see her quite plainly from where he sat, and that tortuous fact, more than anything else, was making his evening an excruciating episode.

Her black hair, piled in a gleaming mass atop her head, looked almost indigo blue in the candlelight of the dining room. She wore the same strands of Roman pearls he'd seen at the ball, and below them, he could see the shadowy cleft between her breasts, for the neck-line of her lavender silk evening gown was cut far too low for his peace of mind. She seemed more beautiful than ever before. He wanted her more than ever before. He ached with it, he burned with it. He felt as if he must be emanating lust.

Had she seemed to be in a state at all similar to his, he might have been able to take the situation in a better spirit. Unfortunately, she seemed to be having the time of her life. Unlike him, she was conversing easily with her dinner companions. He knew that because every time he glanced her way—which happened about every six seconds by his estimation—she was talking and laughing with those around her. He never caught her looking at him, worse luck, and by the time the dessert of raspberry fool had been consumed, he was almost at the end of his tether. When the duchess declared that the ladies would leave the men to their port, he decided he'd had enough.

Once the ladies had gone through, he swallowed down his port in a gulp, murmured an excuse about needing a walk after that delicious meal, and departed for the outdoors, hoping the cool spring air could cool his blood.

Once outside, he strode along the terrace, passed the open French doors that led to where the ladies were gathered in the music room, and went down the steps to the gardens. He made directly for the boxwood maze on the south lawn, for having been through it before dinner, he was reasonably sure he could remember how to find the center. And the center of a maze seemed an excellent place for some privacy, something he badly needed just now.

This situation was intolerable, he thought as he walked between walls of tall boxwood hedge. How could he be anywhere near Belinda for an entire week and not break that stupid, stupid promise? How could he not haul her into his arms and kiss her? How could he not pull her into his arms, caress her, and make love to her?

He took a deep breath, knowing he had to stop torturing himself this way. He focused his mind on finding his way through the maze, forcing out all other considerations, but by the time he reached the center, he was not restored to a rational state of mind.

Bad enough that he wanted her so much he ached

like a randy seventeen-year-old. But the fact that he was here because he needed to find a wife made it all that much worse, for contemplating marriage to any woman when he wanted one he couldn't marry, wanted her beyond all reason, seemed more than he could bear.

In the center of the maze stood a small folly of wrought iron covered with climbing white roses that gleamed in the light of the full moon. He made for the stone bench tucked beneath the roses, but he felt far too keyed up to sit down. Instead, he halted in front of it, staring at the thick tangle of rose canes all around him, and wondered what on earth he was going to do.

What could a man do when he had a passion for a woman who had no use for him at all? Did he write love letters? Compose poetry? He shied away from that possibility and moved on. Send roses? Hell, he didn't even know if Belinda was fond of roses. Most women were, but Belinda was unlike any other woman he'd ever met.

Still, he rather liked the idea of roses. Assuming that she did have a fondness for them, what kind would be her favorite? He considered the question, tilting his head back to study the pristine white blooms above him. He inhaled, but there was so little fragrance to the flowers, they might just as well have been daisies, and he knew that if he ever sent Belinda roses, they wouldn't be like these.

No, they'd be big, red, velvety roses, the kind that were lush and dark and smelled of summer, because Belinda was that kind of woman. Despite her pristine surface, she was heady and passionate. She didn't want to be, he knew, but deny it all she liked, she was a passionate woman. Yes, he decided, for Belinda, only red roses would do.

Nicholas smiled rather ruefully at that. If he sent Belinda roses, he'd probably learn afterward she had a rose allergy. When it came to her, his luck seemed to be running that way.

"Lord Trubridge?"

The sound of a feminine voice broke into his thoughts, but he knew the voice was, unfortunately, not Belinda's. He turned around, and the sight of Rosalie Harlow right in front of him, and the expression of adoration on her face confirmed that his luck was going in the wrong direction, not only with Belinda, but with all women everywhere.

"Miss Harlow?" He cast an uneasy glance over her head. "You shouldn't be out here alone with me."

"I—I saw you go past the music room, so I knew you weren't having port with the other gentlemen. I slipped out and followed you." Her fingers twined together and untwined again, showing her nervousness.

He was damned nervous, too, for he couldn't afford a repeat of the Elizabeth Mayfield episode. He didn't think Rosalie was that sort of girl, but a man could never be too careful. He glanced at the opening in the hedges, hoping Mrs. Harlow wasn't about to arrive on the scene, full of righteous indignation and demanding honor be satisfied.

"You'd best go back at once," he advised. "The ladies will be wondering where you've gone."

"No, they won't. Not for a few minutes yet."

"But surely your mother—"

"Oh, we don't need to worry about her. She thinks I went to the necessary. I don't usually lie to Mama, of course. But I knew I must speak with you privately, and I couldn't think of any other way to manage it."

"Speaking with me privately is not a good thing for an unmarried young lady to be doing." He stepped closer, hoping she would step back and allow him a gentlemanly exit, but she did not move. The thorny branches that lined the sides of the folly prevented him from going around her. "If not your mother, someone else might see us, and it would grieve me if your reputation were damaged because of me."

"I know it is far too bold of me to approach you in this way, but ever since we met, I have been in agony that we are apart, and now that I have seen you again, I must confess my feelings."

He rubbed his fingers over his forehead with an unhappy sigh. "I'd rather you didn't."

She ignored that, of course. "You must allow me to tell you how ardently I admire and love you."

He wondered if she'd uttered those words with conscious intent. He rather doubted it. Girls memorized Austen's Darcy speech as a matter of course, and she'd been reading *Pride and Prejudice* that very afternoon. It was probably stuck in her head as the most romantic words anyone could say.

He stared into the pretty, adoring face before him, and he strove to let her down as gently as possible. "My dear girl, you don't even know me. You can't possibly love me."

"I do love you, I do. I'm mad for you."

"It's a temporary insanity," he assured her. "It will pass."

"You think me transient in my affections? Oh, how can I prove otherwise?"

He once again moved forward, but even though they were almost touching, she still did not move back, and he knew there was no way other than force. He put his hands on her arms to push her back, but she was too quick for him. She pulled free and entwined her arms around his neck.

"This is the only way I can express what I feel," she said, and kissed him.

He reached up at once, curled his fingers around her wrists, and pulled her arms down, but he made the mistake of letting go too soon, and before he could excuse himself and try to move past her, she seized the lapels of his dinner jacket in her fists and rose up on her toes to kiss him again. Perceiving her intent, he managed to evade the move by twisting his head sideways, and as Rosalie's lips grazed his jaw, he saw Belinda standing by the entrance to the maze.

Her face seemed like smooth, polished alabaster in the moonlight, and he knew any minuscule chance he might have had with her had now vanished altogether.

He grasped Rosalie's wrists and pulled, but she tightened her grip on his jacket and would not let go. Before he could begin prying her fingers loose, Sir William also appeared, demonstrating that Nicholas's luck was deteriorating at an alarming rate. It had gone from bad to worse to absolutely hellish in three seconds flat.

"Lord Trubridge," Sir William cried as he strode forward, "remove your hands from Miss Harlow this instant!"

Rosalie gasped and turned to look over her shoulder, loosening her grip, and Nicholas was able to free himself at last. He shoved her backward with as much force as a man could honorably employ against a woman, enabling him to extricate both of them from the prickly confines of the folly.

But he knew by the other man's enraged countenance that he hadn't a prayer of exiting from this situation entirely unscathed. An angry man in the throes of love and jealousy was a dangerous thing, and he wondered if there would be a challenge to his honor and a demand for pistols at dawn. That would be the perfect punctuation to the entire absurd episode, but having been shot once in his life already by a man who was enraged, jealous, and inebriated, he would prefer not to go through that sort of thing again.

"It's not what you think, old chap," he began, then stopped. Though the words were God's truth, the lameness of them made even him grimace, and they certainly did not appease Sir William.

"You bastard." The younger man's left fist slammed into his right cheek before he could duck. The blow sent Nicholas staggering backward into one side of the folly, then his knees seemed to give out, and he felt as if he were sinking.

He heard the rend of fabric as rose canes ripped through the back of his dinner jacket, and he sucked in a sharp breath as thorns pierced the skin of his shoulder. Past the pain of being hit in the face and shredded by thorns, he realized he was still falling, and when his other shoulder hit the turf beside the folly, his last thought before everything went black was that if things kept on this way, finding a wife was going to kill him.

Chapter 13

When Nicholas awoke, his first impression was pain—an ache on the right side of his face and a burning sting in his shoulder. He opened his eyes and overhead he saw the night sky and a carpet of blurry stars. In the air was the scent of grass and boxwood, and he remembered where he was and what had happened.

He wriggled his jaw experimentally, and winced, confirming that he had not been dreaming. Rosalie's kiss, Sir William's powerful left jab, and his own tangle with the rosebushes had all been nothing less than reality.

He sat up and immediately wished he hadn't. His head throbbed, his jaw hurt, and his shoulder felt raw. Worst of all, Belinda was sitting on the grass right in front of him, looking to his dazed mind like Judith about to behead Holofernes. Fortunately, she didn't seem to have a sword in her hands.

He would have lain back down, groaning in pain to perhaps gain a bit of sympathy, but knowing Belinda, he doubted it would do any good. No, he'd probably already been tried, condemned, and sentenced. All that remained was execution.

He looked at her luscious mouth, knowing that his chance of kissing it ever again lay somewhere between none and very, very slim, but he wasn't going to give up on something like that without a fight. "I didn't do it," he said, chagrined at how idiotic that sounded—like a child caught stealing sweets. He tried again. "I came out here to be alone. It wasn't—"

She cut him off by holding up her hand, palm toward him. "You don't have to explain."

"No, I do. I really think I do. I know what it looks like, but I didn't break my promise to you. I didn't kiss her. I mean, we were kissing, obviously, but . . ." His voice trailed off, for there was no way to tell her the truth without putting the blame squarely on the girl, and that was something he would not do. "Hell," he muttered instead, propping his elbows on his bent knees and resting his head in his hands. "Hell."

"Nicholas, I saw what happened."

"You did?" He lifted his head, hope rekindling inside him. Perhaps all was not quite lost.

"Yes, I did. I know Rosalie followed you, because I followed her when she left the drawing room. Over the top of the hedge as I came through the maze, I heard you tell her to leave and her confession of her feelings, and I arrived upon the scene just in time to see her kiss you."

"So you don't blame me?"

"No. Although," she added with a sniff, "I do think you might have pulled her arms down a little bit faster than you did."

"What?" He made a scoffing sound. "That's absurd. I disentangled myself from her as quickly as I could, but it wasn't as easy as it might seem. Belinda, that girl was like an octopus."

Her lips twitched, just a little. He felt another glimmer of hope.

"My lady?"

Both of them turned to find a footman standing in the opening between the boxwood hedges, a glowing lamp in his hand and a tray in the crook of his other arm. "You sent for ice and bandages?" he asked.

"Yes, Henry. Bring them here, if you would."

He came forward, giving Nicholas a nod and glancing with concern at his torn clothing. "I hope you're not seriously injured, my lord. Sir William said you fell into the rosebushes?"

"That's one way of putting it, I suppose," he acknowledged.

The footman turned to Belinda. "Shall I tend His Lordship's wounds, my lady, so that you may return to the party?"

"Thank you, Henry, but that won't be necessary. With fifty people to wait on, you're needed inside more than I am." She gestured to the grass. "Put the tray there," she added as she began pulling off her long evening gloves. "Then you may go."

"Yes, Your Ladyship." The young man obeyed, gave a bow, and departed, leaving them alone once again.

Belinda tossed her gloves aside, rose up on her knees, and lifted the lamp. "Turn a bit," she ordered. "So I can have a better look at your injuries."

He complied, watching her over his shoulder as she held the lamp high and carefully pulled back part of his torn jacket and shirt with her fingers. "It's not too bad," she said after a moment. "The thorns did tear through your jacket and shirt, but for the most part, I think your clothing protected you. Still, there are some punctures as well as scratches, and the wounds will definitely have to be cleaned."

She set the lamp beside her, then picked up a dark brown bottle from the tray, pulled out the cork that capped it, and reached for one of the bandages. "You'll have to remove your shirt."

He grinned at that, sending pain shooting through his jaw, but teasing her was worth it. "Why, Belinda," he murmured, "you naughty girl."

Her answering glance was wry. "Only in your dreams, Trubridge."

"It doesn't happen quite this way in my dreams," he corrected, still watching her face as he shrugged out of his dinner jacket and unbuttoned his waistcoat. "The way I always envision it, I'm taking off *your* clothes first."

In the lamplight, he could see a rosy tint suffuse

her cheeks, but she began saturating the bandage with whatever unguent was in the bottle and didn't reply.

He pulled off his waistcoat and white bow tie, then removed his studs and links and dropped them onto the tray. As he pulled off his shirt and the undershirt beneath, he knew the thorns must have drawn blood, for the linen and silk stuck to his skin as he pulled them off, and when he tossed them aside, he could see the dark red stains on the tattered fabric. "I fear my valet will be very displeased with me over this."

"He isn't the only one. Sir William is none too fond of you either." Belinda rose on her knees behind him and pressed the wet cloth against the bare skin of his shoulder.

He sucked in air between clenched teeth. "God, woman," he said, looking at her over his shoulder. "what's on that cloth? Lemon juice?"

"An antiseptic."

"It stings."

"Oh, don't be such a baby."

"I'm not," he protested, and as if to prove it, he uttered a very manly curse when she pressed the cloth to another part of his shoulder. As she worked, he concentrated on the feel of her bare hands against his skin, and that dissipated any pain.

"How's your face?" she asked.

"Aches a bit."

"There's an ice poultice on the tray."

"I didn't realize Sir William was such an excellent pugilist," he said as he picked up the cloth bag filled with ice chips, but he stopped before applying it to his face. "Speaking of Sir William," he said, and turned to look at her again, "why in heaven's name did you bring him out here with you?"

"I didn't. He must have come outside, seen Rosalie crossing the lawn with me behind her, and followed both of us. That's all I can think. I had no idea he was even there until he strode past me and accosted you."

"Ah," he said, enlightened, and gingerly pressed the poultice to the side of his face. "That does make the most sense, I suppose."

She chuckled suddenly. "I fear your season isn't going too well so far."

"Really?" he countered, but he couldn't help laughing, too, for it was all so terribly absurd. "I hadn't noticed."

He paused, considering, then he said, "I think I should leave tomorrow."

"I hardly think that's necessary. It was embarrassing for all of us, I daresay, but the four of us are the only ones who know what happened. Sir William is discreet and a gentlemen, and speaking of it to anyone would hurt Rosalie's reputation, which he would never do. Rosalie's too embarrassed, I suspect, to reveal any of what happened, and has every reason not to do so. You and I won't discuss it with anyone. So why should you go? You do—" She paused, her hands stilled against his shoulder. "You do still want to find a wife, don't you?"

"What I want has little to do with it," he said, savoring the feel of her touch, even as he reminded himself of why he ought to leave. "Besides, it doesn't matter if none of us speak of it because by tomorrow night, I will probably have a second black eye to match the first, and people are bound to know there's been some sort of scuffle."

"I believe Sir William's version of events is that the two of you had a bit too much to drink and made the mistake of engaging in a discussion of politics. Things became quite heated and resulted in a most unfortunate round of fisticuffs."

"A credible story, I suppose, although anyone who knows me would laugh at it. I would never fight over politics. Still, it's best if I go. It avoids further questions on the subject."

"True," she said and resumed her task. The matter seemed settled, and yet, he didn't want to leave. As intolerable as this situation was, it gave him the chance to be near her, and he wanted that, but he didn't want to find a wife. He wanted Belinda.

He was becoming acutely aware of that fact as she placed a bandage on his shoulder and began wrapping gauze around the pit of his arm to secure it in place. As her warm hands brushed his bare skin, desire began stirring inside him, blotting out the pain of his bruised face and scratched skin as effectively as any anesthetic, and he could only conclude he was hopelessly skirt smitten.

"There," she said at last, and her hands fell away. "Be sure to have your valet look at the wounds in the morning, but the scratches aren't deep, so by tomorrow, I don't believe a replacement bandage will even be necessary."

"I'll tell him." Nicholas moved onto his knees and turned around, facing her.

She spoke again, quickly, before he could. "I should advise you not to wear any wool next to your skin for the next several days. It might be too irritating."

He didn't want to talk about his scratches or his underclothes. He tossed aside the ice poultice. "So you agree I should leave?"

"It's probably for the best," she said, but he thought there might have been a hint of reluctance in her voice. Was that because she was trying to marry him off as quickly as possible or because she might, just might, miss him if he left? He decided to find out.

"But do you *want* me to go?" He leaned a bit closer. "Or do you want me to stay?"

"It hardly matters what I want. Go if you like. Stay if you like. It doesn't affect me."

"I think it does." He reached for her hand, and held it fast when she tried to pull it away. "If I stay, do you think you'll still be able to advise me about which of the women here might make me a suitable wife?"

"I . . ." She paused, and her tongue flicked over her lips, and he found the notion that she was nervous encouraging. "I don't see why not."

"Hard-hearted Belinda." He paused to lift her hand in his. Turning it, he pressed a kiss to her palm, and her shiver in response raised his hopes another notch.

"Don't," she said, and, again, she tried to pull back. Again, he wouldn't let her.

"Don't what?" he asked, brushing his lips along her wrist. "Don't want you? Don't hope that you want me, too?"

"You can't possibly want me," she said, determined

to argue even though she had stopped trying to pull free. "You've been injured."

He laughed, blowing warm air against the soft skin of her wrist. "I'd have to be dead not to want this." He pressed kisses along the inside of her forearm.

"But I don't want it." There was a breathless quality to her voice that told him that was a lie.

"Perhaps I'm deluding myself, but I don't believe you." He let her hand go, but before she could move away, he wrapped his arm around her waist and leaned closer. "I think we both feel the same thing. I say, why fight it?"

"You're making advances," she said, sounding truly desperate now, but she made no struggle to get away. "You're breaking your promise."

"I know, but I can't help myself." His free hand cupped the back of her neck. "I'm such a cad."

He kissed her, keeping his eyes open, watching hers close. But her mouth did not open under his, and he ran his tongue back and forth over the closed seam of her lips, coaxing her to part them.

After a moment, she relented, opening her mouth with a soft moan of surrender. His body responded at once. He tightened one arm around her waist, his free hand raking upward into the silken strands of her hair. His mouth opened wide over hers, and though it hurt his jaw, he didn't care. She tasted of the raspberries they'd had for dessert, warm and sweet, like summer itself.

Time seemed suspended as he explored her mouth— the lush fullness of her lips, the straight line of her teeth, the excitement that flared in his body when her tongue met his. But a kiss wasn't enough.

He broke the contact of their mouths long enough for a breath of air, then tilted his head the other way and kissed her again, and as he did so, his arm tightened around her waist and his other hand slid down from her hair, along the column of her throat, and across the bare skin along the base of her neck. As he tasted deeply of her mouth, his fingertips grazed her skin, moving over the hard bump of her clavicle and down the soft, warm expanse of her bosom.

He cupped his hand over her breast and groaned with pleasure at the lush, round fullness of it against his palm. But he also felt her stiffen in his embrace, and as she broke the kiss, turning away with a gasp, he was forced to pause.

He knew with all the layers of clothing she wore, the thud of her heart against the heel of his hand was only his imagination, but she did not push him away, and as he waited in an agony of suspense, their harsh, mingled breathing was the only sound in the stillness of night.

At last, he moved again, touching his lips to her cheek, her temple, her ear. Her breast still cupped in his hand, he caressed the bare skin above the edge of her gown.

Her breath was coming faster now, and he could feel the desire in her growing hotter, but she made no move to touch him. Her arms stayed at her sides, and con-trary sort of man that he was, he found that more erotic than he'd ever have thought possible. It inflamed not only his desire but also a relentless determination to wring a response from her, to have her as she'd been the first time he'd kissed her, with her arms around him and her hips moving against his.

His arm tightened around her waist, and he fell back and sideways, pulling them both down into the grass with her on top of him. When her lips parted, he kissed her at once, for he didn't want to hear the refusal that might be on her lips.

Lust was like a roar in his ears now, drowning out everything else. His hands grasped folds of fabric, pulling her ball gown up in his fists until he could slip his hands beneath the layers of silk and muslin.

Her hands pressed into the grass on either side of him and she tried to lift herself away, but his hands slid up the backs of her thighs at once, cupping her buttocks to keep her where she was, and when she sank back against him and her hands came up to touch his face, he made a rough sound of triumph into her mouth.

He kissed her, shaping her buttocks with his hands, and her skin seemed to scorch his palms through the thin lawn of her drawers. He wanted her legs spread apart over his hips and he tried to pull the folds of her gown higher, but her skirt was too narrow for that, and he had to content himself with the sweet torture of her sex pressed against his groin. He flexed his hips, and that tiny move was so exquisite, he broke the kiss with a groan.

That was his mistake.

"We have to stop," she gasped against his neck. "We have to stop."

He shook his head in complete rejection of something

so absurd. Stop? When it felt like this? He squeezed her buttocks again, holding her in place as he flexed his hips again, a move that wrung a sob of pleasure from her. But he had no time to relish the sound, for she began to struggle in earnest to extricate herself, her hands pressing into his shoulders to lift her away.

"Nicholas, let me go," she panted. "We can't do this."

His body ached with need. "Don't," he pleaded through clenched teeth. "For God's sake, Belinda, don't stop me. Let's make love, right here in the grass."

"You're mad."

He might well be, but he couldn't see how this sort of insanity was a bad thing. He wanted to caress her, pleasure her until she surrendered completely, but he feared that if he loosened his hold, she'd be off him like a shot, so he tried using words.

"I want you, Belinda, right here, right now. I've wanted you ever since that first day. Even while you were looking me up and down as if I was the most contemptible man you'd ever seen, I wanted you. What can I say? I'm a glutton for punishment."

"You're talking nonsense."

"No," he panted. "Not nonsense. It's desire."

"But that's all it is," she cried, and twisted her body, wrenching free and rolling off him. Before he could gather his wits, she was scrambling backward amid the tangle of her skirts, putting herself out of his reach before he could even sit up. "It's nothing but lust!"

His body was on fire, leaving him unable to dispute that particular point. In truth, he felt as if disputes of any kind were beyond him. His body was in chaos at this moment. His heart was racing, his blood pounding through his veins, his cock aching, and his brains utterly gone.

He bent his legs, resting his elbows on his knees and his head in his hands, taking deep breaths and striving for some semblance of control over a body in complete rebellion. "What the hell is wrong with lust?" he muttered, that response the best he could manage under the circumstances.

He heard the swish of her skirts and looked up to see her rise to her feet. "It's not love!" she said, panting. "That's what's wrong with it."

"Love?" He shook his head, baffled, still caught in the throes of desire, trying to make sense of what seemed senseless.

"Yes, love! I realize that for you, that's not a consideration—not in lovemaking, not in marriage, not in anything." She paused, bending to reach for the train of her gown. "In fact," she added as she straightened, hooking the train loop over her wrist. "I'm not sure you even know what love is."

That unfair accusation was like a match to powder, igniting his already inflamed emotions. "You think I don't know what love is?" He stood up, his body burning, anger flaming as desire cooled. "Believe it or not, Belinda, I was in love once. Only once, I grant you, but I know damned well what love is because I felt it, I had it in my hands, and I lost it."

He never spoke of Kathleen, but he couldn't stop himself from doing it now, for Belinda's words made a mockery of what he'd felt all those years ago, and he couldn't let it pass. "I was a lot like you, I expect. I met the love of my life, I thought it was perfect, beautiful, and right. Like you, I had no doubts, no fears, no questions. I felt a euphoric bliss that caught me up and made me feel that anything in this world was possible. And, yes," he added, the words like acid on his tongue, "like you, I remember the deep, bitter disillusionment of knowing I was never truly loved in return. Of learning that to my beloved, money was more important than I was. Of knowing that everything has a price. My love, I'll have you know, was worth ten thousand pounds, because that is what my father paid the woman I loved to abandon me and disappear. So don't tell me I don't know what love is because I know *exactly* what it is. I also know how it feels to lose it."

Belinda pressed a hand to her bosom, her eyes wide with shock. "Your father bought off the girl you loved?"

Nicholas felt as if he were drowning—smothered by memories, thwarted desire, and his own anger. "Her name was Kathleen Shaughnessey. She was Irish, and Catholic, and poor, and her father was a tenant farmer on Landsdowne's estate in County Kildare. I met her when I stayed there the summer I was nineteen. I was too young and stupid to realize that a girl like that couldn't possibly be allowed to marry the future Duke of Landsdowne."

"What happened?"

"First, he tried to separate me from Kathleen by summoning me home from Ireland before my holiday was up. He kept me at Landsdowne through the autumn and planted a beautiful and acceptable girl in my path."

"Lady Elizabeth Mayfield."

"Yes. Elizabeth and I already knew each other, of course. She's a distant cousin, and our families had always hoped for a match between us. But when I wasn't diverted from Kathleen, he orchestrated the entire episode—the house party, the chance meeting in the conservatory, Elizabeth throwing herself at me, and her mother walking in at just the right moment— all perfectly timed." He gave a humorless laugh. "For a moment tonight, I really thought history was repeating itself, except that Landsdowne would never choose an American."

"Nicholas, you don't think—" She broke off and shook her head. "Rosalie would never devise such a scheme to trap you."

"No, even before you arrived, I'd already guessed Rosalie just had a crush. But if her mother had come walking in instead of you, I might have revised my opinion."

"So how did you learn your father was behind it?"

"Elizabeth's not a very good liar. She broke down and finally admitted Landsdowne had arranged it. Both of them thought I would do the honorable thing, you see, but I refused to be manipulated by him or by her. So, when that plan failed, he went to Kathleen and told her to name her price. She did."

He gave Belinda a grin of self-mockery. "So now you know the true reason for my requirements for a wife. I want just the sort of woman that my father would hate, one who's rich enough to provide an income, yes, but one who is also so rich, so obscenely rich, that Landsdowne will be unable to bribe her to go away."

"So you will make your choice of wife based on all the criteria that will best aggravate and frustrate him?"

"Damned right. After he cut me off, he told me he'd reinstate my income only if I wed, and the girl had to match his precise requirements in every detail. That's typical of him. He thinks of himself as king of all he surveys, controlling everything and everyone."

"And it never occurs to you to change that?"

"How?"

"Talk to him, hold out the olive branch—"

"Olive branch?" He laughed, a sound harsh enough that both of them winced. "You don't understand in the least. For that, I'd have to be a person of flesh and blood to him, and I'm not. I'm not his son. I'm just another means to get him what he wants. And I refuse to play his game."

"My God," she murmured, staring at him as if appalled, "that's the driving force behind everything you do, isn't it? Doing whatever your father does not want. The wild living, the bolstering of your bad reputation, the irresponsible spending of your income, finding a wife he won't approve—all of it as some sort of . . . of revenge?"

"It's not revenge. It's avoiding the chains he has tried to wrap me in my entire life. It's never allowing him to dictate to me or control me or have any power over me, my actions, or my life ever again."

"But that's just it, Nicholas. He does have power over your life. He has all the power."

"What? That's ridiculous."

"No, it's the truth." She shook her head, giving a little

laugh of disbelief as if amazed he didn't see the situation the same way she did. "You live your entire life doing what he doesn't want. You're not free to make choices of your own accord, for all of them are predicated on what his choices would be and doing the opposite. You're not the master of your life at all!"

His anger flared higher with every word she spoke. "Take care, Belinda. You go too far."

"And what role do I play in this game between you?" she demanded, heedless of his words. "While you search for the wife most appropriate for outraging your father, and he works to force you to the woman he wants you to wed, what am I? Your plaything? Your way of passing time until the wedding day?"

"Of course not! I don't think of you that way at all."

"Or perhaps I'm just another outrageous way to get back at him. After all, I'm an American. I might give you a child who's a bastard. He'd hate that, I'll wager. And even if not, I'd still be a mistress, a distraction that prevents you from finding an appropriate duchess. If you had an affair with me, that would aggravate Landsdowne mightily, I expect."

"That bastard has nothing to do with what I feel for you! Nothing."

"How would I know that?"

"How would I prove it? What do you want? Declarations of love? Courtship rituals? A marriage proposal?"

The moment the words were out of his mouth, he knew they'd been the wrong ones to say. Her face hardened into implacable lines. "I will never marry again. And if I did, it certainly wouldn't be you. Why would

I want a man who has no ambition for his life beyond acting like a rebellious youth? A man who always prefers the easy path? I had a man like that, and I don't ever want another."

That cut him, inflicting more pain than any of the other injuries he'd suffered tonight. "That's a lie," he shot back. "I know damn well you want me. You want me as much as I want you. Or do you deny that scarcely five minutes ago, you were as caught up in desire as I was?"

"No, I won't deny it. But desire is all it is, and desire without love and respect is nothing." Her blue eyes glittered in the dim light. "You are a lily of the field, Nicholas, with no desire to change or better your circumstances by your own efforts. I cannot respect a man like that, nor ever truly love him."

Her words felt like a knife slicing open his chest and exposing his soul, and he could only stand there, filled with fury and pain, as she turned and ran, vanishing between the hedges.

Chapter 14

His trunks were packed by half past seven the following morning. By quarter to eight, they were in the foyer, and a carriage was standing in the drive, ready to take him and his valet to the station. The only thing that prevented his departure was his hostess. He was waiting for her to come down so that he could bid her farewell.

Having learned he was leaving, the duchess had sent her maid to beg his indulgence long enough for her to dress and see him off. Nicholas, who needed all the friends he could get, and who found his hostess a delightful woman, complied with her request. He just hoped she didn't take too long. The earliest train for London departed at quarter past eight, and he intended to be on it, for he couldn't bear another moment of being near Belinda and being unable to have her.

It was hard to define what he felt, but he knew now it was more than desire because he'd desired many women before, and if any of them had told him what Belinda had, he'd have shrugged it off without a qualm. He'd never much cared what people thought of him.

Belinda, however, was different from any other woman, and that fact was the main reason he'd been up most of the night. Even now, her blunt words still rang in his ears, the disdain in them as unmistakable as it had been ten hours ago. And the devil of it was that he couldn't refute a single word she'd said.

Oh, he'd tried. He had stayed in the maze last night after she had returned to the party—all night, in fact. At first, he'd been in such high dudgeon that all he'd been able to do was pace round and round the folly, telling himself all the reasons she was utterly wrong, punctuating these enumerations with some of the foulest curses he knew.

When he'd rather worn out that method of dealing with the situation, he'd been forced to admit that perhaps Belinda had a bit of a point. He'd lain down in the grass, staring up at the stars and thinking back over all the moments in his life when he'd chosen a course of action deliberately to oppose what Landsdowne wanted, and this review of his past had proved quite nauseating. Belinda had more than a point. Belinda, he'd been forced to concede, had been exactly right. The question he'd then had to face was what to do about it. How did a man break free of a habit he'd engaged in for most of his life?

There was also the matter of his financial difficulties

to be resolved. Marrying money had seemed the only solution to his problems, and an easy solution at that, but Nicholas thought of his bruised face, his scratched shoulder, and his desperate longing for a woman who didn't want him, and decided there was nothing easy about it.

Besides, finding an heiress to marry was clearly off the table now. A night spent lying in the grass, breathing in the cool spring air, had eased the desire for Belinda raging through his body, but that respite, he knew, was temporary. All he had to do was see her, or give in to his imagination, and those feelings would flare up again quick as lighting a match. He couldn't imagine bedding any woman but her. And marrying her wasn't a solution, either, for even if she had the blunt to solve his financial difficulties, which she didn't, she certainly wouldn't give it to him. Not in a thousand years.

And, truth be told, he wouldn't take it.

You are a lily of the field, Nicholas, with no desire to change or better your circumstances by your own efforts. Why would I want a man who has no ambition for his life beyond acting like a rebellious youth? A man who always prefers the easy path?

In a few razor-sharp sentences, she had described him and his life, and though he didn't like the description, it was a brutally accurate one.

It had been many years since he'd dared to dream of a purpose for his life. He'd even managed to convince himself that he didn't want one. But last night had changed everything. Belinda had made him see the truth about himself, and though he didn't like it, there was no going back. There was no easy path. And now, as he thought of being something more than a lily of the field, he felt hope stirring inside him, something he hadn't had since he was a boy. He wanted to find a purpose for his life.

How he'd set about that still wasn't quite clear. He'd fallen asleep in the grass with no solution in sight, but he'd woken at dawn to the realization that if there was a solution, he wouldn't find it here. He wouldn't find it by marrying a woman he didn't love or by trying to charm his way into Belinda's good graces. Neither of those would gain him her respect, and though he desired her body, he desired her respect even more. Without that, the rest meant nothing. She'd been right about that, too.

Her declaration that she had no respect for him had felt like a knife going in, but somehow during the night, that wound had transformed into determination. There was fear, too, of course. Fear that hovered at the back of his mind like a shadow—fear that there was no solution, fear that he'd never gain her good opinion no matter how he tried, fear that he'd never be truly free of Landsdowne no matter what he did, but Nicholas forced down those unpalatable possibilities. He'd think of an answer because he simply refused to believe otherwise. Besides, as things stood, his situation couldn't get worse than it already was, and he certainly couldn't sink any lower in Belinda's eyes than he'd already sunk, so there was nowhere to go but up.

"Trubridge?"

He turned as the duchess came down the last flight of stairs, looking charming in her morning wrapper of corn-colored cashmere. "I am so distressed that you are leaving already," she said as she halted in front of him.

"It is my regret as well, Duchess," he said with a bow.

"Is this sudden departure due to your injuries of last night?" she asked, as he straightened. "I heard," she added, smiling a little, "that you had a spot of bother with some of my rosebushes."

"The injuries are minor, I assure you. Still, I don't believe it is ever wise to wrestle with a rosebush."

"No, it's rather a losing battle, I imagine." She studied him for a moment, and her smile widened a bit. "And how is your face?"

"A bit sore, but tolerable, though I fear I shall have my second black eye of the season."

"And over fisticuffs with Sir William?" She sighed, shaking her head. "I thought you were trying to rehabilitate your reputation."

"I am." He smiled at her. "I don't seem to be getting on very well."

She laughed and gestured to the door. "Walk with me a bit before you go. It's a lovely morning. Now, don't argue," she added as he opened his mouth to reply. "I know the early train doesn't go for half an hour yet. You've plenty of time."

"I wouldn't dream of arguing," he said, giving in. "I never refuse to take walks with beautiful women."

That made her laugh again. "I'm not, but it's very gallant of you to say so," she said as a footman opened the front door for them and they walked out into the morning sunlight. "And you are such delightful company. I hate that you are going."

"I think it's best. I shouldn't want Sir William to be staring daggers at me for the next week."

"You men, so silly, fighting about politics. Odd, though," she added, "I'd never have taken you for the sort who gets heated about that particular subject. And I'd have said Sir William is far too diplomatic to engage in such arguments." She shot him an inquiring sideways glance, but when he didn't take the bait, she changed tactics.

"I'm sure Sir William regrets his outburst of temper, and the two of you could become friends before the week is out. Also, I have heard that you desire to marry, and if that is so, there are plenty of young ladies here. You see? I'm giving you heaps of reasons to stay longer."

"Perhaps Sir William and I could become more fond, but as to the other . . ." He shook his head. "No, I have come to realize I'm not the sort who can marry for material considerations. There are . . . other things that matter more to me."

"I see. Deuced inconvenient, that."

"Yes," he agreed with feeling. "And given that I have no money of my own, it leaves me rather nowhere."

"Oh, I wouldn't say that. It's amazing what a determined man with good looks, brains, and charm can accomplish."

"You flatter me, Duchess."

"It's not flattery," she said as they started along the path to the gardens. "It's more along the lines of a hint." She paused, smiling a little. "There's one lady here who might be susceptible to those qualities, at least in you."

He pretended obtuseness. "If you are referring to Miss Harlow—"

"I am not." She stopped on the path, causing him to stop as well. "Miss Harlow wasn't the one you were staring at all through dinner."

He forced himself to smile in a deprecating fashion. "I'm sure I don't know what you mean."

"Oh, don't dissemble with me, Trubridge. I'm not blind, you know. Half the time you were ignoring those around you and staring down the table to where Belinda was seated."

His throat felt dry, and there was a sick knot in his stomach at the notion that he had so exposed his feelings. He forced out a laugh. "How rude of me. And how ghastly to know I am so transparent."

"You can't help it, I daresay. Men always look like woeful sheep when they are falling in love."

The knot in his guts twisted. "Duchess, you are mistaken. I'm not—"

"I told you, I'm not blind," she said, cutting right through his denial. "Tactless, perhaps," she added, flashing him a smile, "but not blind. And so, I've just given you a superb reason to stay. Why go back to London when the woman you want is right here?"

This conversation was making him feel far too vulnerable, and as was his usual custom, he tried to make light of it. "As much as you may appreciate all my fine qualities, Duchess, there are women who don't. Belinda is one of them."

"I wouldn't say that."

"Now who's being gallant?" He gave up any attempts at dissembling. "The truth is that Belinda hasn't the time of day for me. I'm too much like her late husband to suit her book. In her eyes, I am nothing but a worthless fortune hunter." It was a hard admission to make, but there was no point in ignoring hard realities.

The duchess tilted her head, looking at him thoughtfully. "I wouldn't have thought a man like you would shy at the difficulties involved in winning a woman."

"I'm not shying away. I intend to change her mind about me, though precisely how I shall accomplish that feat isn't quite clear to me yet. Still, sometimes a strategic retreat is what's needed to win a war. Or a woman."

She laughed. "Good man," she said with approval. "In my opinion, Belinda could be convinced to overlook your flaws if you can find her soft spots. She has them, trust me."

He gave her a rueful grin. "I don't suppose you'd care to tell me what they are?"

She shook her head and turned to start toward the carriage in the drive. "I will say this much—Belinda has forgotten—deliberately—how it feels to be a desirable woman. Despite any painful past experience, every woman longs to feel desirable. Even me," she added with a little smile, "and I'm as jaded as they come. Make Belinda feel desirable again and you'll win her over."

"That may be the most delightful advice anyone's ever given me. Have you any other words of wisdom? Such as how I can support her once I've won her over?"

She turned her head to look at him, her green eyes wide with a surprise he didn't quite understand. "Why would you need to support her?"

"Well, it's no secret I haven't a bean, and Belinda hasn't much more. Featherstone left her very badly off. So—"

"Belinda, badly off?" The duchess began to laugh. "Did she tell you that herself to keep you at bay?"

Taken aback, Nicholas frowned. "No, Jack told me—that is, Lord Featherstone. He said his brother left both of them without a farthing. But Belinda did confirm it."

"Ah, Featherstone. Well, that explains it. If Jack were my brother-in-law, I should tell him the same. He's terribly reckless and irresponsible. I'm sure Belinda's very grateful he lives in Paris. He'd soon learn the truth about her finances if he lived in London, and he'd be after her for a loan quick as lightning. In fact, I'm surprised she's kept her money a secret from him as long as she has. Of course, Belinda doesn't flaunt her wealth, but—"

"Wait." He cut her off, stopped walking, and turned toward her as his mind tried to make sense of what she'd been saying. "Belinda is rich?"

"Rich as Croesus." She laughed. "You seem quite stunned, Trubridge."

Stunned? He felt as if he'd been hit in the head with a cricket bat. "Rather," he murmured. "You've knocked me flat with this news, I admit."

"I don't see why it should be such a surprise. You were staring at her so thoroughly last night, you must have noticed those gorgeous pearls around her throat."

"Roman pearls, surely."

"They're so perfect, you'd think they're false, I agree, but no. Belinda can afford real ones, believe me. In fact, I'd wager she has more money than some of the American heiresses she represents! As I said, she doesn't flaunt it, but still, I can't believe you didn't figure it out. You must have discovered what she charges when you hired her. Do the arithmetic."

"Actually, we never discussed the monetary details of the arrangement," he confessed, still trying to accept the idea of a Belinda with money. "I have no idea what her fees actually are."

"Ten percent of the marriage settlement. When I married Margrave, Belinda's fee was nearly a hundred thousand pounds."

"Good God."

"It is a bit staggering, isn't it?" she said, as they resumed walking toward the carriage. "But American millionaires are happy to pay it if it means social acceptance for their families. My father is exceptionally wealthy, and I was fortunate to have an enormous dowry. Not all Belinda's fees are quite as high as what my father paid, of course, but they're high enough. And Belinda is very frugal. She's partial to her pearls, true enough, and she likes beautiful clothes, but other than that, she lives modestly, saves and invests her money, and doesn't do any lavish entertaining. She doesn't have to. She's invited simply everywhere. I can't imagine what she's worth, but it's a lot. There," she added, laughing, as they paused beside the carriage, "if you marry Belinda, all your problems are solved."

He couldn't laugh with her. "It isn't that simple, I'm afraid. As I said, she hasn't the time of day for me. It's going to be hard going to convince her to want me, much less marry me. And if somehow I do manage to persuade her, her dowry is irrelevant because I wouldn't take it even if she offered it. As I said, material considerations aren't part of this. Not for me. Not with her."

"Your integrity does you credit."

He laughed as he stepped into the carriage. "Duchess," he said, grinning at her through the window, "I believe that is the first time anyone has ever complimented my integrity."

NICHOLAS DIDN'T MISS the train though it was a near shave. Before the carriage had even stopped in front of the station, he could see the steam from its engine curling overhead, a clear indication that it was about to depart. The moment the carriage came to a halt, he was out of the vehicle and beckoning for a porter as he headed to the ticket window. Thankfully, porters paid attention to gentlemen who arrived in the duchess's carriage, and Chalmers received assistance at once while Nicholas purchased tickets.

When the train whistle blew, he shoved his valet's ticket into his hand, grabbed the last suitcase himself and jumped up onto the first-class carriage. He'd barely found his seat before the train jerked into motion, and he could only hope Chalmers had been able to do the same.

Once the rush to make the train was over, however,

and his journey under way, Nicholas's mind turned to what the duchess had told him.

He couldn't blame Belinda for deceiving him as to her financial situation. And the information didn't change his course. As he'd told the duchess, he didn't want Belinda's money. Not only because he was out to gain her respect but also because he wanted to regain his own. That meant making his own way, and that meant earning a living.

But how? That was the crucial question. He resumed his speculations of the night before, but after over an hour, he confessed himself still as unenlightened as before. His education was that of a gentleman, which meant it was of no practical use whatsoever. Not being a second son, he'd never studied law or medicine or engineering or anything remotely useful. Latin and Keats weren't of much commercial value. Had he been able to study the sciences as he would have wished to, that might have made a difference. He felt a hint of bitterness at the thought, but he shoved it aside. That was water under the bridge now, and bitterness was hardly helpful.

Still, the brutal truth was that he had no skills for which anyone would pay. He wasn't trained for anything. No one would hire a duke's son to be a clerk in a bank, especially when the duke would surely come along at some point and queer the pitch. He had good health and brute strength, but he'd guess longshoremen made barely enough to keep body and soul together.

He considered post after post, but as he did, he knew

it was a futile exercise. All other considerations aside, there was no job of any kind that Landsdowne couldn't manage to get him sacked from.

That fact also prevented him from going into diplomatic service. Landsdowne's influence was too great. One word in the proper ears, and he'd find his career in diplomacy over before it began.

If he had capital, he could invest it in funds or shares, but of course, his lack of capital was the heart of his problem. Belinda's words about saving for a rainy day came back to haunt him, and he thought with infinite regret of all the money he'd frittered away on empty pursuits. But like bitterness, regrets were of no use. All he could do in the future was vow to do better than he had in the past.

He'd been over all these same considerations last night, as well as when he'd first been informed his trust had been cut off, and as he contemplated them again now, no new ideas presented themselves. As Belinda had pointed out, he was a lily of the field, but what other fate could there be for a man like him?

The speed of the train slackened, and he glanced up, startled to discover that the two hour journey was nearly over. The train had just crossed Grosvenor Bridge and was nearing Victoria Station, and he stared out the window as it lumbered along beside the canal. Beyond the canal were industrial buildings and blocks of flats for the working classes, with their costermonger carts out front and lorries clogging the streets.

The train's speed slackened even more, almost to a crawl, and Nicholas stood up. He lowered the window and looked out to see if he could determine why they were moving so slowly, but they were on a curve and he could see nothing ahead but the train itself.

He shut the window and sank back into his seat. It made no sense to be impatient. After all, it wasn't as if he had anything useful to do when he arrived. Sitting in a train was as good a way of passing the time as anything else, especially when a man needed to think.

He returned his mind to his situation and wondered about the possibilities of business and commerce. A gentleman who messed about with business affairs was looked down upon as some sort of bad seed by many in society, and though being a bad seed had never bothered him in the least, it didn't alter the fact that what he knew about commerce and trade would fit in a thimble.

The train slowed even more, if that were possible, then for some reason known only to railway engineers and conductors, stopped altogether, still several blocks from Victoria Station. Directly out the window in front of him was a soot-covered brick building with boarded-up windows, a vagrant stretched out across its doorway sleeping in the sun, and weeds sprouting up among the cracked pavements and along the foundation. A sign tacked to one of the boarded-up windows proclaimed the building had once been a brewery, and that it was available for let or for sale.

Nicholas stared at the sign, fragments of conversations and scraps of information swirling through his mind—his discussions with Freebody, the crops at Honeywood, Denys's family—bits and pieces that suddenly coalesced into one simple, straightforward idea. When he glanced again at the abandoned building and saw the name painted above the doorway of the place, he realized the solution to all his problems might just be staring him right in the face.

WHEN HE ARRIVED back at South Audley Street, he learned that Denys was not yet out of bed, but he had no intention of allowing that to stop him. Heaping a tray with eggs, bacon, kidneys, and hot buttered toast from the warming dishes on the dining room sideboard, as well as the entire pot of coffee and two cups, he went up to his friend's room.

Carefully balancing the tray on one forearm, he tapped the door, then opened it without bothering to wait for permission to enter. "Morning, Denys," he said in the voice he usually reserved for his deaf Aunt Sadie as he shifted the tray back to both hands and kicked the door shut behind him.

"What in blazes?" Denys bolted to a sitting position at the bang of the door, flinging back covers. But with one quick glance at the man who'd disturbed his rest, he fell back into the pillows with a groan. "Nick? Good God, man, why the devil are you waking me at this ungodly hour? Do you know what time it is?"

"Half past ten."

"Half past ten?" He groaned again. "No one rises at half past ten! Not in town during the season anyway."

"Scarcely found your bed, have you?"

"While I suppose you haven't been to bed at all?"

"I haven't, actually. Unless turf could be deemed a bed."

"What are you blathering about? And what are you doing in London? Aren't you supposed to be at some house party this week?" Denys stared at him, blinking sleepily for a moment, then he grinned. "And what the devil happened to your face?"

"It's a long story. I shan't bore you with it." He lifted the tray. "I've brought breakfast."

Denys waved aside breakfast, peering at him closely. "Your jaw's swollen and you've a graze on your cheek. I do believe you'll have another black eye," he said, sounding thoroughly pleased. "Who is the splendid fellow who bestowed it? I must meet him and shake his hand."

"I don't have time for explanations this morning." He glanced around, then set the tray on one side of the washstand. "Coffee?" he asked as he poured himself a cup.

"I should love some," Denys replied as he rolled over, turning his back on his friend, "but I don't intend to stay awake long enough to drink it."

Nicholas ignored that and poured a second cup. "Would you like milk and sugar?"

"God have mercy," Denys mumbled and pulled the covers over his head. "Why?" he asked, his voice muffled by sheets and counterpane. "Why do you have to keep reappearing in my life and wreaking havoc?"

"Because that's what friends are for. And I do live here."

That caused Denys to flip back the sheets and glare at him over his shoulder. "Only temporarily."

"Just so. And that's partly what I want to discuss with you." He brought both cups of coffee to the bed. "Come along, Denys. Do sit up, have a coffee, and attend to me. I've something very important to do, and I need your help."

"My help? Haven't I done enough for you already?"

"You've been a brick." He settled himself on the edge of the bed. "And I'm about to ask you for more, I'm afraid. But if it's any consolation, this is something I think you might actually want to help me with because it helps you as well. It might even make us rich. Or at least prosperous."

"Sounds too good to be true."

"Well, there is one sticky wicket. We'll have to obtain a loan, and neither of us has the blunt that's necessary for this venture. I was thinking of your father—"

Denys groaned. "Really, Nick, there are limits to our friendship!"

"Well, we certainly can't go to my father."

"And what is this idea?"

"Beer, Denys. We're going to make beer."

His friend heaved a sigh and sat up, rubbing his sleepy eyes. "Pass me that coffee."

Chapter 15

Belinda didn't learn until almost noon that Nicholas was gone. Most of the night, she'd been plagued by images of him kneeling in front of her without his shirt and tormented by the kisses and caresses of the night before. She'd finally fallen asleep sometime after three o'clock, and when she awoke, it was nearly half past eleven.

Molly, upon bringing her a breakfast tray, was the one who informed her of Lord Trubridge's departure for London on the early train.

So he did leave after all, she thought, staring down at her bacon and eggs. He'd asked her if he ought to stay, and she'd said it didn't matter to her.

Hard-hearted Belinda.

She didn't want to be hard, but how could she be otherwise, given his history? The words she'd said last night were true, she knew that. Yet in the cold light of day, she also knew that she hadn't said them for that reason. She'd lashed out at him purely out of fear. The desires he'd awakened in her made her feel vulnerable and afraid; she had turned him away, and it made no sense to feel let down now because he'd gone. If he'd stayed, she'd have been forced to spend the coming week shoving other women at him, something that seemed equally impossible.

Belinda tried to eat her breakfast, but all she was able to taste was the bitter tinge of disappointment and regret, and she didn't understand herself at all.

A knock on her door interrupted these musings, and Rosalie's voice came to her from the other side. "Auntie Belinda, may I come in?"

She nodded in response to her maid's questioning look, and the servant opened the door. "Thank you, Molly," she added, setting the breakfast tray aside as Rosalie came in. "That will be all for now."

The moment Molly departed, closing the door behind her, Rosalie burst into speech. "Oh, Auntie Belinda, I am so embarrassed! I made an utter fool out of myself last night, didn't I?"

Belinda's mind flashed back to own wayward behavior last night, reminding her that she was hardly in the position to give a lecture on propriety. Instead, she patted the bed, inviting the girl to come sit down.

Rosalie complied, crossing the room to perch herself on the edge of the mattress. "It's so humiliating," she went on, her cheeks as pink as her rose-colored wrapper. "I just want to die. How will I ever face him?"

"You won't have to, dearest. Lord Trubridge is gone. He left this morning."

"Trubridge?" Rosalie gave her a blank stare for a moment, then she shook her head. "No, no, I know Trubridge is gone. My maid told me. I wasn't talking about him. I was talking about Sir William."

"Oh!" Taken aback, it took Belinda a moment to think how to reply. "It isn't so much that you made a fool of yourself," she finally said. "Every girl—every person—does that from time to time. It isn't what happened that matters now. It's that you understand what could have happened had someone less honorable than Sir William witnessed you kissing a man. Your actions put your reputation and Lord Trubridge's at risk. And mine as well," she added, not above using guilt to be sure Rosalie never made such a risky mistake again.

"Yours?" Rosalie looked stricken, telling her that her words had made the proper impact. "But why? You didn't have anything to do with it."

"Nonetheless, people know I have launched you in society, and to some degree, they judge me by your behavior. And your mother, and your father, too, would have been shamed if the episode came out. But that isn't the greatest concern, dearest," she added, softening now that she'd made her point. "Yours is the reputation most endangered by the sort of situation you risked last night. It is vital that you remember modesty and restraint."

Even as Belinda said those words, she thought of Nicholas's hands yanking up her skirts, of his hands shaping her buttocks, and the arousal pulsing through her body. She was a fine one to talk of modesty and restraint.

Amid this flush of hot memories, she barely heard Rosalie's next words. "Don't worry, Auntie Belinda," she said as if from a great distance away, "I won't ever do such a thing again. Heavens, I can't imagine what Sir William must think of me after the shameless way I behaved."

Belinda closed her eyes, unable to disengage her thoughts from her own behavior the night before. It had been something primal, and it shocked her to think she could be like that. Raw lust was something she'd never felt before. Even Charles, even in her first flush of passion for him, had never made her feel like that—hot, carnal, and utterly desperate. She had broken things off in the nick of time, for if a few more seconds had gone by, she'd have passed the point of no return.

"But he was splendid, wasn't he?" Rosalie said in a dreamy, musing voice. "Don't you think he was splendid?"

"Yes," she answered, acknowledging Nicholas's ability to arouse her passions with a resigned sigh. "He was."

Only after she'd said it did she realize she'd spoken aloud, and she once again forced aside her own experiences of the previous night. "Sir William was very splendid, indeed."

"I've never seen him angry before. My goodness, I truly didn't know he could be like that. It was very exciting, and yet, it was reassuring, too, seeing the way he stood up for me and defended my honor."

"You will make it clear to Sir William that he was mistaken in his conclusions and that Lord Trubridge was not to blame?"

She gave an unhappy sigh. "I suppose I must. Though it shall be terribly hard to own up to my behavior. Especially to Sir William. He's such an honorable sort of man. What if he doesn't forgive me?"

"Does it matter so much to you? His forgiveness?"

She nodded, biting her lip. "It matters. I care terribly what he thinks of me, and I didn't even realize it until now."

"I'm so glad you are at last seeing Sir William's fine qualities."

Rosalie's face took on a rueful expression. "You were right all along, Auntie Belinda. And even though I made a complete fool out of myself, perhaps everything has worked out for the best."

For the best?

With Nicholas's departure, there would be no more scenes like last night, with Rosalie flinging herself at him, and Sir William engaging in fisticuffs, and herself turned into some primitive, desperate, carnal creature who'd allow a man to yank up her skirts and relish every second of it.

"Yes," she answered Rosalie's question, forcing herself to say what was true even though it wasn't what she felt. "Everything has worked out for the best."

As Nicholas had predicted, Denys loved his idea, so much so that the two of them had barely finished their coffee before going downstairs in search of Denys's father. But Lord Conyers proved less enthusiastic and much more cautious than the two younger men.

A business venture like a brewery, the earl informed them, was a tricky business, and he had no intention of granting them a loan for the capital or buying any shares without first receiving a detailed proposal, including the location of the brewery, a production schedule, an estimate of the crop yields from both their estates, and a budget that included repayment of the loan and profit estimates for their first three years of operation.

"You see," Denys said, as they left Lord Conyers's study, "this is why I never ask him for money. Even when I was fifteen and wanted to borrow a bit to hold me over until my monthly allowance was paid out, he would demand all the details of why I was short of funds, what I wanted the money for, when I'd pay it back, and what interest rate I was prepared to pay."

Nicholas refused to be discouraged. "That, I suspect, is one of the reasons he's rich. And besides, he's merely asking us for information we would have had to obtain anyway. Look at it this way," he added, clapping his friend on the back. "At least he didn't look down his nose at us for wishing to be captains of industry."

Denys brightened a bit. "True. So to give Papa what he wants, where do we start?"

"I say with the easiest thing. The building."

"And why is that easiest?"

He grinned. "Because I already know where it is."

Half an hour later, the two men were standing in front

of the abandoned brewery Nicholas had seen from the train.

Denys eyed it dubiously. "This is where you want to put the place? The building is rather . . . decrepit, don't you think?"

He couldn't really blame his friend for a lack of enthusiasm. Though the vagrant was gone, the three-story building of sooty brick was every bit as seedy-looking as it had appeared earlier in the day, but he didn't care. "The cosmetics don't matter, Denys. Windows can be replaced, bricks cleaned, and steps whitewashed easily enough. No, what matters is the name."

"The name?"

Nicholas pointed to the faded paint above the door. "Lilyfield's," he read aloud, and began to laugh. "By God, if that's not a sign from the heavens, I don't know what is."

SIX DAYS LATER, upon her return from the house party, Belinda expected to find some word from Nicholas in the pile of correspondence that had accumulated during her absence from town, but though she searched through the letters and invitations on her desk three times, no note from him was among them.

She had no idea what would happen now. After that episode in the maze, would he still wish to carry on looking for a wife and expect her to assist him? She honestly didn't know. She thought he'd been joking when he'd asked for a moment to consider her sarcastic suggestion along that line, but perhaps he hadn't been joking. And if he were serious, what would she do?

During the past week, she had tried again to imagine helping him find a wife, but her brain just couldn't seem to fashion that scenario. But if she refused to assist him in his quest, would he go on without her? He could, for she'd already paved the way for him to return to good society, and he didn't really need her now to find himself a rich bride.

That thought made her feel rather dismal, and not even because of any sort of moral indignation on behalf of rich, innocent heiresses. No, she feared she'd become less altruistic and much more selfish in her motives where that man was concerned. She didn't want him to find a wife because she didn't want another woman to feel with him what she had felt.

And yet, what else could he be expected to do? What financial option was there for him other than to marry? She'd suggested he earn an income, but she was well aware that such a thing wasn't as easy as it sounded, especially here in Britain. And now that she knew the facts about his relationship with Landsdowne, she knew it wasn't likely the duke would reinstate his trust fund unless he married, which brought her thoughts right back to where they'd begun: finding him a rich wife.

I'm rich.

The thought came to her like the whisper of a mischievous imp, but she snuffed it out at once. Marry Nicholas? Heavens, no. She wasn't the sort who ever made the same mistake twice if she could help it, and as she'd so bluntly pointed out the other night, nothing in his behavior thus far demonstrated he was capable of being a responsible man and a good husband. He was charming, yes. Handsome, yes. Desirable—God, yes. But responsible? That was doubtful. She understood the underlying reasons for his behavior better now, but that didn't alter the fact that a man like Nicholas wasn't likely to change his ways.

The only other possibility for them was an affair, and much to her chagrin, she found that a far easier proposition to imagine than marrying him, one she'd been imagining far too often of late. But there was no future in it, not for a woman of her position. If word got out that Lady Featherstone was engaging in an affair, her profession would be in ruins, and for what?

Yes, she desired him, but she didn't love him, nor could she in all good conscience respect him. That wasn't likely to change either, and the only thing to do was what she'd done the first time he'd kissed her— pretend it hadn't happened, put him out of her mind until she heard from him, and carry on.

With renewed determination, she began opening her other correspondence, sure that reading and answering letters would be the perfect distraction, but she soon found she'd been mistaken.

The first letter she opened was from Mrs. Isaiah Hunt, inquiring as to possible dates for inviting Lord Trubridge to dinner. Geraldine, she wrote, hadn't seemed to take to the marquess upon their first meeting, but Mrs. Hunt was certain the girl could be prevailed upon to change her mind. For her part, Mrs. Hunt had thought him a most delightful man, having first met him at Lady Montcrieffe's ball.

"Oh, yes," Belinda mumbled with a sigh. "He's quite

delightful. Unfortunately not in the way a mother would approve."

She set Mrs. Hunt's correspondence aside and continued on, but she'd scarcely gone through three more letters before she came across a note from Nancy, asking how the wife search for Trubridge was going and offering the names of several young ladies who had just arrived from New York that she might consider as possibilities.

Belinda set Nancy's note aside and moved on. Two letters later, she was staring at an envelope with Carlotta Jackson's name on it.

Oh, for heaven's sake.

She tossed aside Carlotta's letter without even opening it. How was she supposed to not think about him when half her letters were about him? Thoroughly exasperated, she reached for a blank sheet of stationery and yanked her pen out of its holder.

She considered for a few moments, inked her pen, and dashed off a short note, asking about his plans and intentions regarding matrimony.

His response came a few days later, and consisted of only one sentence.

Is that a proposal?

She tossed aside his reply with a huff of indignation. Proposal, indeed. He knew perfectly well it was nothing of the sort. Still, a clear and decisive letter clarifying the matter was definitely in order, and she once again pulled out pen and paper.

Lord Trubridge,

My note was most certainly not a proposal. As we discussed only a few days ago—

Belinda stopped, thinking perhaps she shouldn't refer to that night in the maze even if their argument then was germane to the issue. She wadded up the paper, and tried again.

Lord Trubridge,

You seem to be laboring under a misunderstanding about my feelings, feelings which I have always made perfectly clear. I—

Once again, she stopped, for that was an outright lie. Her feelings regarding that man were anything but clear. She felt so muddled up, in fact, that she couldn't even seem to write him a simple letter. Once again, she crumpled her composition into a ball and started over, reminding herself that he was a client, and she needed to respond accordingly.

Lord Trubridge,

In regard to your question, my answer is no, and I regret that my letter may have inadvertently given rise to any other impression. I am simply asking, as your matchmaker, whether or not you wish to continue seeking introductions to young

*ladies of my acquaintance. If so, please inform
me at once.*

> *Yours,
> Lady Featherstone*

She read the letter over, underlined matchmaker
three times, and blotted the ink. She then folded the
letter, slipped it into an envelope, and reached for seal-
ing wax.

There, she thought a short time later as she dropped
her note to him onto the tray in the foyer with the other
letters for Jervis to post. *That ought to be clear enough.
I should be hearing back from him by tomorrow.*

Despite all her determination to put what had happened at Highclyffe out of her mind, the thought of
hearing from him brought a tiny thrill of anticipation.
But she quashed it as best she could and resumed her
efforts to think nothing more about him until she received a reply.

Her resolve lasted a week. Seven days later, when
she'd received no response from him whatsoever but
had received seventeen inquiries about him from various American mothers, fathers, gossip columnists, and
friends, she'd had enough.

Tossing down the afternoon post, she rang for Jervis
to have her carriage brought around, and ten minutes
later, her driver, Davis, was holding the door of the vehicle open for her.

"Twenty-four South Audley Street," she told him and
stepped into the carriage.

"Yes, Your Ladyship." Davis closed the door, tipped his cap, and climbed up on the box.

"If the mountain won't come to Muhammad," she muttered, paraphrasing Francis Bacon as the carriage jerked into motion, "then, Muhammad will just have to go to the mountain."

Chapter 16

Going to the mountain, she soon discovered, was not as easy as it might appear, for no one seemed to know where the mountain in question happened to be. Lord Somerton, the viscount's mother informed her over tea, was with Lord Trubridge, but what lark the two were engaged upon, she had not the slightest clue. All she knew was that it seemed to be taking up all their time, for she hadn't seen either of them in days. Why, she only knew they were alive because their valets had confirmed the fact.

Lady Conyers then shifted the conversation, mentioning her son's woeful intransigence in regard to marriage, and expressed the desire for Lady Featherstone's opinion on how he might be brought round.

"Slowly," Belinda advised. "Very slowly. You don't

want him to dig in his heels. Perhaps," she added before Lady Conyers could delve more deeply into the matter of marrying off her son, "Lord Trubridge's valet might know where they've gone? It's very important I reach Trubridge at once, you see. So many young ladies are asking me about him—and asking about Somerton, too, of course. Will they be at this ball or that rout, you know—and I'm sure you will agree that it isn't right to keep the young ladies in suspense, holding out hope and saving places on their dance cards if the two gentlemen are too busy to attend the events of the season. Somerton will never be brought round to marriage unless he can be brought to earth."

"I understand," the countess said gravely, and reached for the bellpull. "We shall see what we can find out."

Chalmers, Lord Trubridge's valet, was sent for, but he could provide little information as to His Lordship's whereabouts.

"Heavens, Mr. Chalmers," Belinda said, forcing a laugh, "has your master fallen off the edge of the earth?"

Before the valet could even attempt to answer that question, Lord Conyers walked in, whistling. He stopped at the sight of Belinda. "Why, Lady Featherstone, what a pleasure! You grow lovelier every day."

"You flatter me, Conyers."

"Edward," Lady Conyers said, tugging at his coat to tear his attention away from Belinda, "Lady Featherstone is on a hunt for Somerton and Trubridge."

"On their trail, are you?" He gave her a wink. "Poor fellows."

Belinda, accustomed to such witticisms about her profession, laughed as expected, then said, "They are not at their club, so I can only conclude they are off punting or fishing or engaged in some other sport, but I really must—"

"Sport?" Lord Conyers interrupted, and it was his turn to laugh. "Oh, no, my dear lady, you've got it all wrong. They are engaged in business matters."

"Business matters?" the two women said in unison.

"Indeed. I can give you the address where they might be found, though I'm not sure Commercial Road is the most desirable place for ladies to go visiting."

Commercial Road? This situation was growing more intriguing by the moment, so intriguing in fact that Belinda didn't care what neighborhood they were in, she intended to find them and see what they were up to. "I would appreciate that address very much, Lord Conyers. Thank you."

Half an hour later, Belinda was gazing with doubt at a brick building on Chelsea's Commercial Road that had clearly seen better days. What on earth could Nicholas and Somerton be doing down here? Whatever their purpose for this building, part of it involved improving the look of the place, for workmen were swarming over the building like ants, replacing broken windows, repairing the roof, and patching the crumbling brick.

Davis appeared beside the carriage door. "Are you certain you wish to go in, my lady?" he asked. "A construction site isn't quite the nicest place for a lady."

At that moment, Belinda caught a glimpse of Nicholas passing by one of the broken-out windows. "I shall be quite all right, Davis." She waved aside her driver's offer to accompany her and alighted from the carriage. "I shan't be long. Wait for me here."

She crossed the sidewalk, nodded to the pair of workmen scrubbing the brick on either side of the doorway, and passed through the entrance. Coming in from outside, the interior seemed dark despite the many windows, and she blinked several times before her eyes grew accustomed to the dimmer light and she could make out her surroundings.

She was in a single room that took up the entire ground floor of the building. Half a dozen workmen moved amid the reinforcing pillars of the vast space, sweeping up debris from the concrete floor, pulling jagged panes of broken glass from the windows, brushing cobwebs out of corners, and scrubbing down walls. To her right, a plain staircase of rusted wrought iron led to the upper floors, and the only furnishings in the place were a battered oak table in the center of the room flanked by a pair of wooden chairs. The chairs' peeling paint was a contrast to the fine wool jackets draped over them.

Nicholas was leaning over the table in his shirt-sleeves, Lord Somerton and two more workmen with him, and the four were discussing what seemed to be a set of architectural plans laid out on the table.

"We're connected to the main line here," Nicholas was saying as he pointed to a spot on the plans, his voice raised to be heard over the bang of hammers and the clink of glass around and above them. "Westminster has assured us that we're turned on. So why haven't we any water?"

One of the workmen launched into explanations for what repairs needed to be made to the plumbing, and Belinda studied Nicholas as he listened.

His hair, burnished and tawny even in this dim interior, recalled to her the first afternoon he'd come to see her and evoked again the sunshine of some exotic place. The sight of him in his shirtsleeves reminded her of the muscles and sinew she'd seen in the moonlight of the maze. Desire unfurled within her, spreading to every part of her body before she could stop it, and any resolutions she'd made to be coolly professional and indifferent went to the wall.

Suddenly, he seemed to sense he was being watched, and he looked up to see her standing there amid the bustling workmen. He smiled, making her stomach dip with a giddy weightlessness and her heart twist in her chest with a pang so strong that it hurt—for it reminded her forcefully of a shy, tongue-tied girl standing on the verandah of the Grand Union Hotel. She wanted to look away, leave, run for her life, but she couldn't seem to command her body to take any of those actions. She could only stand there, happy and terrified, smiling back at him.

"Somerton," he said without taking his eyes off of her, "we have a visitor."

"A visitor?" his friend echoed, turning to look. "Why, it's Lady Featherstone!"

The viscount's surprise forced her to tear her gaze from Nicholas. "Somerton," she greeted, turning her smile on him. "Your mother will be glad to know you are well and haven't taken off for parts unknown."

"Father knows. He told you, I suppose? How like him not to bother telling Mama about any of it, though. She's always the last to know the family secrets." He smiled back at her. "Worried, is she?"

"Not worried, exactly," Belinda said. "Puzzled might be a more accurate way of putting it. And a bit concerned about what people would say if they knew the two of you were engaged in commerce."

"Poor Papa. He'll be raked over the coals for helping us now."

"I did my best to assure your mother it was perfectly acceptable for titled gentlemen to also have business interests." She glanced around as she approached the table. "I can see the pair of you have been busy, but what is the purpose of all this?"

Before either man could answer, a loud whistle sounded outside that made Belinda clap her gloved hands over her ears with a grimace.

All work stopped at once. Hammers were set down, leather gloves pulled off, brooms laid aside. Clattering on the stairs had her glancing to her right as a line of workmen came marching down from the upper floors. They touched caps to her respectfully as they came down, nodded to Nicholas and Somerton, and flooded toward the door in an inexorable line. The two workmen standing by the table followed suit, and in less than a minute, she and the two gentlemen were the only people in the building.

An awkward silence followed the departure of the workmen as Somerton glanced from Nicholas to her and back again. "Right," he said, rubbing his hands together. "I think I'll be off as well. I must catch the evening train if I'm to go to Kent today, and I'm not even packed. Are you going down to Honeywood on the same train?"

"No, I'm going tomorrow. I want to give a few more instructions to the foreman before I leave since I expect to be away for four to five weeks. How long will you be at Arcady?"

"Only a fortnight. Until I return, we'll put Jenkins in charge of things here, yes?" When Nicholas nodded, Somerton turned to her. "Lady Featherstone."

With that, Somerton pulled his jacket from where it was draped over one of the chairs and departed, leaving her and Nicholas alone.

There was still a smile lingering at the corners of his lips as he looked at her. "It's good to see you, Belinda."

With those words, a bubble of happiness rose up within her, pressing against her chest and making it hard to breathe. She wanted to tell him she was glad to see him, too, but the words caught in her throat, held there by a wave of her girlhood shyness. It suddenly became vital to look away, but though she transferred her attention to her surroundings, she knew he was still watching her.

"So," she said at last, forcing the word out, "this is what you've been doing instead of answering my letters."

"I did answer your letter."

"The first one."

"Have you corresponded with me since?" He gave a laugh. "Sorry, I've been so busy that I've barely had time to eat and sleep this week. I haven't even glanced at my correspondence."

"But what's keeping you so occupied? What is it you and Somerton do here? What is this place?"

"My lord?"

Both of them turned as a gnarled old man in worn tweeds entered through the front door. At the sight of Belinda, he stopped and doffed his cap.

"Ah, Mr. Jenkins," Nicholas greeted, beckoning him forward. "Please tell me you've located our copper brewing kettles?"

"I have, Yer Lordship. They've been sitting dockside at Pimlico Pier the whole time if ye can believe it, but they'll be delivered when we want 'em."

"Excellent." Nicholas gestured to her. "Belinda, this is Mr. Jenkins, who has been the brewing master down at Honeywood for . . . oh, at least thirty years. Mr. Jenkins, this is Lady Featherstone."

"My lady." He gave a bow and glanced again at Nicholas. "I've also found ye a supplier for oak barrels. You'll be wanting oak."

"Yes, indeed." He laughed. "I remember you've always insisted oak was the only acceptable wood for beer barrels."

"Oak and no other, my lord. With your permission, I'll be going over there now to have a look at 'em?"

"Yes, of course. We can't make beer without barrels, can we?"

"No, sir. Ye be leaving for Honeywood tomorrow?"

"Yes. If you simply must reach me, cable me there. Lord Somerton will also be gone, so you'll be in charge here until he returns. Make those men work while we're away, Jenkins," he added with a wink.

"Indeed, I will, sir. Won't allow 'em to shirk just because the master's away." He nodded to Belinda. "Good day, ma'am," he said and departed out the door.

"He's such a slave driver," Nicholas whispered to her, as Jenkins walked toward the door. "You should see him and my land steward supervising the day laborers at Honeywood during hops-picking time. Ruthless, both of them. They only allow those poor day laborers a quarter hour for their lunch rest. I think—" He broke off, pausing until Jenkins was gone, then went on in a normal voice, "I think I'll have to insist upon a half an hour for them now that I'm taking charge of it all. Hops picking's hard work."

Belinda stared at him, trying to take it all in. "You and Somerton are making beer?"

"Well, not yet," he said with a laugh. "We need hops and barley first. But yes, once we have a harvest, we're making beer. It's something I know how to *do*, you see."

"I didn't realize you knew anything about brewing."

"Well, Honeywood grows hops and barley, and the home farm has always had a brewery. Honeywood makes all the ales, bitters, and stouts for Landsdowne's estates, so I've been around beer making all my life. So has Somerton. His estate, Arcady, grows hops and malting grains also. Many estates do in Kent. We've both been selling almost our entire crop every year on the open market, but with agricultural prices so low, there's little profit in the harvest itself. From now on, both our estates will sell all their hops and grain to our own brewery. Fair prices, of course, but the real profit shall be in the beer."

She smiled, appreciating the excitement in his voice. "You sound as if you can't wait to start."

He laughed. "Yes, well, I've always been fascinated by the process. As a child, I was forever following Jenkins around, asking questions, getting in the way, and being a pest generally."

Belinda studied his face, seeing there a hint of the boy who had wanted to study the sciences at Cambridge.

"When Landsdowne cut me off," he went on, "I racked my brains trying to think of something I could do to earn my own living, but I never thought of this, probably because it's never been a business to me. It's always been part of the estate, not a source of income in itself. I'd never thought of turning it into a business for profit until now."

"But you've no capital. Did Somerton fund the entire investment?"

"No, Lord Conyers did. He's agreed to buy ten percent of the shares and to stake us a loan for the rest. We had to give him a detailed prospectus before he'd agree, which is what we've been so occupied with during the past week. We presented our plans to him two days ago, and he agreed to the venture."

"But, when . . . how . . . what made you . . . ?" She stopped and shook her head, laughing at her stuttering attempts to gain explanations. Nicholas's doing something like this was so unexpected, she didn't know what to make of it. "How did the two of you come to decide to do this?"

"It was my idea. I was coming back from Highclyffe, and the train stopped right out there." He paused, pointing toward the open front door, the canal, and the railroad tracks beyond. "It was Providence, Belinda, that the train stopped right there. It was Providence pointing me to a purpose for my life."

"I don't know what to say, Nicholas." She pressed a hand to her chest, laughing, for his exhilaration was infectious. "You've flummoxed me."

"Have I? The cool, self-possessed Lady Featherstone is flummoxed? That's quite a treat for me—having the tables turned this way."

"Table turned? What do you mean?"

"Whenever I'm with you, I'm utterly at sixes and sevens. Hell, half the time, when I look at you, I can't even remember my own name."

She stilled, her laughter fading as her heart gave a leap. "I don't know why," she whispered.

He reached out and cupped her cheek. "Don't you?" he asked tenderly.

She ought to pull away. She didn't want to, but the door was wide open, and they were in full view of anyone who might walk by. She felt as if she could stand here like this with him forever, and though she knew she should withdraw, she didn't want to. He let his hand fall before she had to decide.

"If you don't know why," he said, "then I shan't tell

you. It makes me feel better to know that my *whole* heart isn't sitting on my sleeve."

His words were light, carelessly uttered, but she knew that was not a reliable indication of his true feelings. She never knew what was genuine, not with him. She wanted his heart on his sleeve, she wanted to see it and know what was in it, but she couldn't say that was what she wanted. Not after all the other things she'd said.

"Did you see the sign out front?" he asked.

She blinked at this abrupt change of subject. "What?" she said, and shook her head, knowing she was the one who was at sixes and sevens. "Sign? What sign?"

"I'm glad you didn't notice it. That means I can show it to you myself." He grabbed her hand and pulled her toward the open doorway. "Come on."

She allowed herself to be pulled through the doorway and out to the sidewalk. There, he put his hands on her shoulders and turned her around. "Look," he said, and pointed to the white insignia and name painted over the brick.

"Lilyfield's," she read, and laughed, looking at him. "Lilyfield's?"

He grinned. "Fitting, don't you think?"

"Not for long," she pointed out. "Not if you keep up with all this."

"I told you this was Providence. I was sitting on the train, as I said, still resenting that tongue-lashing you'd given me in the maze the night before when you called me a lily of the field—"

"It was unbearably rude of me to presume—"

"Don't," he cut her off, reaching out to touch her again, pressing his fingertips to her lips right there in the street. "Don't be proper and polite and apologize for being honest. I hated hearing the things you said, but they were true. We both know it."

Once again, his fingers slid away from her mouth. "You made me see that I have to do something with my life, find a purpose for myself. I know if I don't, I'll never earn your respect. And I want that, Belinda. I want it more than I've ever wanted anything in my life."

She tried to remind herself of all the hard truths she'd learned about rakes, of all the insincere things they were capable of uttering without a qualm, but such reminders floated right past and came apart like smoke on the wind.

"You realize what this means, don't you?" He didn't wait for an answer. "It means that I won't be needing you anymore."

Her heart gave a queer, hard thump against her ribs, as if that bubble of happiness had burst. "What . . ." She paused, but then forced herself to ask. "What do you mean?"

"There's only one way to say something like this, and that's straight out." He cupped her cheeks in his hands, lifting her face. "Belinda," he said as he ducked his head beneath the brim of her hat, "you're fired."

He kissed her, but the touch of his mouth was only a light graze against hers, too quick to be anything but a tease.

"You know," he said as he pulled back, his brow creasing in a slight frown as he looked into her up-turned face, "if you insist on flinging yourself at me in this blatant fashion, you really mustn't do it on a public street. What will people say?"

He grabbed her hand again. "Come with me, and I'll show you the rest of the place."

As he pulled her back through the doorway and started up the stairs with her in tow, she felt compelled to set him straight regarding his choice of words. "I did *not* fling myself at you."

"Lady Featherstone, society's shining example of ladylike propriety," he continued as he turned at the landing, his voice conveying that breezy carelessness that always told her he was teasing, "the model for all her fellow Americans of how to be a proper British lady—"

"Oh, that's ridiculous! You make me sound like someone's maiden aunt!"

"And there she was," he went on, undeterred, "kissing a fellow right there on the sidewalk. Why, I'd never have believed it if I hadn't been there myself. Can you imagine what a scandal it would make if the gossip columnists ever got hold of the story? I can't begin to fathom what they'd say."

"I did not fling myself at you," she protested again, as they reached the top of the stairs and entered another large room as empty as the one below.

"You did. I know you did." He turned toward her and eased closer, tilting his head to avoid her hat. He was going to kiss her again, she knew, but he moved so slowly that by the time his lips were a hairsbreadth from hers, she couldn't breathe. "You know how I know?" he whispered.

"How?" she whispered back.

His lips brushed hers. "Because I'm falling like a ninepin," he said, and kissed her.

Chapter 17

Nicholas already knew kissing Belinda was akin to lighting matches in a room full of dynamite. There were sure to be explosions, he just never knew how singed he'd end up. In kissing her moments ago on the sidewalk, he'd figured the best he could hope for was a slap across the face, but when that hadn't happened, he'd figured his chances in private weren't quite as dismal as he'd previously thought. But even here, away from any prying eyes, he'd never expected this.

He hadn't expected her mouth to open under his without any coaxing at all, or her arms to entwine around his neck to pull him closer. And when he tore his mouth from hers and pulled back to gather his wits and make sure this wasn't some smashing, damnably erotic dream, he certainly didn't expect her to grasp his face in her hands, kiss him four times, and frantically gasp, "Don't stop. Don't stop."

Stopping was the last thing he wanted to do, but he felt he had to at least try and be noble. "Belinda—"

"If you keep talking," she interrupted, "I'll start thinking how mad it all is and what the consequences might be. I don't want to think about consequences, Nicholas. Just shut up and kiss me again."

When he didn't move, she rose up on her toes and kissed him, and with that contact, he knew the responsible, dependable man he was trying to become was in serious jeopardy.

"No, no," he said as he broke the kiss, the arousal rushing through his body making him feel a bit desperate. "Think, Belinda, do. Because if you don't, it won't be long before I won't be able to. And at that point, it'll be agony to stop."

"You're a rake," she reminded, brushing his lips with hers as if it was her turn to tease and coax. "Why should you stop?"

He said the first thing that came into his head. "Because you won't respect me in the morning."

She gave a stifled giggle against his mouth.

"Why do you always laugh when I'm *not* making a joke," he muttered against her lips, "and never laugh when I am?" He turned his head away, but he only got far enough for his lips to graze the satiny skin of her cheek before his resolve began weakening again. He compromised, nuzzled her ear, inhaling the intoxicating scent of her perfume. "You think all the wrong things are funny."

"Do I?" She gave a shiver of pleasure as he pressed a kiss to her ear. "Oh," she gasped, a soft, hushed sound in the empty room.

He pulled her earlobe into his mouth, sucking gently, as his hands slid down between them to shape and cup her breasts through her clothes. Any minute now, he thought, she'll come to her senses and tell me to sod off. Any minute now.

She didn't. Her breathing quickened, her head falling back to rest against the wall behind her, and her hips pressed up toward his.

The pleasure of it was almost unbearable, and he clenched his jaw, resisting valiantly, trying to think not about what he wanted but about what was right. "We can't," he said with a groan. "I don't want it this way. Not for us."

Even as he said it, he proved himself a liar, for his hands grasped at the fashionably narrow folds of her skirt, pulling them up to get his hands beneath. She didn't help him, but she didn't stop him either, and he managed it at last on his own. As his palms glided up her thighs, he could feel the heat of her skin through the thin fabric of her knickers.

He was losing his head; his wits went down another notch with every inch his hands went higher. Even so, he tortured himself by moving slowly, exploring the shape of her legs—the dents of muscle along the outside of her thighs, over the undulating curve of her hip, to her behind. Shoving up her bustle, he allowed himself one quick, frantic exploration of her shapely buttocks before sliding his hands to the front.

He wanted to touch her bare skin somewhere, any-where. He slid his hands across her abdomen, wonder-ing why the hell women had to wear so many clothes, then he shoved his fingers up underneath her stiff whalebone corset and curved them inside the waist-bands of petticoats and drawers, and when the backs of his fingers finally touched the soft skin of her belly, his reaction was immediate and unexpected. His knees buckled beneath him.

He groaned, his hand tightening around folds of muslin and his body pressing hers to the wall so that he could stay upright.

It took him a second or two to regain his balance and his equilibrium, but not enough to find the will to stop. "You're killing me, Belinda," he panted, pressing kisses to her face, her throat, and her hair as his knuck-les grazed her belly under her tightly fitted clothes. "Killing me by inches."

He caressed her as best he could, but the tiny little patch of bare skin to which he had access wasn't going to be enough to satisfy either of them. He pulled back, thinking to withdraw, but his resolve crumbled when she gave a moan of protest, and he worked his hands beneath her petticoats to more promising territory.

He shaped her thigh, then eased his hand between her legs, and even though he was probably proving himself to be the very same libertine she'd declared she could never respect, when he turned his hand and cupped her mound, he didn't care.

Her knickers were damp, she was ready, and at the touch of his hand, she cried out. He stifled the sound with a kiss, for though he desperately wanted to hear her cries of pleasure at his touch, he didn't want anyone else to hear, and he didn't think all the broken windows had been replaced.

He kissed her, taking her sounds of pleasure into his mouth, relishing the way her body moved against his hand, but he didn't have the chance to relish it for long. Her hips jerked frantically against him two—three—times, then she cried out, coming in a rush so quick it startled him, her thighs clenching tight around his hand, her subsequent cries of pleasure hushed by his kiss. When she collapsed into the aftermath, breathing hard against his chest, he caught her with an arm around her waist and held her tight, slowly easing his other hand from between her thighs as he pressed kisses to her hair.

He wanted, more than he'd ever wanted anything in his life, to unbutton his trousers, lift that lovely, luscious bum in his hands, and take her; to be inside her and feel her legs wrap around him would be like heaven. But he couldn't do it. He didn't want her like that, against a wall. Not when he was trying to be a better man.

Drawing on willpower he didn't even know he possessed, he tore himself away, extricating himself from muslin and cashmere and sweet-scented woman. Shaking his head, trying to regain some semblance of sanity, he took several steps back, enough steps that she was out of his reach.

"Why—" She broke off, panting, her eyes wide and almost gray in the dusky twilight. Her skirts were still up above her knees, too tight across her hips to fall to the floor on their own. Her bustle and hat were askew. She looked utterly ravished, and though the ache in his groin was a painful reminder that he wasn't, he realized that didn't really matter at all. It was satisfaction enough just to look at her.

"You stopped." It sounded almost like an accusation.

"I had to. If I took you here, now, like this, it would be . . ." He paused, trying to find the words to explain. "It would just be wrong."

He couldn't help laughing at himself as he said it, for he appreciated what an inadequate explanation it was, and one that he'd never made before. In the entire thirty years of his life, he'd never been the one to say stop, but hell, he seemed to be doing all manner of unaccountable things lately.

She ducked her head, and a pink tint washed into her cheeks at the sight of her hem up around her hips. She pushed at the folds of wool and muslin, settling the layers of her dress back into place.

"I don't blame you," she said without looking at him, and her voice was so stiff, he felt as if the floor were opening up beneath his feet. That's what chivalry and responsibility did for a fellow.

"After what happened two weeks ago," she went on, "it's no wonder you're chary. One day I'm shoving you away and ripping you to shreds, and the next, I'm begging you to make love to me." She gave a little laugh, the color in her cheeks deepening. "You must think me the most inconsistent, muddleheaded woman in the world."

"I don't." He stepped forward and caught her arm as

she started to turn for the stairs. "I don't think that at all. But look where we are at this moment. I don't want to take you for the first time against a factory wall with my trousers around my knees."

"Oh." She was scarlet now. "I suppose you're right. I—I didn't think of that."

Despite the damnable situation, he couldn't help a chuckle at that, and he could tell she didn't know what he found so amusing. "In situations such as this," he explained, "it's usually the woman who manages to keep her head."

That earned him a smile though it was a rueful one. That impudent nose of hers wrinkled a bit. "Are you saying I'm not fulfilling my proper womanly role?"

Nicholas glanced down, thinking wistfully of when he'd had her with her skirts up around her waist. Ah, well. He looked back up to meet her gaze again. "I can't imagine you ever being anything but womanly, Belinda."

Her smile widened, losing its rueful quality and revealing how much what he'd said pleased her. It caught him square in the chest, that smile. It lifted him up to the sky, and yet he knew he'd never had his feet more firmly planted on the ground.

"Come down to Kent," he said. "Come to Honeywood and stay with me there. Be with me."

He watched her smile go, and he cursed himself for pushing too fast, too soon. He hadn't meant to say those words; they'd just come tumbling out, and now, there they were, hanging in the air like an awful mistake. She'd say no. What other answer could he expect? Did he think two weeks and one stab at making his own way would be all it took to change her opinion of him?

He watched her open her mouth to reply, and not wanting to hear her refuse, he rushed on, "I'm not expecting anything. I'm *hoping*, of course, but that's not really the same thing, is it? At least, I hope it isn't to you. But . . . but either way, if you came down, I could show you everything. The hops and barley fields, the brewery, the house and all its God-awful furnishings—" He broke off, painfully aware that it was the most inarticulate, unromantic-sounding offer he'd ever made to a woman, and that it was also the most important one. Why would she want to look at barley fields and his family's ghastly paintings? He wanted to kick himself in the head.

She pressed her lips together, and he had no idea if she were about to give him a set down or if she was trying not to smile. He waited, heart in his throat.

"Let me think about it."

Disappointment pierced him, which made no sense, for he hadn't expected her to say yes anyway, but he gave a nod and gestured to the nearby stairs. "It's growing dark. We should go down."

She started to descend, but then she stopped, one hand on the rail. "Nicholas?" When he halted behind her, she turned to look at him over her shoulder. "I didn't say no."

She turned away and continued on down the stairs, missing the grin that spread across his face. That was probably for the best, he reasoned, following her down the stairs. As he'd told her before, a chap couldn't go around wearing his whole heart on his sleeve. Not all the time anyway.

HONEYWOOD WAS EXACTLY as he remembered. The hops still reminded him of Guards of Honor, their support poles pointed skyward like sabers drawn. The cottage gardens still put on a splendid display of color in the month of June, the half-timbering and ivy-covered brick of the house were still charming, and Forbisher, the butler, was still a tall, commanding presence despite his advanced years. The furnishings, unfortunately, were still hideous.

As he paused in the foyer to hand Forbisher his hat and gloves, he stared at the lurid chartreuse and grape papier-mâché tables that flanked the front doors with an affectionate sort of horror—rather as one might regard one's grandmother as she ate her peas off her knife in front of the Prince of Wales.

"And may I say . . ." Forbisher paused a moment, his Adam's apple bobbing a bit as he swallowed hard. Clearing his throat, he tried again, "It is good to see you back at Honeywood again, my lord."

"Why, Forbisher," he said, tickled by the way the old fellow jutted up his chin, "you seem almost . . . moved by my return."

"Moved, my lord?" The butler's eyes widened just a fraction, as if the idea of showing emotion were akin to falling into the pit of hell.

"Forgive me," Nicholas said at once. "I was mistaken."

Pacified, Forbisher gestured to the spare, gaunt figure

in black crepe beside him. "You remember Mrs. Tumblety, of course."

"Indeed, I do." He smiled at the housekeeper. "Not losing your keys nowadays, I hope?"

"That hasn't happened since you were a boy, my lord," she said, an answering smile tipping the corners of her mouth. "It's been a long time since the days when you'd tiptoe up behind me and slip them off the hook."

"A very long time," he agreed, and looked past her. "Mrs. Moore in the kitchens, I assume?"

"No, my lord," Forbisher told him. "Mrs. Moore's knees finally gave out on her last winter, I'm afraid."

"Burroughs gave her a sufficient pension, I hope?"

"Oh, yes, sir. She's in one of the cottages now and has plenty to be comfortable. And I'm sure Your Lordship will find the cooking of her replacement, Mrs. Fraser, quite excellent."

"I'm sure I shall." He returned his attention to the housekeeper. "The tenants found the place satisfactory during their stay?"

"Oh, yes, sir. They wanted to come back in the autumn when they return from Scotland."

There was a question in those words, and Nicholas answered it. "They shall be disappointed, I fear," he told her, and was rewarded with a pleased smile in return before he moved on.

It had been eight years since he'd dealt with a houseful of servants, but as he greeted housemaids and footmen, he was surprised at how easily it came back to him. Rather like slipping into an old smoking jacket and being surprised at how well it still fit.

Later, as he walked through the fields and toured the cottages with Mr. Burroughs, he was aware the land agent might be uncomfortable at finding himself demoted, and he took care to express appreciation for the fine way the other man had taken care of things. He also solicited Burroughs's opinions, especially during those first few days home, but as June rolled into July, he found that resuming the role he'd rejected eight years ago became easier with each passing day.

He'd thought he might feel pain at coming back, for the last time he'd come here, he'd expected Kathleen to be waiting for him, only to find Mr. Freebody there in her place, informing him in that dry, precise, legal voice that Kathleen wouldn't be coming at all.

But to his relief, there was no pain at coming back. He had warm, agreeable memories of young love, a pleasant enough feeling, with no angst, and, strangely, no regrets. Belinda had a great deal to do with that.

He wrote to her every day. She was not quite so assiduous, but that only made the pleasure of each letter all the greater. It was also bittersweet, however, for not once did she mention coming down to Kent.

Those stolen moments in the brewery tormented him more, rather than less, with each day that passed. He couldn't seem to stop remembering how quickly she'd climaxed at his touch, but he knew it wasn't his skill and finesse at lovemaking that had brought her there. Things had happened too fast for that. It was clear she'd been without a man far longer than any woman ought to be, and he was determined that if he had another chance, he'd be sure she fell asleep in his arms, exhausted and fully satisfied. He wanted that more than he'd ever wanted anything in his life, but as tempting as it was to ask her plans, he didn't.

She'd requested time to think things over, and he wanted her to have it. For him, though, no thinking on that score was necessary. He knew his own heart and his own mind, and with each passing day, he only became more certain of what he wanted and more hopeful it was in his grasp. For the first time in years, he dared to believe he truly could control his own destiny.

Fate, however, seemed bent on putting the same obstacle in his path over and over. On a sultry day in mid-July, only a few days before he planned to return to London, his father came to see him. Forbisher let him in, a display of quite poor judgment to Nicholas's way of thinking, but that was hardly Forbisher's fault. Landsdowne was a duke, after all, and even the most faithful butler was bound to cave when a duke came to call.

Nicholas gave a sigh and set the book he'd been reading to one side of his desk. It was bound to happen sooner or later, he supposed. Best to have it over with. "Show him in here, Forbisher."

His butler eyed the disordered chaos of his private study with a hint of alarm. "Here, my lord? But I've put him in the drawing room."

"The drawing room won't do, Forbisher. I'll not stand on ceremony for Landsdowne. Bring him in here."

"As you wish, my lord." The butler bowed and departed, reappearing in the doorway a few moments later. "The Duke of Landsdowne," he announced, rolling it off his tongue with full relish, something Nicholas found rather amusing. Butlers were such snobs.

"Father," he greeted, as Landsdowne came in. "This is unexpected. To what do I owe the pleasure?"

"Don't be coy." The duke came across the room, leaning heavily on his gold-tipped walking stick as he did so. "You know quite well what has brought me here."

"As much as I would dearly love to see inside that Machiavellian mind of yours and read what's there, I can't. I'm afraid you'll have to spell it out. I didn't realize you even remembered the way to Honeywood, much less had any inclination to visit."

"This isn't a social call." Landsdowne eased down in the chair across the desk from him without waiting for it to be offered. "I've come on a matter of business."

"Even more astonishing," Nicholas murmured, and resumed his seat. "I don't think you and I have ever discussed a business matter. Other than the matrimonial sort, that is."

"Do you intend to hold Lady Elizabeth and that Irish chit against me forever?"

He ignored the slight to Kathleen. Given that she'd allowed herself to be bribed, the description seemed appropriate, and even though it came from Landsdowne, it just wasn't worth fighting about. "No," he answered. "To be honest, Father, I just don't care anymore."

The duke didn't seem to believe him, but he didn't care about that much either. Belinda had been right about that; doing the opposite of what Landsdowne wanted was every bit as enslaving as doing his bidding. He was coming to find genuine indifference to Landsdowne's wishes far less aggravating.

"An alarming report came to me a few days ago from Mr. Burroughs," the duke said, tapping his walking stick against the carpet beneath his feet for added emphasis. "The moment I read it, I knew a serious mistake had been made, one that had to be dealt with by me."

"How terrible that my land agent has caused you such inconvenience."

"On the contrary, he thought he was performing a courtesy. He has informed me that you are refusing to provide any of the autumn grain harvest to Jenkins so that he may brew the beer for the estates. I'm told you are sending the crops straight to market for sale."

"You've been misinformed."

"Ah."

He waited until the duke had eased back in the chair and relaxed a bit before he finished. "The crops have already been sold," he added, and couldn't help smiling at the way his father jerked back to ramrod straightness.

"I see." Landsdowne's eyes narrowed as he gave Nicholas that icy ducal stare that had intimidated him as a boy and enraged him as a young man. "And where did you get the notion that selling all Honeywood's crops to someone outside the family is an acceptable practice?"

"Well, they are my crops," Nicholas pointed out, still smiling.

"Half the yield of which is always sold to me. That's been a tradition at Honeywood for many years."

Nicholas gave the other man a look of mock apology. "I'm afraid I don't set much store by the family traditions, Father. You should know that by now. And any decisions regarding Honeywood nowadays are mine to make. They are not Mr. Burroughs's, and they are certainly not yours."

"As if you've ever cared about any of the decisions made at Honeywood! You've always been quite content to allow Burroughs to deal with managing things here, and he's done an excellent job."

"Yes, so he has. But things have changed." He spread his hands in the best deprecating manner he could manage. "I am resolved to have greater control of my own estate. In light of that, one of the decisions I made was to sell my crop to whoever would provide me the greatest measure of profit. That, dear Father, is not you."

"This is ridiculous. I am entitled to have the grain at a lower price than market. Honeywood is in the family."

"I realize the number of things to which you think you are entitled knows no bounds, Father, but, as I'm sure you're aware, Honeywood is entailed to me through Mama, and separate from any Landsdowne holdings."

"You are splitting hairs."

"Regardless, it's still mine. It is also separate from my trust. Therefore, as I explained to Mr. Burroughs when I arrived and took charge, you have nothing to do with what is done here, including to whom I sell my hops, barley, and wheat."

"Landsdowne and Honeywood have an arrangement that goes back centuries. Why, part of the reason your mother and I married was to strengthen the relationship between the two estates."

"How unfortunate for you that her father didn't see it quite that way. He had the good sense to entail it through her in the marriage settlement, not through you. What a bitter pill that must have been to swallow, to know her father didn't trust you enough to let you have it as part of the dowry."

"It wasn't about trust!" the duke snapped, the first sign Nicholas was getting under his skin.

A couple months ago, he might have enjoyed that. Now, he didn't have time for it. "Perhaps not," he said, and gave a shrug. "But the fact remains that I have already sold the crop, so I'm afraid none of it will be available to make beer for you. You'll have to buy grain elsewhere. Was that all you wanted to discuss?"

The duke regained control of his temper, but Nicholas could see that it took the old boy some effort. "I know what this is really about. It's revenge."

"No," he corrected at once, "it's business. I know you think the sun rises and sets around you, but in this case, you'd be wrong. My decision has nothing whatsoever to do with you."

"I don't believe it. You're paying me out because I've forced you to see sense about matrimony and made you stop prevaricating."

"A use of force on your part that has proved singularly unsuccessful."

The old man folded his hands atop the head of his cane in a nauseatingly complacent manner. "That won't last. You can't afford not to marry. I've seen to that. The only question is who the mother of my grandchildren is going to be. Speaking of which, how is the bride search progressing? Lady Featherstone doesn't seem to be doing too well at finding you a wife. I confess I'm surprised. I'd have thought some vulgar American nobody would jump at the chance to become a marchioness and someday get her ambitious little hands on a duchess's coronet. What's wrong, Trubridge? Can't sell yourself for a high enough price to pay for your manner of living?"

Nicholas pressed his tongue against his teeth, striving to keep back the cheeky barb that hovered on his lips. There was no point to it. He wouldn't even enjoy it. "I haven't had much time to think about marriage lately," he said after a moment. "As you can see . . ."

He let his voice trail off and gestured to the piles of magazines, newspapers, books, and letters on his desk. "I'm rather preoccupied these days."

"Hmm." Landsdowne leaned forward and pulled one of the books off the desk. "*Scientific Principles of Brewing*," he read and looked up with a frown. "Why on earth are you studying the subject of beer making? Jenkins knows more about it than any book."

"Yes, Jenkins and I have discussed it quite a bit." He didn't elaborate, reminding himself from long experience that the wisest course with Landsdowne was to say as little as possible on any subject. He shrugged as if beer making was a matter of little consequence. "I'm interested in the subject. Beer making is Honeywood's main purpose, after all."

"You've never taken a shred of interest in the subject before, or Honeywood, for that matter."

"That's not true. I did as a boy. But as I grew up, I

came to believe there was no point, since you always seemed to find a way to counter anything I did or tried to do."

"Blaming me for your failures, are you?"

"No. At least," he amended, "not anymore. The truth is . . ." He paused, considering. The duke would find out before long what he was doing. Hell, he might know already and be toying with him at this moment for some reason of his own. Landsdowne was like that. "The truth is," he said after a moment, "that I'm buying the grain myself."

"Buying your own grain? To what purpose?"

He grinned. Leaning forward, he lifted the book from the desk and held it up. Landsdowne stared at him, looking every bit as appalled as he'd expected, and despite all his newfound resolutions, he rather enjoyed that. Old habits died hard. "I'm going to make beer, Father."

"For . . . for commercial purposes? A Landsdowne engage in trade? In . . . in . . . in commerce? It's unthinkable." The duke was spluttering, and his rather gray complexion was turning a purplish hue. "You can't possibly."

"Can't I?" Nicholas's eyes narrowed, though his mouth still smiled. "Watch me."

"The future Duke of Landsdowne a *brewer*? It's out of the question. Absolutely out of the question."

"Really, Landsdowne, it's quite futile to tell me I cannot embark on an enterprise in which I'm already engaged. But though you have always believed yourself to be God Almighty, there are some things you can't control. One of those things happens to be me."

"Always this need to rebel," Landsdowne muttered. "Bah! You'll never change."

Nicholas was gripping the pencil so hard, he was surprised it didn't snap in his hand. He forced himself to relax his grip. "Best if you give up trying, then," he advised affably.

They stared at each other for a full ten seconds before the duke smiled, indicating a change in tactics was afoot. "My dear boy," he murmured, easing back in the chair, "none of this is necessary. You want to play the local squire and manage Honeywood yourself? Well, all right. Nothing wrong with that. It's yours. Perfectly understandable you'd take an interest. It's a right and gentlemanly thing to do."

"Why, thank you, Father. It means so much to me to know you approve."

The sarcasm beneath the meek words was ignored.

"And if crop prices and land rents are too low to allow you all that a duke's son should have," Landsdowne went on, "then that's all right, too. I can make it right." He paused, and Nicholas waited.

He didn't have to wait long.

"Marry Harriet," Landsdowne said, "or some other acceptable young lady, and all you could ask for is yours. It's that simple. It's always been that simple."

"Ah, but I'm not asking you for anything," he pointed out softly. "I haven't asked you for a single thing since I was twenty years old, and that just sticks in your craw, doesn't it?"

"I don't know what you mean."

"When I was eight, I asked you not to sack Nana. I

begged you," he added, as Landsdowne made a dismissive sound between his teeth. "And I remember quite well how that turned out. I asked you to allow me to attend Cambridge. I asked you for your blessing when I wanted to marry Kathleen. So many times I've asked and been denied for no reason other than what I wanted interfered with your plans for me. After Kathleen, I vowed never to ask again. You enjoy dangling people in uncertainty, waiting for them to ask you for help, naming your price when they do, or taking pleasure in refusing them. I won't play that game with you. I won't ask. Not ever again."

The duke didn't respond with anger. In fact, his expression softened to a patronizing sort of fatherliness. "Yes, you will, my son." The tip of the duke's cane hit the floor, and he rose slowly to his feet. "One day, you will."

Nicholas stood up, and as he watched his father walk out of his study, he felt the old resentment still there, still lurking inside him. He might never be rid of it. All very well to want to turn over a new leaf, and an easy thing to talk about, but he was beginning to appreciate how hard a thing it was to do.

Chapter 18

Belinda read through Nicholas's latest letter for the fifth time, and though she was familiar with every word of it by now, it still made her smile. He had a talent for letters, for he wrote as he spoke, dashing off sentences with an ease and naturalness that made even the most ordinary things amusing.

He told her of the hops fields and the barley, of the servants and the house. He reiterated his opinion that the place was a monstrosity—or, as he put it in his letter, "the love child of the baroque and the bazaar." She wondered if he'd misspelled the latter word, until he described the copper ornaments and carved-stone figures from Persia that adorned the drawing room, along with gilt-framed pastoral landscapes and brocade pillows, and she knew he'd meant just what he said. Still, despite his derision, she perceived behind the glib words a deep affection for the place, one that even he was perhaps unaware of.

He never asked if she was coming down to Kent, and she was grateful for that, for she honestly wouldn't have known what to answer.

She was procrastinating, telling herself over and over that she simply couldn't leave London at the height of the season. It was a valid enough reason, but she couldn't seem to convince herself, for another equally persistent part of her kept thinking of ways to rearrange her schedule.

Her heart and her body wanted to go to him. Ever since he'd issued the invitation that afternoon at the brewery in Chelsea, she'd yearned to take him up on it. Fear was what stopped her.

Belinda had never thought of herself as a coward, but an illicit affair did make her afraid. She believed in the rightness of her profession, and she wasn't sure she dared risk losing it to a love affair. Nicholas had professed no deeper attachment than desire, and if he did, what would she do? If he asked her to marry him, what would she say? She couldn't imagine being married again, for if it proved a mistake, there was no way out. Would it be a mistake?

She thought of him, of his dark gold hair and warm hazel eyes, of the way he made her laugh and the way she felt in his arms, and of the longing of her body when he touched her, and her heart said no, it wouldn't be a mistake. But her head said otherwise, and that was why she stayed in London, procrastinating.

She understood him better now than she had when

he'd first walked through her drawing-room door nearly three months ago, she liked him better, and she wanted him more than she'd ever have dreamed possible, but was that worth risking the life she had made for herself?

She had the flesh-and-blood desires of any woman. Was it wrong to act on them, just once in her life? Was it wrong to make love with a man, sleep with him, and wake up in his arms without the blessings and security of matrimony?

Belinda tossed aside his latest letter and leaned back in her chair. She'd gone over these considerations again and again during the past few weeks, her thoughts spinning in pointless circles, with no satisfactory answer.

What did she want? For perhaps the hundredth time since he left, those heated moments in Chelsea came back to her, when the mere touch of his hand had brought her to climax, and like every other time she recalled the incident, her body burned to feel those sensations again. It had been so long ago and so rare to occur, she'd forgotten how that sort of satisfaction felt. Now, after that small taste of what she'd been missing, she couldn't seem to think about anything else for more than two minutes at a time.

Closing her eyes, she traced her fingertips against her skin above her collar, caressing her own throat and imagining it was his touch instead of her own. Just that tiny moment of fantasy, and her body responded. Her pulses quickened with excitement, and warmth began flooding through her body.

"My lady?"

Belinda jerked upright in her chair at the sound of her butler's voice, but she could not compose herself enough to turn around. "Yes, Jervis?" she asked, reaching for another letter on her pile of correspondence. "What is it?"

"Mrs. Buchanan and her daughter have come to call. Are you at home?"

Belinda breathed a sigh of relief at the timely distraction. "Yes, of course. I asked them to call today. Send them up."

By the time Mrs. Matthew Buchanan and her daughter reached the drawing room, Belinda was in sufficient command of herself to receive them.

Mrs. Buchanan, though rather stout now, her auburn hair streaked with gray, had once been a great beauty, beautiful enough to capture the heart of Britain's richest coal supplier though she herself had been born a farmer's daughter. A widow now, and still extremely rich, with a home in Berkeley Square and a fine house in Newcastle, she had become socially ambitious, ambitious enough to want the acceptance of higher society for herself and for her daughter. It was Belinda's job to make that happen.

On the surface, it hadn't seemed a difficult business, for May was every bit as beautiful as her mother had been, with the same striking coloring, and her dowry was enormous. But it was proving far harder to find a husband for May than it had seemed at first. Though charming in most aspects, when it came to a consideration of the various gentlemen of London, May seemed impossible to satisfy. Belinda had requested this visit to find out why.

"Ladies, would you care for tea?" she asked after greetings had been exchanged.

"Tea would be a grand idea," Mrs. Buchanan said as she sat down on Belinda's settee, and in her voice was a hint of acidity that told Belinda this was not going to be an easy visit. "It might give you enough time, Lady Featherstone, to talk some sense into this hardheaded, rebellious daughter of mine."

May gave a heavy, exasperated sigh and crossed to the opposite end of the room from her mother, turned her back, and pretended vast interest in the view below. She said nothing.

Belinda studied them both for a moment, then turned to the door. "Tea, Jervis, if you please. Strong and hot. And send up sandwiches and cakes as well."

"Yes, my lady." The butler bowed and departed, and Belinda returned her attention to her guests.

"I don't want any tea," May said. "Or cakes. I just want to go home."

"Home? Nonsense." Mrs. Buchanan gave a sniff. "What would we do in Newcastle, I ask you? It's the season. Everyone who matters is here."

May returned her attention to the window. "Not everyone," she muttered.

"Mrs. Buchanan," Belinda said, turning to the stout lady opposite, "it's perfectly understandable that May wants to go home. Homesickness is very natural. Having felt it myself when I was her age, I think I am in a better position to assist her in overcoming it if I might talk with her alone?"

"Alone?" Mrs. Buchanan's voice was filled with surprise, and beneath it, a hint of resentment. "I can't imagine anything you might say to May that I cannot hear."

"Nonetheless," Belinda said pleasantly, "I think it's for the best."

She used the tone a nanny might use to reason with a petulant child, and after a moment, the other woman gave in with a huff. "Very well. I shall have to take the carriage. My knees, you know."

"I shall see that May is delivered safely back to Berkeley Square."

She stood up, waving a hand toward the girl at the window. "If you can do anything with her, Lady Featherstone, I shall be eternally grateful. She doesn't seem to appreciate any of the trouble and expense I've taken for her future, but perhaps you can remind her."

With that, she flounced out, leaving the other two women alone.

Belinda didn't speak, she merely waited, knowing that girls were usually so impatient that her silence would provoke May to speech more effectively than any questions.

The younger woman held out until tea had been brought and the maid had departed. "I won't do it," she said at last and turned from the window. "I won't marry someone I don't want."

"Of course not." Belinda poured tea. "I don't think anyone expects you to do so."

"My mother does."

Belinda smiled. "I doubt that."

"You don't understand!" May cried, and in her voice was a passion that seemed all out of proportion. "I don't want to marry any of these men. I know the man I want, and he's not here. He is in Newcastle."

"Ah." That explained a lot. "And he is not suitable for you, is that it?"

"He is suitable! To my mind, he's suitable in every way. That's what's so frustrating." May came to sit on the sofa, willing now, even eager, to explain. "David is an attorney, and a good, fine man, from a good family. He's not a rake out for my money."

"I'm sure, but your mother is clearly concerned about his suitability for a girl of your station."

"My station?" She gave a laugh. "My grandfather was a miner and my mother the daughter of a farmer. What is our station if it comes to it? But even if I were an earl's daughter, it wouldn't matter. I want David, and David wants me."

"But your mother does not approve."

May gave a derisive snort. "She's got it in her head that I shall marry a lord, and have a fine country house, and throw grand balls and parties, but I don't want it. I don't want any of it. I just want David!"

"I'm sure you think it all very simple—"

"It is simple!" May cried with all the passionate intensity of a girl in love. "I want him. When he kisses me, my knees buckle and my heart races, and when he smiles at me . . . oh, I can't think! I want to be with him every moment of the day and night, and he feels the same. You see? When two people are right for each other, it isn't complicated at all! It's the simplest, clearest, most beautiful thing in the world. It's these silly society conventions and rules and rituals that muddy things up and make everything complicated!"

Belinda froze, her teacup halfway to her mouth, and she stared at the girl across from her, feeling as if everything in her world had just shifted into its proper place. The doubt that had dogged her for weeks lifted like dark clouds blown away, and she knew with sudden, shining clarity that May was right. This wasn't complicated at all.

"Lady Featherstone, are you all right?"

Belinda set her teacup back in its saucer and glanced at the clock on the mantel. Quarter to two. Yes, she had time to make the afternoon train to Kent, if she hurried.

"I'm sorry, my dear," she said and set down her tea. "I fear I've developed a sudden headache. Perhaps we might continue this discussion in a day or two?"

"Yes, of course." May rose. "I hope you understand now, at least a little, how I feel?"

"Yes," Belinda said with feeling. "I do understand. I understand perfectly."

NICHOLAS STOOD WITH Burroughs in one of the hops alleys, eyeing the dark green bines that were climbing along the twelve-foot poles. "The cones look good. At this rate, they should be full of lupulin by early September."

"I agree. A very good crop in the making."

"My lord?"

Nicholas turned to find one of the undergardeners racing toward them down the hops alley. The youth halted in front of him, panting from the exertion of running all the way down from the house. "James, is it?" he asked.

The young man nodded. "Yes, my lord. Mr. Forbisher had me sent down to tell you that you've a visitor."

"A visitor? One of the gentlemen of the county, I presume?"

"No, sir. It's a lady come to see Your Lordship. Lady Featherstone."

"Lady Featherstone?" A grin spread over his face before he'd even finished saying her name. He started back toward the house at a run. "Thank you, Mr. Burroughs," he called over his shoulder. "I'm leaving tomorrow, but I'll be back in two weeks to see how the bines are coming along."

"Very good, Your Lordship," the land agent called back, but Nicholas was already out of the hops alley and making for the home farm, where he'd left his horse earlier in the day. Within five minutes, he was handing the reins of the gelding over to a stableboy and racing for the house.

Once inside, he found Forbisher waiting for him at the foot of the stairs. "Where is she?" Nicholas asked, breathing hard as he came to a skidding halt.

"If you are referring to Lady Featherstone, my lord, she is in the drawing room. She has brought luggage with her, sir," he added, sounding disapproving. "And her maid. She seems to believe she is to stay here as your guest."

"God, I hope so," he replied, laughing even as he worked to catch his breath. "If she came all the way from London only to have tea, that would just be silly."

"If you say so, my lord. I regret that I was unable to prepare for her arrival in advance."

Nicholas feared he'd fallen several notches in the butler's estimation, not so much because he'd brought his mistress to Honeywood but because he'd failed to inform the staff of her arrival beforehand. He grinned. "My fault, Forbisher, but I'm sure you'll be able to make her comfortable, even on such short notice. Have Mrs. Tumblety prepare the Rose Room for her," he added as he went up the stairs. "It's the least hideous room in the house."

Moments later, he was entering the drawing room, his heart pounding in his chest and his heart in his throat. She stood by the mantel, and as she turned toward him, she looked so lovely, he came to a stop just inside the door.

The teal blue coat and skirt she wore made her eyes seem the brilliant blue of aquamarines. She'd removed her hat, and her hair gleamed like a blackbird's wing in the sunlight pouring through the window.

She smiled, gesturing to the mantelpiece and the crude statuettes of carved alabaster that stood there, tucked between an ormolu clock and a small copper coffeepot. "Baroque and bazaar, indeed. I wasn't sure whether or not to believe you."

"Yes, well, you can't say I didn't warn you." He turned to the footman. "That will be all for the moment, Noah."

The footman went out, closing the door behind him. The latch had barely clicked into place before Belinda was across the room and in his arms. She kissed him, her mouth warm and lush and tasting like heaven.

He savored it for a moment, then his hands came up to cup her cheeks, and he pulled back so that he could look at her. "Belinda, what are you doing here? And why didn't you tell me you were coming?" He pressed a quick kiss to her lips, another to her forehead and another to the impudent tip of her nose. "And why in blazes did you take such a long time getting here?"

She laughed, twining her arms around his neck. "I know, I know. But I'm here now."

"And I'm going back to London tomorrow."

"Then let's not waste a moment." She took a deep breath. "Where is your room?"

Chapter 19

Nicholas caught his breath at the question, hardly able to believe this was happening. He'd joked about it several times, about how one day, she'd fling herself into his arms and demand he make love to her. He'd never thought it would actually happen.

He'd figured if he ever were lucky enough to get her into his bed, it would be because he'd somehow managed to seduce his way past her previous experience with men, her morals, and her good sense. But this was something he'd never expected in a thousand years.

"I'm dreaming," he murmured. "I have to be." But even as he said it, he was grabbing her hand and turning to open the door. He led her out of the drawing room, up another flight of stairs, down a long corridor, and into his private suite.

"This is quite different from the rest of the house," she said. "A bit spartan," she added, glancing at the plain white walls, brass bed, and cherrywood furnishings as he closed the door behind them.

"I simply had everything awful removed, and this was what was left," he explained as he began drawing the moss green curtains, not all the way. Enough to cut off the bright sunlight outside, but leaving just enough space between the curtains for there to be light in the room. He didn't want to make love to her in the dark. "Except the bed," he went on as he started toward her. "That's from one of the guest bedrooms. The one in here was this hideous thing of purple mahogany—" He halted in front of her and hauled her into his arms. "I don't want to talk about the damn furniture."

"I don't want to talk at all," she answered, and kissed him, wrapping her arms around his neck. He was already fully aroused, and she must have felt it, even through the many layers of clothing that separated them, for she pressed her body closer, groaning into his mouth, tasting him with her tongue. He felt the desire he'd been banking for weeks flare up as if no time had passed since those moments in the brewery, and he worked to keep it at bay.

He'd wanted her to come here, so that they would have the leisure of low, slow, luscious lovemaking, but for that plan to work, he knew he had to slow things down. He'd waited for this moment, dreamed of it, imagined it over and over, and he intended both of them to savor it. He gentled the kiss, nipping her lower lip, pulling it between both of his, tasting her.

"You go too fast," he told her, and reached up to pull out her hatpin. "It won't do, Belinda."

He plucked off her hat, wove the pin through the crown, and tossed the confection of yellow straw and stuffed bluebirds into a corner. "You see," he said as he reached for her hand and began pulling off her buff-colored kid gloves, "I've imagined undressing you dozens of times by now, and I'll not be deprived of my fun just because you decided to take weeks to come down here and drove both of us to the brink of insanity."

"Dozens?" she murmured, as he pulled off her second glove. "I doubt that."

He let her gloves drop to the floor before he paused to consider. "You're right," he said, and reached for the first button of her teal blue polonaise. "It was probably hundreds."

He untied bows, shoved buttons out of their holes, and slid the jacket of cotton sateen off her shoulders. One toss, and it joined the hat in the far corner of his room. He then lifted his hands to the base of her throat, his fingers searching beneath tiny, pleated layers of pale blue silk for a button or a hook, but her voice made him pause. "Nicholas?"

When he looked up, he found her smiling at him. "The buttons are in the back," she said.

"Well, I don't see how I was supposed to know. You've more layers to you than a French pastry." That fact was confirmed when he turned her around and saw the long row of cloth-covered buttons down her back. "As many times as I imagined this moment, your clothing never had this many fastenings. Why you women wear such intricate garments is beyond my understanding. Makes things deuced difficult for a chap."

"Well, that is rather the point," she said, as he began undoing buttons. "Still, had I thought far enough ahead to realize we would be engaging in a *cinq à sept* the moment I arrived, I'd have worn something less complicated."

"This is not a *cinq à sept*," he told her, taking issue with her choice of words. "Making love to you shall take me much longer than two hours."

She shifted her weight impatiently. "It will if you don't go any faster."

"Speed, my darling, is not the point." He pulled her dress apart and pressed his lips to the bare skin at the nape of her neck, relishing the way she shivered in response. "Why are you in such a hurry?"

"After the shameless way I kissed you when I arrived, how can you ask?"

Those words and the catch in her voice as she said them tempted him to accommodate her wishes and speed things up, but he resisted temptation valiantly. He'd vowed that pleasuring her this time wasn't going to be like the last time, and he intended to keep that vow.

Finished unbuttoning her bodice, he pushed it off her shoulders and down her arms. It caught at her waist, held there by the many hooks that attached it to her skirt. He left it there for now and turned his attention to her hair. One by one, hairpins hit the floor, and a few moments later, locks of raven black silk tumbled down almost to her waist, and he caught the fragrance of her perfume—light, sweet lemon verbena and deep, erotic musk, a combination that never failed to arouse him.

Not that he needed any encouragement there. He was fully, flagrantly aroused, but despite that, he seemed bent on torturing himself. He grasped a handful of blue-black strands in his fist and lifted them, savoring the scent of her and the deepening of his own desire that came with it. He tangled the strands in his fingers, played with them, kissed them, and, finally, pushed them aside. He pressed slow, tender kisses along the side of her neck up to her ear as he glided his fingertips down her bare arms, and he relished how her breath quickened in response.

He turned her around, and the moment he did, she lifted her face in anticipation of a kiss, but he didn't kiss her. Instead, he continued undressing her. He wanted to heighten her anticipation, bring her all the way to the edge before he gave her what she was in such a hurry for. Slowly, he unfastened hooks, undid buttons, and untied ribbons, removing layers of silk, satin, and muslin from her body. One by one, bodice, corset cover, underskirt, corset, three petticoats, and a pair of shoes joined the pile of garments in the corner. By the time he had her down to her chemise and drawers, he was sure he was never going to be able to hold out long enough to make love to her properly.

His body ached for her, but he strove to contain it as he reached for the hem of her chemise. He pulled it up, and when she stretched her hands toward the ceiling, he removed it altogether. But he left her drawers on for now. He needed some sort of barrier, however flimsy, to remind him to keep his desire leashed as long as possible.

To that end, he spread his arms wide. "Your turn."

"You want me to undress you?"

"I told you, I'm not making love to you with my trousers around my knees, remember? Not the first time, anyway."

She reached out, hesitated a few seconds, then unbuttoned his waistcoat and slid it from his shoulders. It fell behind him to the floor, and she set to work on his studs, fumbling a bit with them. She laughed, sounding nervous. "I'm not very good at this. I've never done it."

He frowned, puzzled. "You never undressed your husband?"

"No." She fell silent, and he grasped her wrists, stopping her.

"Are you certain you want to do this? You don't have to."

"I want to." She paused and looked up at him. "I want you, Nicholas."

Those words, stated so simply, did queer things to him, they made him feel dizzy—with relief, and pleasure, and something else he couldn't quite define.

"Thank God," he muttered, taking refuge in teasing as she turned to drop his shirt studs into a crystal dish on the dressing table. "Because if you'd have refused me now, I think I would have had to throw myself off a cliff."

She laughed at that as she pulled his braces off his shoulders and unfastened his cuff links. "Isn't that a bit extreme?"

"That's right, laugh," he said, nodding as she turned away with his cuff links. "Laugh at the fact that I've been mad with lust for you almost from the first moment I walked through your front door, while you haven't cared two straws. It's driven me to the brink."

He pulled his shirt over his head, then his undershirt, but when he looked at her again, she still had her back to him. She was so rigid, so still, it worried him. "What's wrong?"

His cuff links dropped from her hand into the dish, joining his studs with a clink. "Is that really true?" she asked without turning around, "or are you teasing me?"

"I'm not teasing. Well, I am, a little, because I'm nervous as hell, and I always tease you more when I'm nervous." He put his hands on her bare shoulders and turned her around. "But it's still the truth. I've wanted you from the first. It stuns me that you think otherwise."

"Yes, well, there are things you don't know about me." She took a deep breath, then looked down at her fingers, which were twining and untwining nervously. "When I married my husband, I loved him too much, and he didn't love me at all. As a result, he felt smothered, I felt undesirable, and our physical relations were . . . disappointing for both of us."

"Undesirable? You? Stuff." Nicholas made a sound of disbelief. "Was he impotent?"

"With me, yes. Sometimes. With his other women, I don't know."

Still holding her wrists, he leaned forward and kissed her. "I won't be disappointed, Belinda."

She smiled a little. "Don't say that quite yet."

She started to pull her hands away, but he didn't let her. "There is no way on God's earth you could disappoint me because you are lovelier than anything my imagination has ever conjured up, and believe me, I have a very good imagination."

He released her wrists. "Everything about you is desirable to me. Your hair, for instance," he said, smoothing the inky locks with his palm. "It's so black it's almost blue, and it feels like silk. Your eyes— all different shades of blue in the daylight, gray in twilight—stun me every time I look into them. Your skin, your scent intoxicate me. And your figure, well . . ." He paused and grasped her wrists again to spread her arms wide. His throat went dry at the sight of her pale, smooth skin, and her round, full breasts with their pink nipples and darker aureoles. He slid his gaze farther down to her perfectly proportioned hips, and he cursed himself for not taking off her drawers earlier. By the sunlight that peeked between the curtains, he thought he could see the dark triangle of hair at the apex of her thighs, and the desire he'd been holding in check for weeks threatened to flare up out of control. He forced his gaze back to her face, but it still took him a few seconds before he could speak again because her face was every bit as wrenchingly beautiful as her body.

He cleared his throat. "As for your figure," he resumed, "I hope it's all right if I reserve judgment on that for a bit."

"Reserve judgment?" she echoed, and he didn't

know whether what he heard in her voice was disbelief
or fear. Possibly, it was both.

"Yes," he answered. "You see, I think I have to do
quite a bit of research on this particular topic before I
pronounce an opinion. I think I'll begin here."

Still holding her hands apart, he bent his head and
kissed her breast. "Lovely," he said, and grazed her
nipple with his tongue, gratified to hear her sharp
intake of breath. He let her hands go and cupped both
breasts. "Pink and white, and such gorgeous nipples."

He played with her breasts, shaping them. He toyed
with her nipples, relishing how they hardened in response. He pulled one into his mouth and suckled her,
softly at first, then harder, until she was moaning low in
her throat and her hands were raking through his hair
to pull him closer.

He could feel her arousal growing hotter. He wanted
that. It was clear Featherstone had been a piss-poor
lover, and though the other man had clearly had no idea
just how much passion Belinda possessed, he knew,
and he intended to stoke that fire as hot as it could go.

He gently scored her nipple with his teeth, and
she cried out, her knees giving way beneath her. He
wrapped an arm around her to hold her upright, his
tongue still licking her nipple as he guided her body
backward until she hit the brass footboard of the bed.

"Now, where was I?" he murmured, pretending to
think about it. "That's right. I was doing research."

His hands slid to her waist. "Perfect," he said. "I
think you should leave off the corset from now on. You
don't need it at all, and if we do decide we want a *cinq*

à sept, it will be far easier to manage it. Particularly if we're in some farmer's field somewhere tomorrow afternoon."

"In a field? Lovemaking outside, in the open?" She was staring at him as if he'd gone mad.

"I suppose that sort of thing wasn't to Featherstone's taste either?"

She shook her head. Her tongue shot out to lick her lips. "Never. Not even at night."

"Then he was a fool. Anywhere I have you to myself I want you." He grasped her hips and turned her around, then slid his arms around her to grasp the drawstring of her drawers. "Hang on to the bed," he told her.

Belinda did so, curling her fingers around the brass on either side of her hips, but as he undid the bow that secured her drawers, she had no idea what he was going to do. Take her right here?

The air was warm and sultry in the room, but as he slid her drawers off her hips, and they fell to her ankles, she shivered, feeling terribly vulnerable because she was naked and it was daylight and he could see her from this position, but she couldn't see him.

What was he doing?

He knelt behind her. "Lift your feet," he said, tugging at the drawers tangled around her ankles. They joined the rest of her clothes in the corner, along with her stockings and garters, then his palms glided up the outsides of her thighs, scorching hot. Oh, God, she realized, he was staring straight at her bare backside. He kissed her there, his lips warm against her buttock, and she was seized by another paroxysm of her girlhood shyness. She made a sound of protest, moving to turn around, but he wouldn't let her.

"Ssh," he admonished, trailing kisses across the base of her spine. "Let me do this. I want to look at you and touch you. Every . . . single . . . part of you."

The heels of his hands cupped her buttocks, shaped them. "You have the most gorgeous bum," he said. "God, I'm making myself insane."

Abruptly, he stood up and leaned into her, dipping his knees so that his hips pressed hers, and she groaned at the hard ridge of his arousal against her bare bottom. Combined with the rough-textured wool of his trousers, it was unbelievably erotic.

"There now," he said, his breathing ragged as he flexed his hips, sliding his hardness against her buttocks. "I hope we've now settled the question of your desirability? If not, I could keep going."

She shook her head. She didn't want that. She wanted what she'd come here for. She wanted his body on hers and his mouth on hers and his manhood inside her. She ached for it. "No," she gasped. "I believe you."

"Good." He kissed her shoulder, and she was sure he would undo his trousers and come into her now, but he didn't. Instead, keeping his arousal pressed to her bottom, he reached around her, over the footboard and back between the bars to touch her. When the tip of his finger slid between the folds of her sex, she moaned, pleasure fissuring through her, but it wasn't enough. She wanted more.

She tried to wriggle her hips, but his superior weight had her pinned to the footboard, and all she could do was stand there as he caressed her through the bars, a tender, almost delicate caress as he pressed hard against her from the back. It was like nothing else she'd ever felt. His fingertip was a tease, a whisper, a promise of what might be if only she could get closer. And behind her, his manhood was another tease, a harder, deeper promise of something still just out of reach. Caught, she was desperate for a deeper caress, but unless he gave her more, this was all she could have.

It was agony, to have desire held out of reach. It was unbearable. She tried to tell him that, but she couldn't seem to catch her breath, and the only sound she could make was a sob of frustration.

He kissed her ear, flicking his tongue against her lobe and sending shivers through her body, but he didn't bring his hand any closer. He didn't let her go. "Is there something you want?" he whispered. "Tell me."

Tell him? How could she tell him? She couldn't talk. She could barely breathe.

He waited. He didn't deepen the caress. He didn't unbutton his trousers. Instead, his fingers slid away, and she gave a gasp. "Nicholas," she whispered, feeling all the awful shyness of her girlhood coming back. "I can't. I can't."

He turned her around, and sank to his knees in front of her, catching her hands as she frantically tried to cover herself. He entwined their fingers, spread her arms wide, and pressed a kiss to her stomach, making her quiver inside. And then, to her utter shock, he pressed his lips to the hair at the apex of her thigh.

She squealed. She couldn't help it. She felt panicky,

embarrassed, overcome by another wave of shyness. "Oh, don't," she moaned, her hips jerking as if to push him away. "Don't."

"Belinda, you were a married woman," he murmured, his lips caressing her as he spoke. "I can't believe your husband never did this."

"Of course he didn't do this. Nobody does this!"

That made him laugh, warm breath against her curls. "Ah, but they do. They do it quite often, and for good reason." He paused and looked up at her. "I need you to trust me. Do you trust me?"

She bit her lip. "Yes," she said after a moment.

"Then let me kiss you here." He let her hands go, then his fingers touched her, tangling lightly in the curls. "Open your legs for me and let me do this."

"All right," she said in a miserable whisper, and when she allowed him to part her legs, her embarrassment became so great, she felt as if it were burning her from the inside out.

She had to look away. She braced her weight on the footboard behind her, her bottom perched on the edge, her fingers curled tight around the brass and tilted her head back to stare at the ceiling, as his lips brushed her again and she fought the impulse to tear away.

"Look at me, Belinda."

She shook her head, still looking at the ceiling.

He kissed her again. "Look at me."

She forced her gaze down to meet his. "I want this for you," he said, and his eyes locked with hers as he eased his hand between her thighs. "I want you to have this. There's no shame in it."

"I'm not ashamed. I'm just . . . shy. I was, you know, as a girl. I still am, sometimes."

"I didn't know that. You have no reason to be shy, not with me. You're beautiful." He lowered his head to look at her most intimate place. "Everywhere," he added. "I knew you would be."

She stared down at him, at his hair—burnished in the shady dimness of afternoon, at his thick brown lashes—gilded at the tips, at his face—filled with desire as he looked at her, and when he kissed her again, all her shyness seemed to dissolve and float away, no longer of any consequence, like so much flotsam vanishing on a summer breeze.

And then . . . oh, God . . . and then his tongue touched the crease of her sex. She gasped, a gasp of astonished pleasure as his tongue began to lash her with the softest, most incredible caresses she'd ever felt.

She couldn't think, she was lost in sensations beyond anything she'd thought possible. She'd known—at least, she thought she'd known—all about intimate relations. But this? She hadn't ever imagined such a glorious thing as this.

Because of him, all the desires she'd suppressed for years, desires that had diminished and died because of another man's indifference and neglect, came to life again, and she unfolded to him like the petals of a flower opened to sunlight. He was like air and food and light for her parched soul.

She needed to move, and this time, he let her, his arm wrapping around her thighs to hold her as his tongue gave her these carnal kisses. This wasn't at all like that afternoon in Chelsea. That had been a quick, powerful jolt of orgasm, a primitive instinctual response to need. This was something else. It was languid and lovely, but as it deepened and spread, it grew stronger and more powerful, until her body was moving in frantic little jerks, and she was sobbing with the exquisite pleasure of it. She climaxed at last, a powerful wave that flooded every part of her body with sensation. And then, to her amazement, the wave came again, and again, then again. She thrust against his mouth with each wave, savoring each climax, until at last, she collapsed, so overwhelmed by it all that she would have fallen had Nicholas not been holding her.

She blinked, staring down at him in wonder, and when he looked back up at her, he was smiling, just a slight, knowing curve of the lips. "Now you know why people do this."

Belinda shook her head. Never had she experienced orgasm like this. During her marriage, climax had been a quick, frantic coupling in the dark, usually followed by a crushing sense of frustration and disappointment and months of indifference. And even the rare times it had been tender, it had never been like this. Pleasure that came in waves over and over, until one slid off the edge of the earth into utter bliss? Never.

Until now.

"I never knew," she whispered, giving a little laugh. "I . . . I'm stunned."

Nicholas thought that was most gratifying thing anyone had ever said to him. "I'm glad. Very . . ." He paused to press a kiss to her stomach. "Very glad."

When Nicholas lifted his head to look up at her again, his pleasure at her compliment gave way to something deeper. In a shaft of late-afternoon sun that peeked between the draperies, she looked tousled and luscious and thoroughly pleasured. Her smile was radiant. Her long hair fell in waves all around her, and the nipples of her breasts peeked out between ink black locks. Her lips were puffy from his kisses, and her skin was still flushed a delicate pink from the orgasms that had overcome her. He could only stare, knowing that as long as he lived, he would never see anything more beautiful than Belinda was at this moment. "I love you."

He hadn't meant to say it; hell, he hadn't even thought it, not consciously, anyway. It had just come spilling out. It was only the second time in his life he'd said that particular phrase to a woman, but now that the words were out of his mouth, he knew they were the simple truth, and even though her smile vanished at once, and he feared he might have made a serious mistake, he wouldn't ever regret saying those words to her.

Nonetheless, he felt impelled to throw himself back onto solid ground, and he did it the only way he knew how. "Stunned you again, have I?" he said, pasting on a grin. "I wonder how many times I can do that in one afternoon. I say we find out."

He stood up, and as he did, he became aware—painfully aware—of his own banked desires. He was rock-hard, aching for her, and he knew he didn't have much time before his self-discipline was utterly exhausted.

He undressed, yanking off his shoes and stripping off

trousers and linen as quickly as he could. Taking her hand, he led her around to the side of the bed, falling back into the mattress and pulling her down beside him.

But still, he didn't move to enter her. Instead, he rolled onto his side, and his fingers eased between her legs again, spreading the moisture of her arousal, over velvety folds and silken curls, across her clitoris and just inside her opening, over and over. Beneath his hand, he could feel her arousal rising again, her pleasure thickening, and the depths of her hunger made him realize just how starved for tender lovemaking she was. Good thing Featherstone was dead, or Nicholas just might have had to go off and shoot the son of a bitch.

He stroked her, his finger sliding up and down in the way that seemed to please her most until each pant was a sob.

"Want me?" he asked, but she couldn't reply. All she could do was give a frantic nod, and, thankfully, that seemed enough.

He withdrew his hand, and as he moved on top of her, her legs opened beneath him. He wanted to go slowly still, but as the head of his penis touched her warm, silken folds, he just couldn't do it, and he thrust hard into her.

She came almost at once, crying out as she clenched tight around him, and the pulsing sensations of her climax were just too much to bear. With a force he could no longer contain, he thrust deeply into her, again and again, losing himself in her softness and her scent and her passionate cries, and when at last he climaxed, the pleasure was explosive, so acute and intense it was like pain, shattering him to bits.

He collapsed atop her in complete release, his arms sliding beneath her to hold her tight, his panting breaths mingling with hers in the hush of afternoon. He kissed her lips, her hair, her throat—anywhere he could reach without pulling out of her. "Are you all right?"

She didn't answer, and he pulled back to look at her, resting his weight on his forearms, his hands beneath her back, his penis still inside her. "Belinda, are you all right?"

"Oh, God," she whispered and her eyes looked into his, wide with wonder. "Oh, my God. I never knew making love was like this."

He laughed, and a wave of satisfaction better than any orgasm rose up inside him, filling his chest, squeezing his heart, pouring joy through his veins, and he knew he believed in love again. For the first time in years, by heaven, he believed in love. What a ripping miracle.

Chapter 20

They came down for dinner, took a walk in the gardens, and made love again that night, but she didn't sleep with him. He wanted her to, but she hated the idea of servants coming in to find her in his bed. He pointed out, quite reasonably, that they already knew what was afoot. Servants always knew that sort of thing. Nonetheless, Belinda had her own sense of propriety about things, and she slept in her own bedroom. But she also hugged her pillow all night and pretended it was he.

The next day, he wasn't in the morning room when she came down for breakfast, and when she inquired as to his whereabouts, Forbisher informed her that His Lordship had already gone out. He was in the hops fields with his land agent, Mr. Burroughs.

"Do you wish to attend Sunday services, my lady?"

the butler asked her. "If so, Robson can take you to Maidstone in the gig."

She did not want to go into Maidstone. And considering what had happened yesterday, church was a bit hypocritical. "No, I don't think so, Forbisher."

"Very good, my lady. His Lordship proposes that you join him for luncheon, and as the day is quite fine, he recommends a picnic. If you agree, I am to have Mrs. Fraser prepare one."

"Yes, thank you. That would be lovely."

"His Lordship also suggested that you pack before you join him since the two of you are taking the five o'clock train for London."

She felt a stab of disappointment at that reminder how short their time was here, but she nodded. "Have my maid pack my things, if you would," she told the butler. "I'm going for a walk after breakfast."

"Very good, my lady."

Belinda ate her breakfast, then occupied her time with a tour of the house and grounds. It was a charming house, at least on the outside. The inside, as Nicholas had told her, was rather awful. But the rooms were well proportioned, and with a bit of ingenuity and some work, they could be made quite attractive. Outside, there were lovely cottage gardens and herbaceous borders, and a forest of birch trees to the north. To the east was the home farm, and past it, the tenant cottages and farms. To the south and west, the hops and barley fields rolled out to the horizon in lush, green waves.

Honeywood was a warm and pretty place, not like Featherstone Castle. That house had always seemed like a mausoleum, a cold lump of granite and marble in the middle of Yorkshire. She had hated it there.

Belinda found a garden bench with a view of the hops. Even from here, she could smell them, a fresh, herbal scent that reminded her a bit of evergreen needles. She breathed in the scented air, so much nicer than London, and gazed out at the fields, but in her mind, she was thinking of Nicholas, and yesterday. It had been amazing and erotic and the most wonderful experience of her life. She wanted to do it all again—be undressed by him, held and kissed by him, made love to by him. And not just that—she wanted to simply be with him. It made her happy, happier than she could ever remember being, and she wanted to kick herself for taking so long to make up her mind to come to him. As May Buchanan had said, love was really pretty simple.

Love. There it was. That word, the one she hadn't let herself think about. It had been years since she'd thought of love in conjunction with her own life. Until now, she'd been content, but she hadn't been aware of the loneliness beneath that contentment. But leaving him last night, lying alone, hugging her pillow, she'd been painfully aware of the void that had been inside her for years—perhaps for her entire life. Could Nicholas fill that void? Was she willing to trust him, to let him? Was she falling in love with him?

If so, it wasn't like her love for Charles. It was far more erotic, for one thing. She thought of Nicholas's eyes, of the way he'd looked at her when she'd been naked in front of him, a way Charles had never looked at her. But was that love? Her feeling for Charles had been a crush, an infatuation that she knew now could never have grown into a deeper love because Charles had been incapable of that. He had not been, she realized now, a man who could truly love anyone.

Nicholas, as he'd pointed out to her back in May, was not Charles. She knew that now, and she believed his declaration of love last night was genuine. She was less certain about her own feelings.

Time was probably the only way she could be sure of what she felt. She was always cautioning her clients to take their time, and yet, she knew she did not have that luxury. The longer this affair went on, the more risk to her reputation. And it wasn't even as if Nicholas's declaration had included a proposal of marriage. Without marriage, a woman in love had nothing but shame and social ruin waiting for her down the road. On the other hand, if Nicholas asked her to marry him, would she agree? What if all he wanted was an affair? Could that be enough for her?

Her mind couldn't help going over these questions again and again throughout the morning, and when a footman led her down to meet Nicholas that afternoon with a picnic basket, she still had no answers, but when she saw him, standing by the hops fields, she knew it didn't matter. The only thing that mattered was now.

He was talking with another, older gentleman when she arrived, seeming wholly at ease as the two men discussed the crop, and she realized in some surprise that country life suited him. He wore no hat, and his hair gleamed like amber honey in the sun. The simple clothing he wore—linen shirt, tweed trousers, and riding boots—fitted his body even more perfectly than the tailored morning coats and dinner jackets of town. As if to confirm that fact, he lifted his arm in a sweeping gesture across the hops fields before him, and the bright sunlight showed the silhouette of his torso through the linen. Yes, she thought, appreciating the sight, country life suited him very well indeed.

She'd never had thoughts like this about a man before, but now, as she lowered her gaze to his narrow hips and remembered what he looked like without his trousers, she realized how much she liked this sort of thinking, and it was a realization that made her smile. Heavens, what would society think if they knew that Lady Featherstone was capable of such lascivious thoughts, especially about the Marquess of Trubridge? What a sensation that would make.

As if he sensed her watching, he turned, and when he caught sight of her standing with the footman, he smiled back at her and brought his conversation with the older gentleman to an immediate end. "Thank you, Mr. Burroughs. My apologies for making you miss church services."

"No apologies necessary, my lord. I know you're leaving for London today. And don't tell my wife, but I'll not regret giving services a miss. Our vicar is a bit long-winded."

Nicholas laughed. "Well then, go on to the pub and enjoy the rest of your Sunday. I've kept you long enough." As the other man was walking away, Nicholas turned to the footman and took the picnic basket. "Thank you, Noah. You may go."

"Very good, Your Lordship." He bowed to her. "My lady."

As Noah departed back up the path to the house, Nicholas turned to her. "What are you thinking about that's making you smile like a cat in the cream jug?" he asked, and leaned closer. "I hope it's the same thing I'm thinking about."

Her smile widened. "I was thinking how much country dress suits you."

"I was rather hoping you were remembering what I look like undressed."

"Maybe I was," she blurted out before she could stop herself.

His smile vanished, and she thought she heard him catch his breath, but when he spoke, his voice was carelessly light. "My, my, how naughty you've become," he murmured, and pressed a kiss to her mouth, then he turned away before she could reply and gestured to a nearby meadow. "I thought we might dine over there."

She agreed, and soon they had trampled down a space of knee-high grass and daisies, spread out their blanket, and sat down with the picnic basket.

"Let's see what's in here, shall we?" Nicholas opened the basket and began pulling out various foodstuffs as he laid them on the blanket between them. "We have bread, ham, two cheeses, pickles, a pot of mustard, and blackberries. Hmm, no wine?" He took another look in the basket. "Ah, she gave us beer."

He pulled out two bottles, but when he held one out to her, she shook her head. "I don't drink."

"What?" He looked at her askance. "Belinda, I make beer. Are you never going to drink any?"

She shook her head again, laughing at his chagrin. "I don't like the taste."

"Worse and worse!" He flipped the top of the bottle, letting the stopper fall back against the glass with a clink, and took a swallow. "It's not your morals that stop you, but your palate?"

She made a face at him. "Oh, very well, when you make all these hops into beer, I'll taste it. I won't promise to like it, mind you, but I'll taste it."

"That's my girl." He leaned across the foodstuffs between them and kissed her again, a kiss that tasted of beer, but somehow, she didn't quite mind the taste on his lips.

He sat back, took another look in the picnic basket, and heaved a sigh. "No poetry? Dash it, I told Mrs. Fraser to toss a book or two in with the sandwiches."

She frowned in bewilderment. "But you don't like poetry."

"Stuff." He plucked a blackberry from its woven basket and popped one into his mouth. "Where did you ever get such a notion? I'm English, my darling. I adore poetry. And I wanted to read you some Shelley today. Every man should read Shelley to his lover over a picnic. Or Byron—women always like him better. You'd fall straight into my arms and make mad, passionate love to me right here in the grass if I read you Byron."

She felt her cheeks heating at those words. In fact, her whole body was growing hot, but she felt impelled to correct him. "I never fall straight into your arms."

"More's the pity. I'd adore it if you would."

"I still don't understand about the poetry," she said, deciding it was safest to stick to that subject. "You said you like the sciences."

"So I do. I also like poetry. I am a multifaceted man, my darling. What?" he added, laughing at her confounded expression. "I can't like both?"

"But that day when we discussed what sort of woman you wanted, you said you didn't like poetry."

"No," he corrected. "To the best of my recollection, what I said was that I hate worrying about tercets and quatrains. And that's true. It's because of Eton, you see."

"Eton?" She shook her head, laughing. He really was the most unaccountable man. "I haven't any idea what you're talking about."

"When I was a boy at Eton, they were constantly at us to compose poetry, and forever chastising us if our compositions didn't use the proper form for the assignment."

He frowned at her. "No, no, no, Trubridge," he said in the severe, lecturing voice a professor at Eton might have employed, "that isn't a *haiku*. A *haiku* has seventeen morae. You've used eighteen." He ate another blackberry. "I like poetry, and I like science, but they aren't the same, and they can't be approached the same way. In science, one must use precise measurements, all one should worry about in regard to a poem is if it sounds right."

"So, it wasn't Blake you disliked that day at the National Gallery, but Geraldine Hunt's recitation of it?"

He groaned. "She was almost as bad at reciting Blake as my schoolmates. Can you imagine listening

328 Laura Lee Guhrke

to thirteen-year-old boys standing up in front of you reading *Songs of Innocence and Experience*? It was torture."

"You were thirteen, too," she pointed out.

He grinned and took another swallow of beer. "Yes, well, I was better at reciting poetry than other boys."

She laughed. "Or perhaps you just like to think so."

"Why don't you be the judge?" He pulled a few more blackberries from the basket and leaned back, resting his weight on his forearm and hip. He studied her for a few moments, eating berries, then he said, "As breath to life, she is to me; as springtime sun to winter's icy dart. A stab by knife, her frown to see; her smile one of summer to a January heart."

Belinda's breath caught, not only at what he said, but the tender way he looked at her as he said it. "I . . ." She paused, her voice failing. She cleared her throat and tried again. "I've never heard that poem before."

"I shouldn't think so," he said, and popped another berry into his mouth. "Since I just made it up."

"What? Just now?" When he nodded, she shook her head, amazed. "It was beautiful."

"Thank you, but an Etonian professor wouldn't agree. I'm sure I missed a syllable or two in there somewhere."

"I didn't notice," she assured him. "I thought it was lovely."

"Thank you, but I don't compose much now that I don't have to."

"You should."

"Yes, well, perhaps with you as my muse, I shall take it up again. But enough about me." He rolled over, settled onto his stomach, resting his weight on his fore-arms as he looked up at her. "Let's talk about you."

She shrugged in a deprecating way, hoping not to have to talk about herself. "There isn't much to tell that you don't already know, I imagine."

"I disagree. I know almost nothing about you."

She stirred on the grass, uncomfortable. She hated talking about herself. "What do you want to know?"

"Where you grew up. Your parents. School."

"I was born in Ohio. Like yours, my mother died when I was very young. My father is still alive. For school, I had a governess."

"You didn't go to away to school?"

"No, but then, many girls don't."

"True. What's your father like?"

"A ne'er-do-well."

"And where is he now?"

"Nevada somewhere. Silver-mine concessions. I don't really know where."

He waited, but when she said nothing more, he sat up, looking at her as if quite aggrieved. "Belinda, really! This is like pulling secrets from the Sphinx."

"I don't talk about myself much." She took a deep breath. "The truth is I'm quite shy. I told you so . . . last night."

"Yes, I remember, but many women are shy when their clothes come off."

She wondered how many women gave him reason to know. She didn't ask, but she knew there were probably quite a few.

"Still," he went on, forcing her to put aside petty

speculations about the other women he'd bedded. "I would never have thought you shy in conversation."

"I've learned to hide it. I had to after I married Charles. A countess is expected to entertain, to be the hostess of house parties, to supervise servants. I had to learn to cope." She gave a little laugh. "It was rather in the manner of sink or swim. Charles wasn't . . . much help. He—"

She stopped. Perhaps she shouldn't talk about her husband.

"What about him?" Nicholas asked when she didn't go on.

"I loved him. He knew that. I mean, I said it once before we married, but he didn't say it back. He didn't say anything. He just smiled and changed the subject. I thought he was like me."

"Shy? Featherstone?"

"Not, shy, no, but like me in the sense that perhaps he found it hard to say how he felt when it was important. I'm like that. The important things always make me the most tongue-tied."

"Everyone's like that to some extent. My shields of choice are to be witty and careless and pretend I don't care. Yours are silence and propriety."

"Charles's was indifference. I mean, he was charming to me before we married, but afterward . . ." She stopped and swallowed hard. "I told him again that I loved him the morning after we were married, after he . . . after we . . . he said—" She stopped again. "This is difficult," she said after a moment.

Nicholas reached over to cup her face, make her look at him. "What did he say?"

Belinda made herself tell him. "He said, 'Let's not pretend, shall we? We both know love isn't the reason I married you. We'll have a much easier time of it if you don't insist upon declarations of affection or demand of me feelings which I don't possess.'"

"Good God." He blinked, staring at her in disbelief.

"You're shocked."

"Shocked? I'm nauseated." He moved to sit beside her and took her in his arms, held her close, kissed her mouth. "My darling. I can't begin to imagine how that must have hurt."

"Can't you?" She lifted her head from his shoulder, turned her head to look up at him. "What about the girl you loved? The one your father bribed to go away? Didn't that hurt?"

"Well, yes, but Kathleen was just weak. She wasn't deliberately cruel. Hell, she was an angel compared to your husband." He pressed a kiss to hair. "And I had no idea. I never saw a cruel streak in him. I mean, I didn't know him well, of course, but whenever he came to see Jack, he always seemed an amiable sort of man to me."

"Oh, yes," she agreed. "Very amiable. He was always quite amiable to me, too . . . in public. In private, he didn't bother. In fact, he seldom spoke to me at all. I think he often forgot I was even there. But then, he was almost never home. And I was already so insecure, all that made me more so."

"You must have felt unbelievably lonely."

"I was. Nancy was who really helped me. Lady Montcrieffe. We became friends, and she taught me ways to overcome my shyness with others. She used the same trick her governesses used on her. When we were both in town or together at some house party, we'd go for long walks. At every corner or every ten arborvitaes, or something along that line, I'd have to ask her a question."

"Ah. Forcing you to make conversation."

"Yes. If I couldn't think of anything to ask, I had to recite, 'I am a thistle sifter,' to the next person we met, no matter who it was, be it shopgirl, housemaid, or chimney sweep. Once, I had to say it to a duchess."

He laughed at that. "They all probably thought you mad."

"Exactly so. It was so awful a prospect, that I soon had an entire repertoire of questions I could fall back on, so no one ever had to endure my long silences at dinner. And I began to realize that if I got other people to talk about themselves, I wouldn't have to talk about myself. And I have a knack for observation—so many years of sitting in a corner watching and listening to others, I suppose."

"All of which helps you be a matchmaker, I should imagine."

"Yes. It's much easier for me to talk to people nowadays, and I'm more self-assured than I was as a girl. But underneath it all, I'm still shy. I have to be in the grip of very powerful forces, I think, before I can reveal my true feelings."

That made him a laugh a little. "Then I obviously

spark very strong forces in you because you've never held back speaking your mind to me."

She smiled at that. "That's true. But that's the thing. I have a tendency to hold things in, and hold them in, and hold them in; and then the dam breaks, and my true feelings just come spilling out, usually at the wrong time, or to the wrong person."

"Like that night at the ball, when you first told me about Featherstone. And that night in the maze."

"Yes. When I've been angry with you, it was usually because I thought you were like him."

"God, you don't still think that, do you?"

"No. You were right to say you're nothing like him. You're not, and I know that now. Underneath all his surface charm, Charles was a cold man, and you're not . . . you're charming, but you're not . . . cold. You don't have any idea how much difference that makes to me."

"Then I don't see why you should be shy about answering my questions. People have surely asked you to talk about yourself before."

"Yes, but I can usually deflect people from asking about me. It's harder with you, though, now that I can't put you in the same category of man as Charles. And, of course, now that we . . ." Her voice trailed off.

He caught her chin with one finger, gently forcing her to look at him again. "Now that we're lovers?"

She could feel the blush in her face deepening. "Yes. I . . . I care about you now, you see. I care what you think, and it makes me self-conscious."

"You care what I think?" He grinned.

"You seem terribly pleased by that."

334 Laura Lee Guhrke

"So I am! Six weeks ago, you shredded me to bits, and now you care about my opinion. That's progress."

"Progress?"

He met her gaze, and something in his eyes was so steady, so resolved, she caught her breath. Her heart seemed to stop. "I told you I want your respect, Belinda, and if you care what I think, that means I'm making progress."

He sat back, and she watched him as he began to gather up the picnic things, and she thought again of him kneeling in front of her, and the declaration that had come from his lips. She desperately wanted to hear it again, when she knew it wasn't in the passion of lovemaking.

When he moved as if to stand up, she blurted it out. "Did you mean it? What you said last night?"

He went still. He didn't ask what she was referring to. His eyes stared into hers, unblinking, as if he was considering it very carefully before he spoke, and it seemed an eternity before he finally replied. "I love you," he said at last, and not only the words, but the quiet sureness of them made her heart sing. Joy was suddenly like a tangible thing, for it opened around her, enfolded her, sank into her bones.

He leaned closer. "I meant it when I said it. I mean it now." He kissed her. "I'll always mean it."

Abruptly, he pulled back. "C'mon," he said, and grabbed her hand.

"Where are we going?"

He grabbed the picnic basket in his free hand and

stood up, pulling her with him. "I want to show you the hops fields before we go back. And we don't have much time if we're to make our train."

She sighed, looking around as he led her back through the tall grass and daisies to the hops fields beyond. "It's beautiful here. I wish we could stay longer."

"So do I, but someone—and it was not me—insisted on procrastinating and keeping us both in suspense for weeks—"

"I know, I know," she interrupted, making a face at him. "But still, can't we go back to London tomorrow? Or the next day?"

"No. I'm trying to be a responsible fellow these days, and I have work to do in London. But," he added, and stopped at the edge of the meadow. His free arm slid around her waist and he pulled her close. "I have to come back in a few weeks, and you can come with me then."

"I'd like that," she admitted. "But it's a risk for both of us."

His lashes, gilt-tipped, glinted in the sun as he lowered them to her mouth. "Then we'll have to be sure no one catches us."

He brushed her lips and turned away, leading her between two rows of lushly growing hops, and as she followed, trailing stems brushed her shoulders. "Where on earth are you taking me?" she asked as they plunged deeper and deeper into the thickness of the hops alley.

"I want to show you something." He didn't say anything more, and he didn't stop until they were in what seemed the center of the field.

"There," he said, stopping and turning to face her, forcing her to a stop as well. "I think we're in about the right place."

"For what?" She glanced around. "What is it you want to show me? The hops? We could have seen them just as easily from the edge of the field—"

"No," he cut her off. "That's not it."

"What, then?"

The picnic basket dropped to the ground. "I want to show you that there's no reason you'll ever have to be shy with me."

"I don't understand," she whispered even though she was afraid she did.

"I want you," he said and kissed her. "Right here. Right now. And as we go along, I want you to tell me what you want and how you feel."

She shook her head, desperate, and tried to laugh. "And if I don't? Are you going to force me to say 'I am a thistle sifter'?"

That made him grin. "I have other much more delightful punishments than that." He put a hand on her waist and immediately gave a groan. "A corset? Belinda, I told you not to wear one today."

She licked her dry lips. "I didn't think you were serious!"

"Making love with you is serious, my darling." He kissed her again, but deeper this time, longer, hotter. As he did, his fingertips caressed her cheeks, her jaw, and her throat. By the time he pulled away, she was quivering inside.

"You didn't really care about showing me the hops fields," she accused, as his hands slid to her hips and grasped folds of her skirt. "You had this in mind all along."

"No, actually, I had the meadow in mind, but I decided the hops would be better cover for us." He nipped at her lips. "Because you're shy."

"We can't," she whispered, as he began lifting her skirts. But even as she said it, desire was rising inside her, desire and apprehension in equal measure. "Someone will see us."

"Who?" He nuzzled her ear, working one hand under skirts and petticoats as his other hand unbuttoned his trousers. "We're in the middle of a hops field."

"Someone could walk by the rows."

"It's Sunday afternoon. No one comes out to the hops fields on a Sunday afternoon." His hands curved over her hips, and he turned her around.

"Oh, Nicholas, no," she groaned softly over her shoulder, as he began unbuttoning the back flap of her drawers. "Oh, no."

He ignored that, probably because she sounded as firm as a custard. The flap of her drawers came undone, and he slid his hand beneath her bare buttocks and between her thighs as his other hand spread across her stomach.

She was wet for him already, she knew that, and he made a sound of appreciation against her ear. "You're so soft," he murmured as he began to stroke her. "Do you want me to do this? Touch you here?"

Her excitement rose with each word he spoke. It pressed against her chest and clenched all her muscles, and she couldn't answer.

"Belinda, you have to tell me what you want. If you want me to stop, say stop. If you want me to touch you, say, 'touch me.' It's easy. I'll show you."

As he spoke, his excitement was rising, too. She could hear it in his voice. She could feel it in his shaft, a hot, hard ridge against her hip. "I want you," he said, his fingers touching her so softly, she almost couldn't stand it. "I want to touch you, and make you come and be inside you."

She ought to say "stop," but she couldn't. His naughty words inflamed her desire even as she felt overwhelmed by embarrassment, and the conflict of the two was an exquisite torment, unbelievably erotic.

"See how easy this is?" He kissed her ear. "You try it. Do you want me to stop?"

She shook her head. "N—no," she managed.

" 'Don't stop, Nicholas.' Say it, Belinda."

His fingertip slid around and around the nub where all her pleasure centered, spreading her moisture. The very tenderness of it was relentless, so much so that it forced the words out of her. "Don't stop, Nicholas." She moaned again, and buried her hot face against her arm to stifle the sounds of pleasure he was tearing from her. "Don't stop, don't stop."

Her own words seemed even more erotic than his had been, and lust blazed through her body like fire. Her hips were moving in rhythm with the slide of his finger.

"Do you want me?" he asked.

She didn't answer, and her silence only seemed to make him more determined. "Lean forward."

She complied, grasping the hops poles on either side of her to keep her balance, and as she did, the tip of his shaft nudged her opening, ready to enter her the moment she gave him what he wanted.

"You're so wet, my love," he murmured, his fingers still caressing her in front. "So ready. You must want me. Can't you say it?"

She pushed her hips back, wiggling her bottom, wanting him to come into her, end this torment. She wanted to say it, but she couldn't. Between her tight corset and the sensations he was evoking, she couldn't seem to get enough air. Each breath was a pant, desire was overwhelming her, and her body was moving in little jerks against his hand. "Want," she gasped. It was all she could manage.

"Not good enough," he said, his fingers moving faster, and she could feel her orgasm coming. Oh, God, she could feel it coming.

"I love you," he said, his breathing now as ragged as hers. "I love you, and I want to be inside you. But first you have to tell me you want me, too."

One more stroke of his hand, and she was there. "Yes!" she sobbed as she climaxed, her voice ringing out over the hops fields, but she was too overwhelmed to care if the entire world heard her declaration. "I want you, I want you. Yes, yes, yes!"

That was all he needed. He entered her, thrusting

deep, and she came again, then again, and each time seemed to shatter her into pieces and break chains that had been in place her whole life. Into this maelstrom, she heard him cry out, and she felt the spasms of his orgasm as he thrust into her several more times. Then he stilled, his arm still tight around her waist. There seemed nothing else in the world, his breathing and hers the only sound in the soft stillness of the afternoon.

At last, he eased back, relaxing his hold. He lowered her skirts, smoothing them back into place, then turned her around. He kissed her, then tipped her chin up to look into her eyes. "Glad you finally said it," he said, giving a hoarse chuckle as he cupped her flushed cheeks. "I'm not sure how much longer I could have held out." He kissed her mouth, a long sweet kiss, full of tenderness. "I love you."

He looked at her, waiting, and she knew what he wanted, but she wasn't ready. She wasn't sure. She couldn't think.

He kissed her again, and let her go. He turned away, picked up the picnic basket, and started down the hops alley, but when she didn't follow, he stopped and looked at her over his shoulder. "Well, aren't you coming? We have a train to catch, you know."

Chapter 21

They didn't talk much on the train, for they were surrounded by people. At Victoria Station, they separated, taking different hansom cabs home. In love affairs, one had to be discreet, especially in town. But Nicholas had to know when he would see her again, and as he assisted her to step into her waiting cab, he stopped her.

"Belinda?" When she turned, one foot on the step, her hand in his, he squeezed her fingers. "I have to see you. Meet me tomorrow."

"Where?"

"Your house? A hotel? Anywhere."

"How about Claridge's?" She smiled. "For tea?"

He groaned. "I meant a room," he muttered, "and not the tearoom."

She shook her head. Glancing around, she whispered,

"I can't. Too many Americans in the hotels. Someone might recognize me, in the foyer or in a corridor . . . I can't risk it."

"Your house?" When she shook her head again, he began to feel desperate. There had to be somewhere. "Lilyfield's. Quarter past five? Everyone will be gone by then."

"All right," she whispered.

He kissed her gloved hand, and stepped back, watching as her cab pulled away, merging into the traffic that clogged the narrow exit onto Victoria Street.

"My lord?"

He turned to find Chalmers behind him. "Your hansom is waiting. The luggage is loaded."

"Let's be off, then."

It was just past six o'clock, and at this hour of the day during the season, traffic in London was fairly light. Gentlemen commuting home from the City had already arrived home, and for society, this was that brief lull in activity between tea and dinner. Nicholas was back at South Audley Street by quarter to seven.

But he'd barely made it upstairs and ordered his valet to draw him a bath before there was a knock on his bedroom door. "It's Denys," the voice said from the other side of the door. "May I come in?"

"Of course," he called back, undoing the knot of his four-in-hand tie. But his fingers stilled as his friend came in, for the look on Denys's face told him something was very wrong. "What is it?" he asked. "What's happened?"

"If you hadn't been coming back today, I'd have had

to cable you." Denys closed the door behind him, leaning back against it with a sigh. "It's off. The whole thing's off."

"What whole thing?"

"The brewery, of course. It's finished. We can't do it."

"Why not? Good God, Denys," he added, as his friend didn't answer. "This suspense is killing me. Spit it out, man."

His friend took a deep breath before he spoke. "My father has withdrawn from the venture. He won't fund it or buy shares."

"What?" The word was a guttural sound, for he felt as if he'd just been kicked in the stomach. Panic followed, but he worked to shove it down. "Why? Do you know?"

Denys shook his head. "I don't. All I know is . . ." He paused, cleared his throat, and looked at him with an expression that said things were about to get even worse. "All I know is that yesterday, Landsdowne came to see him. I don't know what was said, but afterward, the old man called me in. He was white to the lips. He said he was sorry, but he couldn't back us."

"Landsdowne," Nicholas muttered, rubbing his hands over his face. "I should have known."

"I can't imagine what was said," Denys went on. "Conyers refused to discuss it, so whatever it was, I know it was bad."

"You may not be able to imagine it, but I can."

"If you're thinking of a bribe, I can assure you that my father—"

"No, not bribery. Your father has plenty of money.

Landsdowne knows that. He wouldn't even waste his time trying that."

"Then what?"

"Blackmail. Or some other threat," he added when his friend protested. "Landsdowne is capable of finding anyone's weakness and using it against him."

He sat down on the edge of his bed, feeling as if everything good and right and wonderful had just been sucked out of him. "I should have known this would happen," he muttered. "He came to see me at Honeywood a few days ago. He found out what we were doing, and he said he wouldn't allow it. I shouldn't be surprised he's managed to stop it."

"I'm sorry, Nick."

"It's not your fault." Nicholas sat there a moment, thinking, then he stood up and began reknotting his tie. "There's only one thing to do."

"What?"

"Find the money elsewhere."

"Do you think you'll be able to find another investor?"

"I don't know. But I know I have to try." An image of Belinda at Honeywood, surrounded by meadow grass and daisies, came into his mind, reminding him of his vow to earn her respect. Yes, he had to try.

THE FOLLOWING AFTERNOON, Belinda was at Lilyfield's, just as she and Nicholas had arranged. She'd been anticipating their time together the previous evening, lying in bed last night, all day today. The hours had seemed to pass with interminable slowness, but at last, the time had almost arrived.

In her eagerness, she'd come a bit too early, and she waited in her carriage across the street, watching as the workers filed out with the five o'clock whistle, and a few moments later, she saw Somerton emerge. He stopped in the doorway when he saw her alight from her carriage and start across the street.

"Lady Featherstone," he greeted, doffing his hat with a bow as she halted in front of him. "What are you doing here?"

"I came to see Nicholas. Lord Trubridge," she amended at once. "We arranged to meet here. To . . . um . . . to . . ." She stopped, for she hadn't prepared some sort of excuse.

"You needn't be discreet," Somerton said. "He told me ages ago he wanted to marry and was seeking your assistance."

"Oh." That would do. "Yes, right. I . . . um . . . didn't know if you knew."

"I knew. And it's a good thing. He'll have to find himself a rich wife, especially now."

She frowned, feeling a shiver, as if someone had just walked over her grave. "What do you mean?"

He sighed. "I suppose the news will be common knowledge within a day or two." He gestured to the brewery behind him. "We're not doing the brewery. We're closing down."

"What?" she gasped, dismayed. "But why? You were both so keen."

"My father's pulled the funds. Without financial backing, we can't afford to carry on. Nick's trying to find someone else to back us, but I doubt he'll succeed. His father is very powerful."

"Landsdowne? What's he to do with it?" But even as she asked the question, she understood. "He doesn't want his son engaging in trade, does he?"

"I would imagine that's his motive. Brewing beer? Landsdowne would think that far beneath the son of a duke."

Belinda felt sick, for she knew Nicholas must be devastated by this. "How is he? Where is he?"

"I don't know. I haven't seen him since I broke the news to him yesterday. He didn't even come home last night."

"Oh, God." She pressed a hand to her mouth, truly worried.

"I'm sure he's all right," Denys hastened to assure her. "Nick always bounces back. He always finds a way to let his father's schemes roll off his back like water off a duck. He'll be all right."

"Will he? Are you sure?"

"Well, he already told me he's determined to carry on with this somehow though between us, Lady Featherstone, I don't see how he'll manage it. Unless he marries, of course. Find him a rich American girl, would you? One who won't mind being hated by her father-in-law, smeared and reviled?" He gave a humorless laugh. "Good luck."

No wonder Nicholas had spent his whole life rebelling against his father. She'd thought it was for revenge, but no. It was so that he wouldn't have his dreams crushed. She thought of her words to him in the maze in a new, much more bitter light. They seemed so cruel.

But not as cruel as Landsdowne. Rage rose up

within her, rage so great, it displaced her worry for the moment. It choked her, it smothered her, it made her for the first time in her life genuinely want to kill someone. Because that man, that odious, awful man, was grinding Nicholas's dreams to dust. Again.

And that was how she knew.

She loved him. She loved him more than her good name, more than her profession, more than her money, more than her friends, more than anything in the world. She would give up everything, all she had, even her life, if it meant saving him a moment of pain, at his father's hands or anyone else's. She loved him that much.

"Lady Featherstone?"

She started at the sound of Somerton's voice. "Sorry," she said, pasting on the polite smile that came from years of hiding her true feelings. "I was woolgathering. Did you ask me a question?"

"Yes. I asked if you have any idea what Nicholas might do?"

"No." She paused, her polite smile vanishing. "But I know exactly what I'm going to do."

NICHOLAS SAT DOWN on one of the wrought-iron benches of Park Lane and stared at the immense mansion across the street. Night had fallen, and the gaslights inside the house had been lit, illuminating the luxurious interiors for all the world to see. Outside, the streetlights along Park Lane lit the house's equally luxurious exterior of marble columns, white limestone, and large, perfectly manicured lawns. The fountain in front, a statue of Zeus carved from Siena marble, must have cost thousands of pounds all by itself. Its water glistened and sparkled in the light of more gaslights, strategically placed to show it off even at night.

He'd played in that fountain once as a boy, he remembered. After he'd been caught, he hadn't been allowed at Landsdowne House for over a year.

He leaned back, exhausted. He hadn't slept last night. Wanting to be completely alone, he'd gone to a hotel and obtained a room, but he hadn't slept. He'd lain in the dark, staring at the ceiling, striving to think of connections, men who might have money to invest— schoolfellows from Eton and Oxford, their fathers, their friends.

This morning, he'd taken the prospectus they'd drawn up for Conyers to other men he thought might be open to the investment, but though some had expressed an interest, all had asked him if Landsdowne had approved of his venture into commerce. And when given a negative answer, one and all had refused to participate.

By the end of the day, the sick knot in his guts told him he was fooling himself. Even if he found someone who was willing to have a go without Landsdowne's goodwill, he knew what happened to Conyers would happen again. There was no one Landsdowne couldn't bribe, or smear, or blackmail into pulling out.

I can make it right.

The old man's words came back as if to mock him because here he was, trying to work up the courage to go in there and do what he vowed he'd never do again in his life. He was here to ask for something.

It would probably be futile, but he couldn't lose Belinda without a fight. He was here to ask, to plead—to beg if he had to—for his father to accept Belinda as his choice of wife and to reinstate his trust fund. Without that, he had no income to support Belinda, and he would never ask her to bring her money to their marriage. That would make him the very sort of fortune hunter she despised, and he couldn't sink to that level in her eyes, not again. If he did, he wouldn't be able to bear it.

So here he was, in front of Landsdowne House, readying himself to do what he had to do. He tried to think of what might persuade his father to agree.

Belinda did meet a few of Landsdowne's criteria. She was a respected lady of British society, with a sterling reputation. She was Church of England, having converted upon her marriage to Featherstone. And she was wealthy, too, able to bring a dowry into the family. His father didn't have to know he had no intention of allowing a penny of Belinda's money into Landsdowne coffers. Her background and her nationality were the biggest stumbling blocks. He just couldn't see Landsdowne allowing an American to be the future duchess. Most of British society had accepted her long ago; indeed, most didn't care that she'd once been a New Money nobody from Ohio. But Nicholas knew his father would never forget a thing like that, and he'd be only slightly less appalled by the prospect of an American daughter-in-law than he'd been about an Irish one.

If that wasn't enough to make Nicholas's chances utterly dismal, there was also the fact that he had no idea if Belinda would ever agree to marry him. In all the passionate cries he'd wrung from her the previous afternoon in the hops field, a declaration of love had not been one of them.

Still, he had to try. Nicholas stood up, took a deep breath, and started across the street, trying to prepare himself for the hardest thing he'd ever had to do in his life.

Wilton was still the butler at Landsdowne House, and as unflappable and proper a butler as any duke could want, but upon the sight of Nicholas, even Wilton gave way to a slight display of surprise. He raised one bushy gray eyebrow. His mouth opened, then closed. He cleared his throat. "Lord Trubridge," he said at last, giving a bow.

"Wilton. How are you?"

"Very well, my lord, thank you."

"I'm glad to hear it. Is the duke at home?"

"I—I'm not certain, my lord."

"Find out, would you? I wish to see him."

"Very good, my lord." Wilton bowed and left him in the foyer.

He glanced around as he waited. Nothing had changed. No awful artworks here. Most of those had been consigned to Honeywood. Like Landsdowne Park in Sussex, Landsdowne House was to his father's tastes, through and through. Polished white marble, classical sculpture, walls and woodwork of white-on-white. A cold house. It had always been a cold house. He shivered.

Wilton's footsteps on the limestone steps of the wide,

sweeping staircase sounded behind him, and he turned. "Well?" he asked. "Shall I be granted an audience?"

Wilton remained his usual dignified self. "If you will follow me, my lord."

The butler took him to Landsdowne's study, another room that hadn't changed since he was a boy. Like the foyer below, it was white-on-white, accented by black ebony bookcases containing leather-bound volumes the old man had never opened and more classical sculptures. The fact that it looked exactly the same took Nicholas even more forcibly back to his childhood. He'd only ever been summoned to the study when he was in serious trouble. The choice of this room, he supposed, was meant to instill fear, the same terrifying fears of his boyhood. But he wasn't afraid. Desperate, yes, but not afraid.

Still, best if Landsdowne didn't sense his desperation, for that would be like the scent of meat to a hungry dog. Instead, he strove to paste on his mask of blithe indifference as he stepped into the study. It was harder than it used to be.

"The Marquess of Trubridge," Wilton announced and stepped aside for Nicholas to enter the ducal presence.

Nicholas came in, doffing his hat, and as he came toward the desk, Landsdowne didn't even bother to stand up. Odd, that, for it wasn't at all like the duke to allow good manners to lapse, no matter the circumstances.

"Duke," Nicholas greeted him, halting before the desk and offering a bow, and when he straightened, he found his father scowling at him.

Another surprise. After winning Conyers's capitulation, the old man ought to be smirking with satisfaction, not glaring at him as if he wanted to wring his neck.

"Why are you here?" Landsdowne demanded, his bitter mouth curving into a sneer. "Come to gloat, have you?"

Nicholas blinked, and despite all the evidence to the contrary, he wondered if he had somehow wandered into the wrong house. "Sorry?" he murmured. "I'm not quite sure I un—"

"Don't play games with me, boy. I already know all about your plans, and I refuse to sanction them. I already said as much to that American chit when she came here."

American chit? Nicholas felt a jolt of hope, and joy, and incredulity, a jolt so powerful, it made him dizzy. But long practice dealing with his father enabled him to reveal nothing of what he felt in his expression. "To whom are you referring?"

"As if you don't know."

There was no sensible reply to that. So, wisely, he made none.

His silence goaded Landsdowne more than any words would have done. "Impudent woman. Coming here and telling me the two of you are engaged to be married. Not asking me for my permission, nor even my blessing upon your union! Oh, no. Telling me about it, and how I shall have to accept it, acting as if she's some sort of queen issuing royal edicts, and I'm the nobody from nowhere. God," he choked, "I never dreamed Lady Featherstone to have such bad manners, even for an American."

Nicholas laughed, laughed out loud. He couldn't help it, for the hope and joy inside him could not be suppressed. It surged up like a rising flood.

Oh, Belinda, he thought. *My darling. My love.*

The sound of his laughter enraged Landsdowne further, and the duke slammed his fist on his desk. "I won't have it, do you hear?" he roared, more out of control than Nicholas had ever seen him. "That woman will never be the Duchess of Landsdowne. Never."

Nicholas laughed again. "As Belinda already told you, we're not asking your permission. We shall be married, and there is nothing you can do about it."

"I'll ruin her. I'll smear her name in every gutter rag from here down to Land's End and up to John O'Groats before you've even reached the altar."

His joy stopped, smothered by rage. "You do, and by God, I will kill you. You take one move in that direction, Landsdowne, and I will take you by the throat and squeeze the life out of you."

Landsdowne was many things, but he was not a physical coward. "Do it, then," he challenged. "Go ahead." When Nicholas didn't move, it was his turn to laugh.

"There, now," his father said, and now, the smirk came out. "That's put you in your place, hasn't it, my boy?"

Tempting as it was, patricide was not an option. Nicholas swallowed, forcing down his rage, thinking fast. "I suppose you already informed Belinda you would besmirch her reputation if she consented to marry me?"

"I did."

"And?" He caught something—an annoyance, an uneasiness—something that caused the smirk on

Landsdowne's face to falter just a bit. "And," Nicholas prompted again, "when you told her your intentions, what did she say?"

"There's no reasoning with her any more than there is with you."

All his joy and relief came rushing back, and he grinned. "Told you to go to the devil, did she? God, I love that woman!"

"You won't get a penny of your trust if you marry her. You'll get nothing from me at all. Nothing."

"I'm not asking for anything from you, Father." No need for Landsdowne to know he'd come to do exactly that. He didn't know how he'd support them, but perhaps she had a plan. He hoped so, because the bridges were burning. "I know you want everyone in your power, Father, and everyone at your mercy, but it's just not possible. Belinda and I shall be married, whether you like it or not, so unless you want to shred the reputation of the future Duchess of Landsdowne to no purpose, I suggest you accept the situation gracefully. The last move in this game's been made, and you've lost. Checkmate, Father."

With that, he turned his back, leaving the old man spluttering with impotent rage.

"Well done, Belinda," he muttered under his breath as he walked out the door. "Well done."

AFTER LEAVING LILYFIELD's, Belinda had first gone to her attorneys in the Marylebone Road. There, she had requested that certain documents be drawn up at once, then she'd gone on to Landsdowne House in Park Lane.

Her meeting with the duke having gone exactly as she'd anticipated, she'd returned to her attorneys, picked up the documents, and gone to South Audley Street, but to her dismay, Nicholas had not been there, nor had anyone even seen him.

By the time she reached home, Belinda was terribly worried, and she sent her footman, Samuel, in search of Nicholas. "Go to White's first," she instructed. "If you still can't find him, go to the other clubs and inquire if anyone's seen him. If you still can't locate him, return to South Audley Street and inquire if they've received word. And when you find him, tell him to come to me. I need to see him at once."

She wanted to tell him what she'd done before he did something desperate, like go to a moneylender. She wouldn't blame him for it if he did, for Landsdowne was a horrible, vicious man who was capable of anything. Her meeting with the duke had told her everything she needed to know about him, and she hoped she never had the misfortune to encounter him again.

Thankfully, she'd been angry, too angry to feel any shyness or trepidation about confronting him. Even the fact that he'd made her wait twenty minutes before agreeing to see her hadn't cooled her fury one bit. From her conversations with Nicholas, she'd had a good idea of what to expect, and things had gone just as she'd anticipated.

She'd laughed at his bribery attempt and informed him she had money enough, thank you. His threat to ruin her she'd treated with scorn as well as ridicule. Not because she didn't think he'd do it. He probably would, and he might succeed, but what he'd failed to grasp was that she didn't care.

He'd finally burst out at her in a rage to leave his house and never darken his door again, and she'd happily gone. Everything she'd planned was in place if only she could locate Nicholas.

She paced her drawing room. She refused dinner. And when nine o'clock came and went with no word, she actually poured herself a drink. She swallowed the brandy in two shuddering gulps.

She was about ready to head out into Mayfair and search for him herself when the doorbell rang. She raced for the stairs, and upon looking down to the foyer, she almost sank to her knees with relief, for Nicholas was standing there with Jervis.

She ducked back into the drawing room before he could look up and see her. She pulled out the documents from her attorneys and set them on the tea table, smoothed her hair, and sat down to wait as she heard Jervis bringing him up the stairs.

She knew what she was going to say, she had a little speech all prepared, but the moment he walked in, she forgot every word. She was so happy to see him, and so relieved, she came running with a sob and hurled herself into his arms.

"My darling," he muttered, pressing kisses to her hair, his voice so fierce it made her heart sing. "My beautiful darling."

"I was so worried about you. I heard what happened."

"Yes, I know." He pulled back, grasping her by the

arms. "What have you done?" he demanded, half-laughing as he looked at her. "You went to see Landsdowne? I don't know whether to kiss you or shake you."

She stared at him, astonished. "You know?"

He nodded, cupping her face. "Are you mad? Why did you do it?" He kissed her mouth, her cheeks, her forehead, her nose. "Why?"

She didn't answer that. "I did you an injustice," she said instead. "That night in the maze when I lashed out at you about your father, I had no idea what he was really like."

"And after meeting with him, after being offered a bribe and having him threaten your reputation, what's your opinion of him now?"

"How do you know what took place? In fact, how do you know I was there at all?"

"Because I just came from there."

"What? You went to see Landsdowne? Why?"

He smiled a little, caressing her cheek with his thumb. "Can't you guess?"

She shook her head. "No, I can't, because after meeting with him myself, I completely understand why you spent eight years in Paris, doing everything you possibly could to annoy and aggravate him."

Nicholas laughed. "My loyal darling."

"What an odious man. I had no idea. Really, if he'd been my father, I think I'd have had to shoot him."

"The idea of strangling him did occur to me," he admitted ruefully. "After he told me he intended to ruin you if you married me, I almost went for his throat."

"But why were you there at all?"

"To ask him for help."

"What?" She stared at him in dismay. "Oh, Nicholas, no. You didn't."

"That was my intention, but it didn't happen. The moment I walked through the door, he started flaying me about you. I found out you'd been there, and thrown his bribes in his face, and told him to go to hell." He kissed her. "And I know that I love you even more than I did before, even though I didn't dream that was possible. And he demanded I give you up. I refused, of course. By the way, I understand I am now engaged to be married?"

"Well . . ." She gave a cough. "You did hire me to find you a wife, so I did. I think she's the perfect wife for you."

"Indeed?" He smiled a little, smoothing her hair. "Tell me about her."

"Well, she's rich, for one thing."

"Yes, I believe I did hear a rumor to that effect."

"You did?" Belinda stared at him, nonplussed, and to be honest, she felt a bit let down to have her surprise partly quashed. "But . . . but who told you about my . . . her money?"

"The duchess. At the house party, the morning I left for London. But it doesn't matter because I don't want my wife's money."

Belinda looked up him, at the tenderness on his face, at the warm hazel eyes that stared steadily into hers, and happiness squeezed her heart, so much happiness, she couldn't even smile. She almost couldn't speak. But she knew she had to. "Y . . . yes, well," she managed, after a moment, "that's neither here nor there. She insists on bringing a dowry with her."

He opened his mouth as if to object, but she rushed on, "We can discuss monetary details in a moment, but there are other things you need to know about her. You'll be pleased to know she's American, which I believe you preferred?"

"Yes." He kissed her. "Most definitely."

"She is Church of England, though, and I know you didn't want that."

His lips brushed back and forth over hers. "I believe I would be willing to compromise on that point."

"She's . . ." Belinda swallowed hard. "She's a bit shy."

"I like that. It means she won't chatter nineteen to the dozen or recite poetry spontaneously in public places."

Belinda laughed against his mouth. "She will never do either. And she doesn't care in the least about tercets and quatrains or if you ever write a perfect poem. Oh, and she always wants the fox to get away."

He smiled and pulled back a little, brushing a loose tendril of her hair from her face and tucking it behind her ear. "Anything else?"

"Well . . . I know that . . . that . . ." She paused, feeling her cheeks growing hot, but knowing she had to say it all. "I know that when you look at her, you do always seem to want to yank her into your arms and kiss her breathless and tear her clothes off."

"True." His arm tightened around her, and he slid his free hand down her neck. He bent his head and kissed her, a long, deep kiss. Then he pulled back again, and she wasn't the only one a little breathless. "I think you're right," he said after a moment. "She sounds perfect for me. But there's more I need to know before I can decide."

"Such as?"

He cupped her face, his fingertips caressing her cheeks. "Does she respect me? Does she know she can trust me?"

"Yes. You've proved the worth of your character to her. She trusts you."

"How do I know? How can I be sure?"

"I believe the marriage settlement will tell you everything you need to know." She reached for the sheaf of papers on the table beside them. "I had my attorneys draw one up this afternoon."

"Very wise of you," he said gravely, taking it. "But how does this help me know she can trust me?"

"You'll know if you read it."

He glanced through it, and he only needed to reach the middle of the first page to know what she meant. He looked up, clearly stunned. "This gives me all your . . . er . . . her money. All of it. No conditions."

"Yes. Her estate is worth seven hundred forty-two thousand pounds. Give or take a pound or two." Belinda's heart constricted, for she loved him so much, and she wanted that money for him, and she was terribly afraid that he was going to refuse it.

"I already told you, I won't take it," he said, confirming her guess.

"She won't marry you unless you accept it. She wants you to have it, so you don't have a choice. That is if . . . if you want to marry her." She entwined her fingers together, more scared than she'd ever been in her life, and more hopeful and more in love. "Do you?" she whispered.

"I don't know yet." He tossed the marriage settlement to the floor, then he took her hands. Gently, he pulled them apart, held them fast in his. "There's one more thing I need to know."

"What's that?"

"Does she love me?" He sank to his knees, looking up at her just the same way he had that blissful afternoon two days ago. "Because I love her. I love her more than my life."

"Yes," Belinda said on a sob. "She loves you."

"I think she has to tell me that herself. She has to say it."

"I love you." Belinda fell to her knees and wrapped her arms around his neck, pressing kisses to his face. "I love you, I love you, I love you."

When she finished, he bent his head to take her lips for a deeper kiss, but she didn't want that. She wanted an answer. "Damn it, Nicholas," she said, pulling back, "are you going to marry me, or aren't you?"

"I believe . . ." He paused, and she watched in disbelief as he picked up the marriage settlement and ripped it in half. "Yes, Belinda, I will."

"Finally! You took long enough to decide. And my attorneys did a great deal of work this afternoon when they drafted that document, by the way," she added, nodding to the torn fragments in his hands. "Now they'll have to write a new one. And as much as I appreciate the gesture you've just made—and I do appreciate it, honestly—we have to be practical. If you don't take my dowry, what will we live on?"

"I do have an idea." He tossed the marital settlement into the air and slid his arms around her, pulling her close as the pieces of paper floated down around them. "How would you feel about investing in a brewery?"

She laughed. "I hear it's a sound investment."

"Very sound." He kissed her mouth. "When shall we have the wedding?"

She kissed him back. "Next week?"

"Next week?" He shook his head. "No, no, that won't do. These things can't be rushed." He gave her a wicked grin. "To do things properly, I believe we shall have to have a long engagement."

She groaned, and wrapped her arms around his neck. "No long engagement," she said firmly.

"But Belinda, courtship rituals are important."

"There's only one that's important to us." She stood up, pulling him with her. "Take me upstairs, Trubridge," she ordered, "kiss me breathless, tear my clothes off, and make passionate love to me, or this wedding's off."

"Oh, very well, if you insist upon flinging yourself at me in this shameless way, I suppose I must capitulate." He wrapped one arm around her back and hooked the other beneath her knees. He lifted her into his arms. "I do have one more question," he said as he carried her toward the door.

"What's that?"

"Is it proper form for a marquess to marry his match-maker?"

"Who cares?" she said, and kissed him.

Continue reading for a sneak peek

at the next novel in Laura Lee Guhrke's

An American Heiress in London series

How to Lose a Duke in Ten Days

Available in Spring 2014

from

Avon Books

Roberts had barely brought the carriage to a halt before Edie was out of the vehicle and racing toward the station. "Bring the luggage, Roberts, would you?" she called over her shoulder as she ran up the steps and opened the door. Without waiting for an answer, she went inside, passed through the small station building, and emerged out the opposite side onto the platform. It was empty, save one man who leaned back against the pillar behind him in a careless pose, hat pulled low. Surrounded by stacks of luggage, he seemed to have no inclination to board the train, and Edie could only presume he had just disembarked from the first-class carriage beside him and was waiting for a porter.

Foreign, she thought at once, and passed him without a second glance or another thought, making for the ticket window. There, Mr. Jones was bent over that morning's *Clyffeton Gazette*, and she gave a cough, causing him to look up.

"Your Grace," he said and straightened to respectful

attention at once, shoving aside the local newspaper. "How may I be of service?"

"My sister and her governess are to take this train to Kent, but we are terribly late. Could you perhaps persuade the conductor to delay departure until they have time to board?"

"I will try, Your Grace." The clerk bowed with a tug of his cap, stepped out from behind the ticket window, and bustled off to board the train and find the conductor. Edie glanced back over her shoulder, but the others had not yet followed her to the platform, and because she did not want to think about her sister's impending departure, she occupied her mind by giving the stranger nearby a more thorough study.

Definitely foreign, she decided, although she didn't know quite why he gave her that impression. He was dressed for the country in well-cut, typical English tweeds, but nonetheless, there was something un-English about him. Perhaps it was his negligent pose, or the way his brown felt hat was pulled sleepily over his eyes. Or perhaps it was the mahogany and ivory walking stick in his hand, or the worn portmanteau of crocodile leather by his feet, or the brass-studded trunks stacked nearby. Or perhaps it was merely the steam from the train that swirled around him like mist. But something about the man spoke of exotic places far away from this sleepy little corner of England.

Her curiosity was aroused. None of the families in the county were entertaining this week and she couldn't imagine what reason a foreigner would have for coming here, but she supposed she'd know before the day was out.

Clyffeton was a picturesque little village on the Norfolk coast at the top of The Wash, a place of strategic importance when Vikings were plundering England's coastline, but nowadays it was nothing more than a sleepy by-water. Even its boast of having a ducal seat couldn't save it from being quaint, insular, and hopelessly old-fashioned. Here in Clyffeton, a man like this would stick out like a pair of red knickers on a vicar's washing line. Within an hour, she guessed, the village would be buzzing like bees about this stranger's arrival. Within two, his bona fides would be established, his background unearthed, his intentions known. By teatime, her maid would probably be able to tell her all about him.

"You stopped it from leaving."

Joanna's voice, dismayed and accusatory, interrupted her speculations, and Edie turned, the stranger forgotten. "Of course," she answered, pasting on a smile for her sister's benefit. "Wonderful thing, being a duchess. They delay trains for me."

"Of course they do," Joanna muttered in disgust. "I should have known they would."

Mrs. Simmons came bustling up. "I've secured a porter. He and Roberts are loading the luggage." She lifted the pair of tickets in her black-gloved hand. "Best we go aboard and not keep the train waiting on us any longer."

"All right, then." Joanna lifted her chin, trying to put

on an indifferent air about it all. "I suppose I have to go, since you're both so determined."

Beneath the nonchalance, there was fear. Edie sensed it, and though it tore at her heart, she could not give in to it. Desperate, she turned to the governess. "Watch over her. See that she's settled in and has everything she needs before . . ." She paused and took a deep breath. "Before you leave her."

The governess gave a nod. "Of course I will, Your Grace. Come, Joanna."

The girl's face twisted, broke up. Her defiance crumbled. "Edie, don't make me go!"

Mrs. Simmons' brisk voice intervened. "None of this, now, Joanna. You are the sister of a duchess and a young lady of good society. Behave accordingly."

Joanna didn't seem inclined to behave like a lady. She wrapped her arms around Edie, clinging to her like a barnacle. "Don't send me away."

"Hush, now." She rubbed her sister's back, striving to keep her own emotions in control as Joanna gave a sob against her shoulder. "They'll take good care of you at Willowbank."

"Not as good as you."

Edie gently began to pull back, and though it was one of the hardest things she'd ever done, she extricated herself from her sister's embrace. "Go on, now. Be brave, my darling. And I shall see you at Christmas."

"That's forever away." Joanna wiped at her face and turned angrily away to follow the governess onto the train. She boarded without a backward glance, but it wasn't more than a moment later before she was sliding down the first window and sticking her head out. "Can't you come visit me before Christmas?" she asked, folding her arms atop the open window as Mrs. Simmons continued on toward their seats further down the car.

"We'll see. I want you to settle in without any distraction from me, but we'll see. In the meantime, write to me and tell me everything. Who you meet and what your schoolmistresses are like, and all about your lessons."

"It would serve you right if I don't send you a single letter." Joanna scowled, her face still damp with tears. "I shan't write a word. I'll keep you in suspense all year long, wondering what I'm doing. No, wait," she amended. "I'll do better than that. I shall cause so much havoc, they'll expel me and send me home."

"And here I thought you'd want a season in London when you turn eighteen," Edie retorted, her voice shaking with the effort not to break into tears herself. "If you're expelled from Willowbank, the only season you'll get will be a place far more remote than Kent. I'll send you to some convent in Ireland."

"Empty threat," Joanna muttered, wiping at her face. "We're not Catholic. And besides, knowing you, I doubt I'll ever have a season. It'd be too much for your nerves."

"You'll have a season." Even as she gave the assurance, she found the idea of safeguarding her sister by putting her in a convent far more appealing. "If you manage to behave yourself."

Joanna sniffed. "I knew you weren't above black-mail."

The whistle blew, signaling the train was about to

pull out, and as her sister stretched out her hand, Edie reached up to give it a quick squeeze. "Be good, my darling, and please, for once in your life, do what you're told. And I shall see you at Christmas. Maybe before."

She knew she ought to stay until the train was gone, but another moment, and she'd fall apart. So she waved brightly to her sister and turned to leave before she started bawling like a baby.

Her escape, however, proved very short-lived. As she started back across the platform, the voice of the stranger calling her name stopped her in her tracks.

"Hullo, Edie."

Even her beloved sister was momentarily forgotten as she turned to the man on the platform. Strangers did not speak to duchesses, and Edie had been a duchess long enough to be astonished by the fact that this one had spoken to her. So astonished, in fact, that she couldn't think of a reply. And when he lifted his head and pushed back his hat to reveal his eyes—piercing, brilliant gray eyes that seemed to see straight through her—her astonishment deepened into shock. This man was no foreign stranger.

This man was her husband.

"Stuart?" His name was a startled cry torn from her throat, but he didn't seem to notice that in it was none of the joy that a reunion between husband and wife ought to convey. He doffed the hat and inclined his head a bit, though it was hardly a bow. He didn't bother to straighten away from the pillar, and that almost impudent gesture only served to confirm the ghastly truth that her husband was here, a mere half dozen feet from her, and not the thousands of miles away he was supposed to be.

Good manners dictated a greeting of some sort beyond the mere cry of his name, but though she opened her mouth, no words came out. Unable to speak, Edie could only stare at the man she'd married five years ago and hadn't seen since.

Africa, she appreciated at once, was a hard continent. That fact was evident in every aspect of his appearance. It was in his tanned skin, in the faint creases that edged his eyes and his mouth, and in the sun-torched glints of gold and amber in his dark brown hair. It was in the harsh, lean planes of his face and in the long, strong lines of his body. It was in the exotic walking stick in his hand and in the assessing look in his eyes. He was studying her rather as a hunter might study possible prey, reminding her forcibly of his profession.

During the years of his absence, she'd wondered on occasion what Africa was like. Now she knew, for in the man before her she could see many aspects of that particular continent—its relentless nature, its wild, adventurous spirit, and the uncompromising toll it took on those who were merely human.

Gone was the carefree, handsome young man who'd blithely married a girl he didn't even know, left that girl in charge of his entire retinue of estates, and gone off for parts unknown with happy insouciance. Returning in his place was someone completely different, someone so different that she'd passed right by him without so much as a glimmer of recognition. Never would she have thought five years could change a man so much.

But what was he doing here? She glanced past him to the black leather trunks stacked on the platform, to the suitcases and portmanteaus around his feet, and the implications of all that luggage hit her with sudden force. When she looked at him again and saw his mouth tighten, that tiny movement confirmed the awful suspicion forming in her mind more effectively than any words.

Home is the hunter, she thought wildly, and her dismay deepened into dread as she realized the perfect life she'd created for herself five years ago might have just crumbled into dust.

Next month, don't miss these exciting new love stories only from Avon Books

The Pirate Bride by Sandra Hill

Medana Elsadottir, known as the Sea Scourge, needs a few virile Vikings to help grow her female-only tribe. When eight strapping Norsemen come into her hands—and her ship's hold—she doesn't mind reaping the benefits, especially with a godly specimen like Thork Tykirsson. Thork doesn't mind being kidnapped by a beautiful pirate, but that doesn't mean he'll give in easily.

Wildest Dreams by Toni Blake

Advertising executive Stephanie Grant knows how to sell an idea, but she's never had to sell *herself* before. Walking into The Big Easy's most exclusive bordello, she's prepared to do just that—until she meets *him*. Jake Broussard knows this sexy blonde isn't who she says she is, and that she's playing with fire. Good thing he likes it hot . . .

Suddenly Royal by Nichole Chase

As crown prince of Lilaria, Alex D'Lynsal is used to notoriety, but the latest scandal has sent him packing to America and forced him to swear off women. That is, until he meets Samantha Rousseau. She's stubborn, feisty, and incredibly sexy. Not to mention heiress to an estate in his country. Sam can navigate the sudden changes to her life, but can she dodge her growing feelings for Alex?

At Avon Books, we know your passion for romance—once you finish one of our novels, you find yourself wanting more.

May we tempt you with . . .

- **Excerpts** from our upcoming releases.

- Entertaining **extras**, including authors' personal photo albums and book lists.

- Behind-the-scenes **scoop** on your favorite characters and series.

- **Sweepstakes** for the chance to win free books, romantic getaways, and other fun prizes.

- Writing **tips** from our authors and editors.

- **Blog** with our authors and find out why they love to write romance.

- **Exclusive content** that's not contained within the pages of our novels.

Join us at
www.avonbooks.com